Functionalism, exchange and theoretical strategy

Functionalism, exchange and theoretical strategy

M. J. Mulkay

SCHOCKEN BOOKS · *NEW YORK*

First published in U.S.A. in 1971
by Schocken Books Inc.
67 Park Avenue, New York, N.Y. 10016

© M. J. Mulkay, 1971

Library of Congress Catalog Card No. 70-144783

Printed in Great Britain

For Lucy, Anna and Lisa

Contents

	Preface	*page* ix
1	Introduction	1
2	A general theory of society: Pareto	9
3	Structural-functionalism as a theoretical alternative: Parsons	36
4	An assessment of Parsons' scheme	66
5	A second functional alternative: Merton	94
6	Functionalism rejected: Homans	122
7	A theory of social exchange: Homans	146
8	A conceptual elaboration of exchange theory: Blau	179
9	Sociological theory and theoretical strategy	213
	Notes	241
	Bibliography	253
	Index	257

Preface

The approach adopted in this book to the presentation of sociological theory was devised in a series of lectures given at Simon Fraser University, British Columbia, and developed further at the University of Aberdeen. Versions of the work have been read by Gordon Horobin and Tony Giddens, whom I wish to thank. Thanks are also due to Pat Rennie, who was a great help.

1 Introduction

This is a study of the development of certain sociological ideas. More specifically, it is an attempt to describe the recent growth of functional and exchange theory by interpreting the work of five important theorists, in chronological order, and by examining some of the intellectual connections between their theories. The study is undertaken from a definite perspective which both controls and limits the exposition of the theories and the account offered of their interrelations. For the sake of clarity, this perspective must be described briefly at the outset.

In the chapters to come a distinction is made between theoretical goal, theoretical strategy and theoretical content. By 'theoretical goal' is meant the long-term objective toward which a theorist is striving. The term 'theoretical strategy' refers to the general policies which a theorist adopts as a means of ensuring that his work makes a valuable contribution to his long-run theoretical goal. The substantive conceptions and propositions which are put forward to depict social phenomena, in accordance with a particular strategy and in pursuit of a long-term objective, constitute the content of a theory.

The theorists discussed here share a common goal. They all want to contribute to the construction of a comprehensive and scientific theory of social life. Their strategies, however, differ considerably. For example, where one theorist decides that a general sociological theory can be formulated only after extensive conceptual elaboration at a most abstract level, another approaches the problem by keeping his conceptual apparatus to a minimum, by reducing the level of abstraction, and by concentrating on explanation rather than conceptualization. Such divergent strategies, when implemented with reasonable consistency, produce theoretical schemes with quite different content. This tendency for theoretical content to be moulded by theoretical strategy provides the focus of the present study. Consequently, each theoretical opus is presented in three stages. First, the theorist's long-term goal is specified, along with his theoretical strategy and the resultant short-run objectives. Secondly, the theoretical content is expounded as an attempt to contribute to the theoretical goal by means of the given strategy. Thirdly, the strengths and weaknesses of each body of theory and its associated strategy are assessed in relation to the ultimate theoretical objective.

It may be objected that this method of presentation oversimplifies the relationship between content and strategy in the development of theoretical schemes. For theoretical strategies are seldom worked out fully, in advance of all substantive notions. We must accept, therefore, that in many cases there is a reciprocal interplay between strategy and substantive theory. Nevertheless, we are justified in beginning the exposition of each theoretical scheme with an account of its accompanying strategy for several reasons: first, because all but the last of the theorists discussed below made an early strategical statement which guided their later work; secondly, because, whether or not strategy preceded content in time, many aspects of their work can best be understood as attempts to apply *logically* prior strategical decisions; and, thirdly, because many of the deficiencies of their schemes are due to the character of their theoretical strategies.

Theoretical strategies are regarded as important here, partly because they shape theoretical content and partly because they are a source of theoretical defects. A second, and related, reason for emphasizing theoretical strategy is that the five schemes to be studied are historically linked together through their strategies. Each theorist to be examined below is connected with prior theory and particularly with the work of his immediate predecessor, in a negative as well as a positive fashion. On the one hand, each theorist inevitably retains many of the substantive notions of previous theory. This is the positive link. On the other hand, each theorist uses these notions differently, owing to his choice of a strategy designed to avoid the faults of prior theory. This is the negative link. Because the method of exposition adopted here stresses the strategical component of each theory, more attention will be paid to the strategical differences between theories than to the more obvious substantive resemblances. Thus the guiding theme of subsequent chapters will be that, despite broad agreement about theoretical goals and despite considerable continuity in theoretical content, *each theorist is forced to devise a new strategy as a direct response to the demonstrably unsuccessful strategies of his predecessors.*

In this essay the recent growth of functionalism and exchange theory in sociology is viewed as a dialectical process. Theoretical development is regarded as being neither continuous nor, in any direct way, cumulative. Instead, it is seen as arising from a number of discrete and intermittent theoretical reorganizations, which centre upon new strategies devised as replacements for the unsuccessful policies adopted by prior theory. The main concern here is with the emergence of exchange theory as a reaction against the strategy and, consequently, much of the content of functionalism. At the same time, however, an attempt is made to show how a similar dialectical process is evident in the genesis of structural-functionalism itself and also how the dialectic operates within each 'school' of thought.

Although functionalism and exchange analysis can be identified as distinct sociological perspectives, neither constitutes a single coherent theoretical system. There are many varieties of functional analysis and several versions of exchange theory. In order to ensure, therefore, that the discussion is as concrete as possible I have chosen to concentrate on a small number of particular theorists, instead of trying to deal in general terms with the entire range of functional and exchange theory. Parsons is taken as the major exponent of structural-functionalism, with Merton's work being viewed as an attempt to combine functional analysis with a strategy designed to avoid the worst defects of Parsons' approach. Homans is treated as the main exponent of exchange theory, which he adopts in the course of a reaction against the strategies of Parsons, Merton and other functionalists. Blau's exchange framework is regarded as an attempt to develop further Homans' theoretical content while abandoning the confines of the latter's strategy. These theorists have been selected because they are widely recognized as important and influential, because they exemplify a variety of theoretical strategies, and because it is among these theorists that the strategical dialectic is most evident.

The kernel of the analysis presented below consists of an examination of the development and theoretical logic of certain recent variants of functional and exchange theory, with special reference to theoretical strategy. The study begins, however, with an appraisal of the work of Pareto, who not only produced his general theory of society some fifty years ago and can hardly, therefore, be called 'recent', but who in addition was neither a functionalist nor a proponent of exchange theory. Nevertheless, this opening is appropriate for several reasons. To begin with, Pareto's major treatise, although first published in 1916, made its greatest impact upon the main line of theoretical development during the 1930s—that is, just before the flowering of sociological functionalism. Pareto's work was in fact an important factor contributing to the intellectual ferment which eventually gave structural-functionalism a central position in sociological theory. Thus any study of functionalism could justify the inclusion of Pareto's scheme on the grounds that it introduced into sociology such concepts as 'social system' and 'social equilibrium' which became integral parts of functional analysis. In this study, however, much greater emphasis is placed upon what could be called Pareto's *negative* contribution to the development of functionalism. Paretian theory is included here because functional analysis was adopted by certain influential theorists *as a means of avoiding the kind of theoretical strategy used by Pareto*. Because functionalism became prominent in sociology as an alternative to the type of strategy advocated by Pareto, we will understand the strategy of functional analysis better if we examine the main characteristics and deficiencies of Paretian theory. Of course, several theories other than that of Pareto could have been used in this fashion. But Pareto is the only theorist whose work has strong links, in relation to both strategy and content, with our second major concern in this study—namely, exchange theory. An examination of Pareto's general theory of society provides, therefore, a suitable introduction to this study of the theoretical logic and development of functionalism and exchange.

Pareto believed that sociology's immediate theoretical goal should be the construction of a rigorous 'logico-deductive system' capable of predicting and explaining a wide range of social events. The leading functionalists included in this essay, although sharing Pareto's ideal, decided that it was unsuitable as a short-term theoretical objective. Early in their theoretical writings both Parsons and Merton argued, in view of the manifest inadequacies of speculations, like those of Pareto himself and of other European theorists, that sociology was clearly not yet ready for the direct formulation of general theoretical systems. They agreed that some kind of preparatory work was required. However, Parsons' departure from the Paretian theoretical strategy was more a compromise than a total repudiation. It did involve him in a limited retreat from the ambitious attempt to construct directly an operational and large-scale explanatory system. But Parsons' self-appointed task of preparing the way for a general theory of society by building up a comprehensive conceptual scheme was scarcely less demanding. He maintained, however, that much of the required material was already available and needed only to be combined in a systematic fashion. Furthermore, in his view completion of this task was a necessary preliminary to the successful formulation of a general sociological theory on the lines of the advanced sciences. Merton's rejection of speculative general theory was more definite than that of Parsons, though still far from total, and led him to advocate that sociological analysis should operate primarily at the level of middle-range rather than general theory. But despite their adoption of radically different strategies in response to the failure of prior theory, both these theorists had one requirement in common—they needed a framework of ideas which would guide their theoretical preparations and which gave some promise of generating in due course a satisfactory theory of society. They both found this framework in functional analysis, which, during the 1930s, was proving highly effective in the study of biological organisms and which had been applied with some success by anthropologists to the study of simple societies. The basic assumption of functional analysis is that the systems to which it is applied have defined structures with built-in tendencies to self-maintenance; and that relationships between items within such structures can be elucidated by examining how they operate either to perpetuate the structure or to bring about its development in a predictable direction. Although both Parsons and Merton were guided by this functional principle, they used it, in accordance with their theoretical strategies, in quite distinct ways. Nevertheless, both theorists saw functionalism as the only framework capable of simplifying complex sociological data to the point where satisfactory theoretical analysis could be undertaken. Thus Pareto's attempt to formulate a system of explanatory propositions about human society in general was replaced by a more modest concern with preparing the ground for such a theoretical system by the use of functional analysis.

During the 1940s and 1950s sociological theory, particularly in the United States, became increasingly committed to one variety or another of structural-functionalism. But in the same way that Paretian theory had been subjected to critical appraisal during the 1930s, so functionalism, after its widespread acceptance, underwent continuous scrutiny both by sociologists and by philosophers of science;[1] and just as functionalism had been introduced as a way of avoiding the defects of prior work, so exchange theory emerged, in turn, as an attempt to remedy the perceived deficiencies of functionalism. Use of the notion of exchange had not been confined to critics of functionalism, but had been shared even by those most committed to the functional framework. For example, where the functional conceptual scheme was elaborated most comprehensively, as in Parsons' work, an increasingly important role had been assigned to the concept of exchange; and, as can be seen in Merton's analyses, where functionalism was more concerned with accounting for concrete phenomena the notion of social exchange had often been implied. But, despite this tendency for the idea of social exchange to recur in functional analyses, it necessarily remained a supplementary rather than a central concept. Functional analysis was so intricately organized around the concept of social function that its adherents necessarily failed to develop all the theoretical implications of the idea of social exchange. As a consequence, explicit exchange theory—that is, the theoretical framework which uses the notion of exchange as its central organizing principle—was eventually formulated only by those openly critical of functionalism.

Exchange theory, as seen in the work of Homans and Blau, did not, of course, involve a rejection of the whole functional framework, any more than functionalism required the total rejection of Pareto's approach. It was, none the less, an important change of emphasis within the functional tradition and a change which reintroduced certain central features of the Paretian strategy. Homans began by challenging the basic functionalist assumption that sociology must for the time being concentrate on various kinds of theoretical preparation. Like Pareto, Homans maintained that the fundamental purpose of theoretical construction must be to provide explanations and that theories must be formulated with this goal constantly in mind. He claimed that the functionalists, having recognized certain valid difficulties facing any attempt to construct extensive explanatory schemes, had reacted unjustifiably by retreating altogether from the basic task of explaining the social world. Homans was convinced that, although functional analysis might be able to provide simplified descriptions, it could not produce those explanations which are the final justification for any theory. According to this view, functionalism had become a hindrance to the proper development of sociological theory and an alternative was required which would restore concern with the construction of an explanatory theoretical system. Once Homans had repudiated the idea that sociological analysis must at present concentrate on preparatory work within a functional framework, he found it possible to turn to that principle of exchange which had been developed extensively in psychology and which already underlay, in practice, so much sociological thinking. Using this principle, he attempted to construct a deductive system along lines broadly similar to those envisaged by Pareto.

Blau has so far made two contributions to the development of exchange theory. In the first place, he has brought together much disparate research capable of formulation in terms of social exchange. He has also attempted to extend the framework so that it covers not only such areas as social control and social differentiation, which have always been examined intensively by functionalists, but also such phenomena as power and radical social change which both

Homans and the functionalists have tended to avoid. In the course of extending the conceptual scope of exchange analysis, Blau, unlike Homans, has come to include much that is indistinguishable from functionalism. Nevertheless, basic differences in theoretical perspective remain. For instance, in its concern with 'causal explanation' rather than 'functional analysis' exchange theory more closely resembles the approach adopted by Pareto. Similarly, where functionalism tends to *assume* the existence of complex social systems and to study how units within the system influence its stability or development, exchange analysis is concerned to show, in a way reminiscent of Pareto, how such complex structures *emerge* out of networks of simple transactions. Furthermore, both Pareto and the exchange theorists differ from the proponents of functional analysis in regarding psychological factors as the true 'sociological universals'. Exchange theory, having explicitly adopted social exchange as its organizing principle in order to remedy the deficiencies of functionalism without resurrecting those of Paretian theory, has developed a distinct type of analysis which, however, combines selected facets of both its predecessors.

Perhaps the most important resemblance between Blau's version of exchange theory and functional analysis is its theoretical strategy. For Blau abandons Homans' attempt to construct a systematic deductive system and reverts to the Parsonian strategy of preparing the way for a genuine theory of society. But Blau's use of this strategy is no more successful than that of Parsons. Indeed, I shall argue that none of the strategies examined in this study give clear evidence of theoretical improvement and that, consequently, the search for the correct strategy continues. In the last chapter, therefore, I shall examine the various approaches used by the theorists included in this study as the basis for a discussion of the proper strategy for sociological theory.

Before proceeding with the analysis, certain of its limitations should be mentioned. In the first place, although the theories to be discussed are presented in temporal sequence, my main concern is to show how each strategy produces a particular theoretical scheme with specific defects and also how each scheme and its defects provide a point of departure for subsequent theoretical development. Consequently, no attempt is made to specify *all* the intellectual sources from which the theorists under study have drawn their ideas. Secondly, although the approach adopted is necessarily critical, viewing as it does each theory as a response to the deficiencies of prior theory, no attempt is made to offer 'complete' assessments. Instead, attention is focused on those inadequacies closely associated with each theorist's strategy and directly relevant to the reaction of his successors. Finally, it is not argued that all theoretical

INTRODUCTION

development in sociology takes a dialectical form. No attempt is made to investigate the wider relevance of the thesis put forward here solely in relation to the development of specific theories of functionalism and exchange.

2 A general theory of society: Pareto

I

Human societies are studied by a wide variety of disciplines, most of which attend in detail to a limited range of social phenomena. In Pareto's view, sociology differs from these specialized disciplines in being concerned with all societies in their entirety. Thus the central task of sociology is to compile a broad synthesis of knowledge about human society. Pareto does not expect all sociologists to be directly and continuously involved in constructing this synthesis. But his own predilection lies in this direction and, as a result, he takes as his goal the formulation of a comprehensive or general theory of society.

For Pareto such a theory must be scientific—that is, it must be based upon direct experience and observation of relevant data and must link together, with consistent logic, a wide range of established social facts. A theory of society must map accurately the general contours of the social world. This does not mean, however, that there can be only one correct map. The concepts through which we view society are, in Pareto's opinion, arbitrary constructs in the sense that different conceptual schemes and theories can fit the facts equally well. He makes little attempt, therefore, to build a conceptual apparatus which is 'exactly right' for the analysis of social life. He suggests instead that our main concern must be to *use* our concepts to formulate theoretical systems which explain and predict an extensive range of social facts. As Pareto himself puts it: 'All sciences have advanced when, instead of quarrelling over first principles, people have considered results.'[1] Concepts and theories can be regarded as adequate in so far as they generate accurate explanations and predictions of empirical phenomena.

The disciplines which have been most successful in producing the kind of results which Pareto prefers are such physical sciences as astronomy and physics. He chooses, therefore, to construct a general sociology using these disciplines as his model. The 'theory of the solar system' provides an example of what he has in mind. The basic components of this theory are certain facts based on experience and observation; in this instance the facts are provided by a multitude of specific statements about observed relationships between sun and planets. These empirical statements are summarized in a smaller number of more abstract propositions; for example, the law that in equal time planets sweep out equal areas around the sun. These in turn are subsumed under even more abstract principles, the most fundamental of which is that of universal gravitation. Such a theoretical system is arrived at, Pareto argues, primarily by induction—that is, statements of observed fact come first and are then summarized in the form of abstract laws. However, although Pareto believes that theories are produced inductively, he stresses that, when complete, they constitute deductive systems which can be tested by deducing entirely new low-level empirical propositions, as well as by deducing and thereby explaining known phenomena. If theoretical predictions are verified, as when an unknown but predicted planet is subsequently observed, the theory can be regarded as further validated. But if, in contrast, predictions are inaccurate some theoretical reformulation is required.

These theoretical goals and their accompanying theoretical strategy have, in Pareto's view, been firmly established by the advanced physical sciences and must be accepted by all would-be sciences, such as sociology. Sociological theory must, therefore, proceed along the following lines: the great diversity of social facts must first be grouped into classes on the basis of observed similarities. After this any regular relationships between the various classes of facts must be established. These social uniformities should then be summarized in the form of sociological laws, which, in turn, should be brought under more general summarizing principles. Any one theory formulated in this way will have been stated within the limits of a particular set of concepts. Because conceptual schemes are partly conventional, it may be possible to apply several theories to the known facts. The worth of rival theories can, however, be judged, as in the physical sciences, by reference to the theories' simplicity, the range of facts covered and the capacity to predict previously unobserved relationships:

> Social facts are the elements of our study. Our first effort will be to classify them for the purpose of attaining the one and only objective we have in view; the discovery, namely, of uniformities (laws) in the relations between

them. When we have so classified kindred facts, a certain number of uniformities will come to the surface by induction; and after going a good distance along that primarily inductive path, we shall turn to another where more room will be found for deduction. So we shall verify the uniformities to which induction has carried us, give them a less empirical, more theoretical form, and see just what their implications are, just what picture they give of society. . . .[2] Since no theory absolutely commands acceptance, of the theories among which we are free to select we shall prefer the one that diverges least from the facts of the past, which best enables us to foresee the facts of the future, and which, in addition, embraces the greatest number of facts.[3]

The predictions and explanations generated by sociological theory should refer unambiguously to the social world. If our theories are to achieve this kind of scientific clarity, we must ensure that our concepts are clearly linked to observable phenomena. As we have seen, the actual scope of a concept is, in Pareto's view, the product of an arbitrary decision and relatively unimportant. However, once the meaning of a concept has been established it must be referred consistently to the same class of facts. Only if theoretical propositions regularly relate the same aspects of the empirical world will they provide reliable explanations and predictions. But even if our theory does produce reliable results its scope must always remain limited. Scientific explanations involve formulating laws which summarize repeated events. History, however, is made up of events which in their totality are unique and, therefore, inexplicable in scientific terms. Consequently, a scientific theory of society will always exclude a residue of unexplained and perhaps inexplicable social facts. In the initial stages of theory construction this residue is bound to be large. Pareto accepts that his general theory of society will begin as no more than a crude approximation to the complex realities of human history. In his opinion, however, there is no reason to doubt that the methods applied so fruitfully in the physical sciences will, in the long run, yield similar results for sociology.

Despite his guarded optimism about the eventual success of scientific methods in sociology, Pareto recognizes that two fundamental and related difficulties hinder their application. The first is that of unravelling an immensely complex network of empirical relationships. The second is the sociologists' inability to measure important variables. Lack of measurement is particularly inconvenient because Pareto believes that complex data are best analysed by the use of simultaneous equations, as in physics and astronomy. A theory which uses differential equations avoids dealing with complicated causal chains. It enables the theorist to regard the area under study as a network or *system* of interrelated elements. At any one point in time, all factors within the system can be taken to be linked together in a manner described by the equations. If certain variables are measured, it is possible, by fitting their values into the equations, to deduce the values of other variables without tracing complicated patterns of cause and effect. Pareto is convinced that this method would be specially useful in sociology, owing to the excessive complexity of its data. However, the method is applicable only where the elements within the system can be measured accurately and consistently; and unfortunately quantification of the variables regarded as significant by most sociological theorists, including those stressed by Pareto, has proved impossible. Thus the one eminently suitable means of describing complex sociological data is not available. As a consequence, Pareto is forced, at this preliminary stage in his theoretical work, to depart radically from the methods of the advanced physical sciences and to devise an alternative approach which he calls the analysis of 'cycles of interdependence'.

Let us assume that any society can be viewed as an isolated system made up of just four interrelated and variable factors A, B, C and D. We can examine the state of this social system at any given moment by investigating four sets of actions and reactions. We can study how:

1   A is acting upon B, C, D.
2   B is acting upon A, C, D.
3   C is acting upon A, B, D.
4   D is acting upon A, B, C.

When all four cycles have been compiled we have a complete description of causal relationships within the social system. This analysis is not, however, quantitative. It can tell us, at least in principle, whether a change in factor A will produce changes in factors B, C, and D; but it cannot measure these variations and cannot be expressed in terms of simultaneous equations. Pareto has accepted that our inability to measure sociological variables will force us to engage in laborious qualitative examination of causal networks. This is the price we must pay for recognizing that societies constitute systems of interdependent elements in exactly the same way as physical systems. Pareto suggests that most prior sociological theories have oversimplified by regarding one class of social facts as 'cause' and the remainder as 'effects'. This is true, for example, of that variety of Marxism which sees economic factors as the sole determinants of social structures. Undoubtedly economic elements are important influences upon the general form of society. But, suggests Pareto, the causal relationships operate in both directions. The various classes of non-economic factors are themselves interdependent and are all capable of affecting the economic sphere. By basing sociological analysis on the examination of cycles of interdependence we can avoid the simplistic assumptions of mono-causal theories and make full allowance for the complex causal relationships which exist within human societies. The introduction of cycles of interdependence as a method of sociological investigation enables Pareto to retain the conception of society as a *system* in which all elements are interdependent, despite his having to reject the kind of mathematical formulation which accompanies systems-analysis in the physical sciences.

Pareto's adoption of the concept 'social system' leads him to take over one further important conception from the physical sciences —namely, that of 'equilibrium'. The equations of mechanics tend to be applied to systems which, like the solar system, are in equilibrium. Such physical systems are said to be in equilibrium when any 'artificial' change introduced into the system from outside would engender a reaction tending to bring the system back to its original state. These artificial changes do not normally occur. They are merely hypothetical changes, introduced by the physicist into his equations to show that the elements in the system are interdependent in such a way that they act to minimize change. Pareto suggests that social systems often have this same tendency to maintain equilibrium states by reducing the impact of external influences and illustrates his point with some rather general examples:

> Somewhat similar to the artificial changes mentioned are those occasional changes which result from some element that suddenly appears, has its influence for a brief period upon a system, occasioning some slight disturbance in the state of equilibrium, and then passes away. [For example,] short wars, epidemics. . . .[4]

At the same time Pareto puts forward a more formal account of equilibrium.

> The real state . . . of the system is determined by its conditions. Let us imagine some modification in its form is induced artificially. At once a reaction will take place, tending to restore the changing form to its original state. . . . If that were not the case, the form, with its normal changes, would not be determined but would be a mere matter of chance.[5]
> . . . society cannot of itself assume any form other than form X [its real state], and . . . if it were made artificially

13

to vary from that form, it would tend to resume it; for otherwise its form would not be entirely determined, as was assumed, by the elements considered.[6]

The formal definition of equilibrium appears to be no more than a restatement of the theoretical assumption that the elements within a social system are interdependent and that the relationships between them will consequently determine the system's structure or form. But if we combine the definition with the more concrete examples we can see that, for Pareto, societies are in equilibrium when their component elements are interdependent *in such a way that* departures from the existing state, or the existing line of development, automatically generate responses tending to limit or control these departures.

Equilibrium analysis is used by the advanced sciences when a set of equations can be formulated showing what compensating changes would occur if specific system values were altered from outside. These equations enable the physicist to describe in a precise manner both the equilibrium state of the system and the mechanisms which work to maintain that state. Pareto is clearly unable to supply such conclusive evidence for the suitability of equilibrium analysis in sociology. In the quotation above he does refer to instances where societies have successfully withstood the impact of disrupting influences. But these are crude examples of *actual* departures from equilibrium rather than mathematical expressions of *hypothetical* changes in system structure. It would in fact be just as easy to cite instances where apparently trivial events have sparked off massive structural change—for example, Sarajevo and the First World War—and to argue that social systems must be assumed to be in continual disequilibrium. There is undoubtedly an enormous gap between the physicist's demonstration of the extent to which the elements within a physical system maintain its structure against hypothetical encroachment from outside and Pareto's assumption that, because some societies recover from disturbances, social systems in general can be regarded as self-maintaining. Pareto introduces the idea of social equilibrium not because it is required by the facts, but because he is convinced that social and physical systems are, at a general level, identical and amenable to the same broad type of theoretical treatment.

So far we have been concerned with Pareto's theoretical prologue. We have examined his theoretical aims and his theoretical strategy; and we have seen that he has come not only to model his theory on those of the physical sciences but also to think of societies in terms of a direct analogue with physical systems. Systems in mechanics are composed of interdependent physical units the relations between which can be described by sets of differential equations formulated as deductive theoretical systems. Human societies for Pareto constitute another type of system composed of interdependent social units. The relations between the elements of social systems can also be described by deductive theories which, however, owing to difficulties of complexity and measurement, must be formulated in terms of cycles of interdependence instead of mathematical equations. Both types of system tend to achieve an internal balance of forces which makes them resistant to external pressures. The tendency of physical systems to self-maintenance can be demonstrated by introducing hypothetical changes into the equations describing the state of the system. Although social equilibrium is more difficult to demonstrate in practice, its existence must be inferred from our assumption that societies are determinate systems. Thus the differences between physical and social systems, and between the methods used in their investigation, are differences in degree, but not in kind. That they exist at all is a result primarily of the extreme complexity of sociological data.

This model of society and its accompanying theoretical assumptions are open to criticism at several points. However, Pareto is emphatic that concepts, methodological principles and so on can be judged only by their results. If we accept this argument then we must delay evaluation until we have followed through his analysis of the social system and gained some idea of just how productive Pareto's theoretical strategy is.

II

Pareto's first substantive theoretical problem is that of deciding which elements to include in his analysis of the social system. He has already stressed the complexity of the influences which determine the general state of society. He divides these influences into three classes:

1   Geographical and geological factors, e.g. soil, climate.
2   External social influences, i.e. influences from other societies and the society under investigation at some earlier period in time.
3   Internal social factors.

For purposes of an initial crude analysis, in order to make his immensely complex problems manageable, Pareto excludes the first two classes. However, sociological analysis remains very complicated even when we consider only those factors which are operating within one society at one point in time. For example, Pareto mentions on various occasions such elements as economic conditions, customs, law, religions, intellectual conditions, scientific knowledge, technological capacity, level of education, and so on. Out of this complexity he selects the following factors:

A   Residues
B   Derivations
C   Interests
D   Social heterogeneity

These four elements correspond to the factors A, B, C, and D discussed above in relation to cycles of interdependence and are to be studied by the application of that method. Unlike the highly abstract conceptions of social system and equilibrium, these concepts are based upon an inductive survey of social facts and are designed to reflect in a more concrete fashion the social world around us. Pareto is aware that concentration upon four factors involves a drastic simplification. He claims, however, that it is justified because most other influences upon the general state of society make themselves felt by affecting one or more of the variables he has chosen to stress. We must therefore examine these concepts and how Pareto arrives at their formulation.

We have seen that Pareto is committed to constructing a theory based upon an impartial examination of social facts. These facts, however, are not easily accessible to the sociologist. In the first place, geographically and historically distant societies are not directly observable. Furthermore, even within our immediate social milieu, we have no *direct* access to the states of mind which underlie human action. Pareto attempts to overcome these difficulties by making use of the verbal statements with which the members of all societies have tried to interpret their physical and social environments.

> Current in any given group of people are a number of propositions, descriptive, preceptive or otherwise.... Such propositions, combined by logical or pseudo-logical nexuses and amplified with factual narrations of various sorts, constitute theories ... the image of social activity is stamped on the majority of such propositions and theories, and often it is through them alone that we manage to gain some knowledge of the forces which are at work in society—that is, of the tendencies and inclinations of human beings.[7]

People's 'theories', whether moral, metaphysical, religious, or whatever, are to be studied to provide insight into those human 'tendencies and inclinations' which determine the general form of society. Some of these theories are scientific. They combine established facts in a rational manner. But in Pareto's view such theories are far outnumbered by those in which the facts are suspect or the reasoning specious. The predominance of such non-logical theories, which he documents with many examples, indicates to Pareto that the investigation of non-logical thinking must be our first concern. He therefore undertakes an inductive survey of non-logical or non-scientific theories in the hope that this will provide a means of understanding non-logical conduct.

An examination of the history of human thought leads Pareto to suggest that all non-scientific theories contain an element which remains constant over long periods of time as well as a more variable element. For example, although in all societies we find expressed the idea that people should be willing to die for their country, the reasons given to justify this sentiment vary from one group to another. In ancient Rome it was 'sweet to die for one's country'. In Japan it was a matter of honour. In classical Greece it was the responsibility of every able-bodied citizen. In the West today self-sacrifice is often justified on the grounds that it is needed to 'save our country from the threat of Communist domination'. If we ignore the variable element of justification contained in these theories we are left with a constant 'residue', which in this case expresses support of extreme patriotism. According to Pareto's interpretation, the constancy of this verbal residue indicates the existence of a corresponding sentiment which is common to large numbers of people and which changes very slowly, if at all. Pareto examines many such linguistic expressions and their accompanying sentiments. He concludes that it is the sentiments which generate both actual conduct and verbal expression. Thus what we actually *do* is to fight and die in defence of our national frontiers, and we do it because of an internal impulse. The *reasons* we give to explain our actions vary widely from one society to another and are, therefore, Pareto argues, largely irrelevant to actual conduct. Pareto calls these rationalizations of non-rational actions 'derivations'. They are essentially a by-product of man's need for at least the appearance of rationality in human affairs.

Corresponding to his classification of theories into logico-experimental and non-logico-experimental, or scientific and non-scientific, Pareto introduces a classification of human actions. *Logical action* is action which is directed toward the attainment of a goal and which, in the view of an informed observer, uses efficient means to attain that goal. Logical action is confined on the whole to the spheres of scientific and economic endeavour. It is therefore already studied in large part by the science of economics, and Pareto consequently pays it little explicit attention in his analysis of social systems. *Non-logical action* refers to all human actions which are not logical actions. Much non-logical action will be rational for the subject being investigated, but non-logical for the observer. For example, the primitive praying to his god for rain presumably believes in the existence of a god and that the god is amenable to persuasion. Subjectively his supplications are rational; they are perceived as likely to produce realization of his goal. To an observer concerned only with concrete facts, however, there is no evidence that the god exists or that appeals to him have any effect on the occurrence of rain. The act of praying for rain is not based on a rational appraisal of relevant facts, but is merely an expression of the primitive's hopes and fears. It is, in Pareto's terms, non-logical:

> Logical actions are at least in large part results of processes of reasoning. Non-logical actions originate chiefly in definite psychic states, sentiments, subconscious feelings, and the like. It is the province of psychology to investigate such psychic states. Here we start with them as data of fact, without going beyond that.[8]

The central conclusion of Pareto's historical survey is that human conduct is primarily non-logical—that is, determined by internal impulses. Strictly speaking, the term 'residue' refers solely to the verbal expressions of these impulses or sentiments, but he uses it loosely to cover in addition the impulses themselves and the actions which they generate:

> The residues must not be confused with the sentiments or instincts to which they correspond. The residues are manifestations of sentiments and instincts just as the rising of the mercury in a thermometer is a manifestation of the rise in temperature. Only elliptically and for the sake of brevity do we say that residues, along with appetites, interests, etc., are the main factors determining the social equilibrium . . . the completed statements would be: 'The sentiments or instincts that correspond to residues, along with those corresponding to appetites, interests, etc., are the main factors in determining the social equilibrium.'[9]

When these sentiments are expressed in words they are usually accompanied by rationalizing 'derivations'. Derivations *can* influence behaviour, but only marginally. Thus, as most actions are seen as non-logical, the concept of 'residue' must be, for Pareto, the fulcrum of any sociological theory. Because this concept is so important, we must briefly examine Pareto's classification of residues. It is as a classification of human sentiments rather than their verbal formulations that the following categories are important for Pareto's sociological analysis. In the following outline all sub-categories, of which there are many, have been omitted:

1 *Residues of Combinations.* 'Figuring as a residue in vast numbers of phenomena is an inclination to combine certain things with certain other things.'[10] People act as a result of this residue to combine like with unlike, rare things with unusual events, true theories with beneficial results, etc. There is a general belief in the efficacy of combinations which is due, not to rational judgment, but to a basic human propensity.

2 *Persistence of Aggregates.* This category refers to the tendency for beliefs and sentiments to become customary and to persist through time. Once certain states of mind have become linked together and established within a human group, 'an instinct very often comes into play that tends with varying energy to prevent the things so combined from being disjoined, and which, if disintegration cannot be avoided, strives to dissemble it by preserving the outer physiognomy of the aggregate. This instinct may be compared roughly to mechanical inertia: it tends to resist the movement imparted by other instincts.'[11] Pareto illustrates these two residues by suggesting that stable Rome was characterized by persistence of aggregates, whereas the instability of Athens was a result of a preponderance of combinations.

3 *Need for Activity.* Pareto suggests that human beings have a strong, innate tendency to express powerful sentiments in activity of one form or another. In some instances the resulting actions bear no relation to the sentiments involved, but simply satisfy the need for action. Many religious ecstasies, dances, chants and so on can be explained by reference to this residue.

4 *Sociability.* There are many sub-categories within this class of residues. Pareto suggests that men tend to have strong needs to belong to specific groups, to receive the approval of others, to conform to the expectations of others, and so on. He argues that the 'residue finds expression in virtually pure form in the temporary uniformities imposed by fashion',[12] which arise out of the fundamental need of human beings to imitate each other.

5 *Integrity of the Individual and His Possessions.* Despite mankind's need for social relations, individual men tend to have a strong desire to defend their own personality and possessions against the depredations of others. These residues are important in maintaining social equilibrium because disturbances in equilibrium are experienced by each individual as threats to his current satisfactions. Thus residues of individual integrity motivate people to react against disturbing social influences.

6 *Sexuality.* Pareto's evidence for the influence of sexual factors in social life is drawn from 'theories' rather than from direct observation of conduct. Thus he can classify sexual sentiments only in so far as they enter verbal statements and are subject to the

usual human tendency to rationalize. He writes that 'mere sexual appetite, though powerfully active in the human race, is no concern of ours here.... We are interested in it only in so far as it influences theories, modes of thinking . . . as a residue'.[13]

So far in this section we have examined two of the four classes of factors which influence the general form of society—namely, residues and derivations. We must now turn to interests and social heterogeneity. The nearest that Pareto comes to a definition of interests is in the following statement:

> Individuals and communities are spurred by instinct and reason to acquire possession of material goods that are useful—or merely pleasurable—for purposes of living as well as to seek consideration and honours. Such impulses, which may be called 'interests', play in the mass a very important part in determining social equilibrium.[14]

Although this definition indicates that interests are essentially states of mind which drive men to strive for the maintenance of life, the attainment of pleasure and happiness, and the acquisition of respect and honour, Pareto uses the term loosely to refer also to the actions undertaken in the attempt to realize such goals as well as the goals themselves. It is not clear whether Pareto wishes to make a conceptual distinction between interests and residues because they operate in different ways or simply because 'the mass of interests falls in very considerable part within the purview of the science of economics'[15] and, in consequence, have already been subjected to extensive theoretical analysis. There do, however, seem to be definite differences between these two sources of conduct. Whereas residues are internal impulses which drive us in directions which we try subsequently to justify through the use of derivations, interests appear to involve a much more rational balancing of means to achieve goals as yet unrealized. We can be fairly certain of the nature of residues because Pareto discusses them separately and in great detail. Our account of interests must be more tentative because he offers no systematic examination apart from that implied in the final substantive analysis of cycles of interdependence. Nevertheless, it is clear that the conception of interests in particular, and logical action in general, pictures man as adapting to his environment so as to achieve preconceived goals, as well as simply acting out impulses. But it is also clear from the following statement that for Pareto the goal-orientated and relatively rational facet of human conduct is not the sole nor even the most important factor determining the character of social life.

> Given certain creatures who have appetites or tastes

[interests] and who encounter certain obstacles in their attempt to satisfy them, what is going to happen? The question is answered by pure economics, and it is a science of great scope, owing to the no scant variety in tastes and the enormously great variety of obstacles. The results that it achieves form an integral and not unimportant part of sociology, but only a part; and in certain situations it may even be a slight and negligible part, a part at any rate that must be taken in conjunction with other parts to yield the picture of what happens in reality.[16]

The three elements of the social system examined above appear to be firmly located within the individual members of society. The sentiments corresponding to residues are states of individuals' minds. Interests are either impulses within the individual or the envisaged satisfactions which guide his conduct. Derivations are more like a social product than the other two, varying as they do from group to group, but they also have the least impact upon the social equilibrium. The fourth element, social heterogeneity, although dependent on individual characteristics, is more nearly a dimension of the social system itself.

Pareto regards it as obvious that people are 'physically, morally, and intellectually different'[17] and that this fact is highly significant for the operation of any society. In order to make some allowance for it within his scheme, he introduces the terms 'élite' and 'non-élite'. A society's social élite is defined as that group of persons who have attained the highest indices of achievement in their branch of activity; for example, cabinet ministers, chess champions, royalty and mistresses of royalty are all members of the élite. Although this rather broad notion may prove useful for certain kinds of sociological analysis, Pareto suggests that most aspects of society are moulded primarily by that small section of the élite in which political power is vested. Thus the social élite must itself be divided into two groupings: on the one hand we have a *governing élite*, 'comprising individuals who directly or indirectly play some considerable part in government', and, on the other hand, 'a *non-governing élite*, comprising the rest'.[18] For Pareto the character of the governing élite, or, more specifically, the kind of residues to be found among that élite, is the most important single factor in determining the general state of society. It is by no means the only factor, however, and the state of any social system can be described only by interpreting systematically the relationships between residues, derivations, interests and social heterogeneity in terms of cycles of interdependence.

III

Pareto's theoretical scheme is designed to furnish a broad account of the operation of human societies. In achieving this central theoretical goal, however, he also formulates analyses which are partial in the sense that they apply to a limited number of societies or to a restricted sphere of social life. We shall now examine one such middle-range theory before moving on to the general theory of society. Pareto's 'theory of industrial protection' is presented in terms of cycles of interdependence. The analysis begins with the assumption that a policy of industrial protection has been introduced within a given society. Such protection falls under the heading of 'interests' because it involves a change in the means used to further economic goals. The initial purely economic effect of this kind of policy is to destroy wealth by diminishing international trade and by bringing about a less efficient international division of labour. However, the full impact of industrial protection can be understood only if we consider the whole range of social consequences. To do this we must examine how:

1. interests influence residues, derivations and social heterogeneity;
2. social heterogeneity influences residues, derivations and interests;
3. residues influence derivations, interests and social heterogeneity;
4. derivations influence residues, interests and social heterogeneity.

Although the change in interests brought about by the policy of industrial protection does not affect residues directly, for the latter remain stable over long periods, it does alter the distribution of residues in society; in other words, it changes the character of social heterogeneity. Owing to reduced economic competition from abroad, opportunities are opened up for those members of society with technical and financial abilities and for those businessmen and politicians capable of manœuvring protectionist favours. Those who rush to take advantage of such opportunities tend to have an excess of Class I residues—that is, residues of combinations. Such men rise to positions of affluence and power, while those in whom residues of group aggregates are strong, bound as they are to the old ways and unable to scheme with the mental agility of combinations-men, are pushed down the social scale. Thus there occurs within the economic and governing élites a concentration of persons highly endowed with sentiments corresponding to residues of combinations. This change in social heterogeneity reacts back upon the sphere of interests as the whole country is influenced by its élite towards greater concern with economic success. For example, there is marked alteration in derivations as new economic theories are formulated which justify industrial protection and which facilitate the rise of the new men to positions of eminence. If this situation persists for a long time the sentiments common throughout society may change, producing a permanent redistribution in favour of those associated with residues of combinations.

This cycle of actions and reactions is unavoidably described as if it were a sequence of events, although many of the relationships involved are in fact contemporaneous. The impression of temporal sequence is created partly by the need to describe in turn selected sets of interactions, instead of formulating one inclusive series of simultaneous equations. Nevertheless, Pareto claims that the effects of introducing a protectionist economic policy, or, indeed, the effects of any major social change in the social system, do tend to accumulate over time:

> ... through a sequence of actions and reactions, an equilibrium is established in which economic production and class-circulation become more intense, and the composition of the governing class profoundly modified.
>
> The increase in economic production may be great enough to exceed the destruction of wealth caused by protection, so that, sum total, protection may yield a profit and not a loss in wealth.... If no counter-forces stood in the way, and the cycle of actions and reactions were to go on indefinitely, economic protection and its effects ought to become progressively greater; and that is what is actually observable in many countries during the nineteenth century. But as a matter of fact counter-forces do develop, and increasingly so.[19]

An irreversible and cumulative industrial expansion would sooner or later disrupt society. It would create a situation of social disequilibrium. There are, however, mechanisms which automatically work to prevent this degree of imbalance. Thus movement into the élite, although fostered by protection, does not continue indefinitely in one direction, but is modified by the very nature of the elements which make up the social system. Capable men of the 'sturdy impulsive type, richly endowed with instincts of group-persistence', resist economic and political exploitation and the rapid changes which appear to them to be transforming society. In due course they form groups organized to prevent social change and to replace the existing élite with men of their own kind. At this point Pareto's analysis of industrial protection begins to merge with his general theory of society, to which we must now turn.

This résumé of Pareto's analysis of industrial protection gives some indication of how societies can be investigated by means of cycles of interdependence. Pareto's advocacy of the inductive method would seem to require him, before constructing his general theory, to examine numerous societies intensively and systematically in terms of such cycles. Yet in practice he does not proceed in this way. After having examined the effects of industrial protection in several specific societies, as well as in general, he moves immediately to the general dynamics which mould societies. Clearly this approach makes his task much easier as well as, perhaps, less convincing. In addition, as in the middle-range theory of economic protection, Pareto further simplifies his problems by including in the general theory only two of the six classes of residues—namely, those of combinations and persistence of aggregates. He suggests that the analysis will remain adequate because these two types of residues account for the great majority of social actions, without appearing to recognize that this assertion seems to belie his formulation of such a complex classification of residues. Nevertheless, the reduction of the number of factors to be considered does ensure that the core of the theory is simple and easily summarized.

Pareto begins his general analysis of social systems by examining the distribution of persons characterized by the two classes of residues within the governing élite of a hypothetical society. If the governing élite is composed predominantly of 'combinations-men', called 'foxes' for short, their actions will display strong tendencies toward innovation, inventiveness, scheming, cunning and the use of fraud. This is so simply because the sentiments corresponding to such residues impel men to act in this fashion. On the other hand, if the governing élite are 'persistence of aggregates men', called 'lions' for short, their actions will display stability, steadfastness, directness, traditionalism and willingness to accept open conflict and the use of force. These two types of governing élite embody the two basic principles of government, force and fraud. The ruling élite can govern either by coercing its subordinates into subjection or by tricking them into submission. Which principle the élite chooses will depend solely upon the residues of its members. If a governing élite could be found which combined recourse to force and fraud at the same time, political stability could be attained and thereby permanent stability of the whole social system. But the character of residues makes such a combination impossible. Men who are direct, reliable and of unquestioning faith cannot also be indirect, scheming and fraudulent. Because these two opposite sets of characteristics cannot be merged within one governing élite, final social stability is unattainable. Either the ruling élite is composed of men with versatile minds but reluctant to use force, or it is made up of men quite willing to use force but unable to adapt quickly to a changing social environment, or it is undergoing a transition from one stage to the other. Thus changes within the governing élite are cyclical, as the lions give way to the foxes, who, in turn, are replaced by the lions.

The élite cycle can be most conveniently described if we start with the accession to power of the lions. These men are conservative and tend to be committed to some ultimate political or religious ideal. They are also tough-minded and forceful. Their success is often achieved through violence, which is used to remove the foxes, who tend to become weak and irresolute in the face of this kind of political action. Force is useful, often essential, in the struggle for power, but it cannot be made the basis of constructive adaptation to changing political circumstances. Sooner or later, therefore, the lions find it necessary to recruit foxes from the non-governing élite. Once within the élite, the foxes use their fertile minds to further their influence. At the same time, the lions become increasingly corrupted by power. Their faith in ultimate values declines and their willingness to use force atrophies. Gradually the governing élite becomes an élite of foxes, speculating, manipulating and seeking satisfaction through self-interest rather than realization of any social or religious ideal. The cunning of the foxes blocks opportunities for upward social mobility into the governing élite on the part of the lions, who, as their frustration mounts, come to see revolution as the only viable strategy. Cohesive opposition groups are formed which formulate ideologies justifying their opposition and their use of force. This situation is fundamentally unstable and in due course reverts back to stage one—that is, the accession to power by the lions—and the whole cycle begins again.

Pareto's examination of the general form of society is in large measure devoted to an extensive analysis of the political cycles outlined above. After outlining the dynamics of the political sphere, he describes the economic concomitants of the various types of government. He suggests, for example, that the foxes create economic opportunities for an entrepreneurial type whose strong sentiments of combinations stimulate economic innovations and speculation. In contrast, the conservative policies of the lions tend to favour the *rentiers*—that is, those who derive their incomes from sources other than speculation. Thus social life is described initially as emanating throughout society from a political centre. As government undergoes its cyclical transformations, so the rest of society is drawn in its train. And as the élite is transformed, so change percolates through the whole social structure. But this is only one aspect of the total picture. Pareto stresses that causal interdependence in societies is highly complex and, as we have seen in the analysis of industrial protection, he accepts that economic developments can, and usually do, react back upon the political sphere as they influence the circulation élites:

> Periods of rapid increase in economic prosperity are favourable to speculators, who grow rich and win places in the governing class if they do not already belong to it, but unfavourable to people who live on incomes more or less fixed. . . . It follows that when periods of rapid increase in economic prosperity are more the rule than periods of depression, the governing class gets richer and richer in speculators, who contribute Class I residues to it in powerful dosage. . . . That change in the composition of the governing class tends to incline a people more and more to economic enterprise and to increase economic prosperity until new forces come into play and check the movement.[20]

These new forces—namely, the gradual organization of those with strong sentiments of group-persistence into protest groups—we have already examined. Once again the analysis has turned full circle. Wherever we begin our exposition of the general form of society we eventually return to our point of departure. Thus Pareto begins with the distribution of residues within the governing élite, not because it is the sole determinant of social change and stability, but because it is the most influential single factor within a complex network of interdependent social facts.

This completes the basic set of generalizations which, in Pareto's view, can be used to deduce and thereby explain many aspects of social life in all human societies. Pareto recognizes that these abstractions do not represent society in all its detailed richness. But this can never be achieved by any science of society. In fact, he argues, concern with sociological minutiae may well obscure the fundamental underlying uniformities. Thus the aim of sociology must be to abstract from social life 'ideal phenomena that are simpler, that we may so arrive at something more nearly constant than the complex and ever-shifting thing we have before us in the concrete'.[21] Pareto's investigations have led him to conclude that the 'ideal phenomena' represented by residues, derivations, interests and social heterogeneity can be used to provide a model of society which corresponds with an extensive range of historical facts. Yet, despite his belief that his description of the social system in these terms is firmly founded on social fact, it does retain a striking resemblance to the classical scientific view of physical systems. The resemblance between physical and social systems which was suggested in Pareto's theoretical prologue has simply been made more definite in the course of his substantive analysis of human societies.

The elements which make up physical systems are particles or bodies, such as planets. In social systems the units are individual persons whom Pareto sometimes refers to as the 'molecules' of the social system. Where particles have mass and velocity, individuals bear residues, interests, derivations and the resulting tendencies to action. In the same way that the general state of a physical system varies as its units change their relative positions, so the general state of a social system alters in line with the distribution of persons within the governing and non-governing élites. The movement of particles is controlled by a positive process of attraction and by a negative process of repulsion. Within social systems Class I and Class II residues are mutually exclusive. This provides the element of repulsion, the negative factor. But at the same time, carriers of both classes of residues strive to occupy positions in the governing élite. This corresponds to the force of attraction. In both types of system these opposing forces generate periodic fluctuations which permeate the whole system, yet which operate within specifiable limits. In the solar system, for example, once the underlying uniformities have been revealed, these cycles can be clearly perceived and accurately predicted. In the social system, although the situation is too complex to allow such a degree of theoretical precision, periodicities can be observed in the circulation of élites, in the economic cycle from depression to prosperity, and so on. External forces can temporarily disrupt these cycles in both kinds of system, but the internal balance of forces tends to reduce the impact of such outside influences and to return the system to its prior cycle.

IV

Pareto's theoretical strategy consists of five guiding principles: that sociological theory should be based on a wide-ranging and systematic review of empirical data; that concepts should be given clear empirical content; that, in order to cope with abundant and complex factual material, considerable selection, simplification and abstraction should be employed; that generalizations and statements of fact should be combined in a deductive system capable of providing an extensive range of explanations and predictions; and that certain conceptions and methods originating in physical science should be applied in the social sciences. The adequacy of Pareto's theory can be judged in relation to this strategy and the theoretical standards which it entails.[22]

Pareto undertakes an inductive survey in order to establish the character of the most important sociological variables and the broad relationships between them. In this way he produces a series of statements about residues, derivations, interests and social heterogeneity, which he then combines to deduce the dynamic processes which underlie social activity in all human societies. The purpose of the survey is to ensure that the theoretical generalizations are firmly supported by empirical evidence. Consequently, if the survey is at all suspect, the validity of the generalizations must be called in question. Pareto's survey is, in fact, far from satisfactory.

In the first place, Pareto's review of empirical data is neither comprehensive nor systematic; he merely cites a relatively small number of non-logical theories selected arbitrarily from the storehouse of human history. At the very least, then, Pareto's evidence is incomplete. Moreover, although Pareto is undoubtedly correct in arguing that we have access to verbal statements from a wide range of societies, and that, to this extent, theories are *convenient* sources of information, this does not make them good sociological material. Pareto uses the theories current in various groups because 'the image of social activity is stamped . . . on such theories'.[23] But the *way* in which theories reflect social activity will vary from one group to another. Pareto may well discount the fact that theories vary in accordance with their authors' cultural background and the audience for which they are intended, on the grounds that the variable element in theories is largely irrelevant to conduct. But he can hardly dismiss the fact that the theories which happen to be available to us from any one group may be entirely unrepresentative of the views held in that group. And if the theories which Pareto uses to probe the sentiments of group members *are* unrepresentative, then his inferences about sentiments are likely to be misleading. Without underestimating the difficulties of interpreting the information gathered by modern survey and observational techniques, it seems likely that the questionnaire and the random sample are required before we can even begin to claim knowledge of the distribution and relative importance of the sentiments operating in specific groups.[24] It is, of course, true that such techniques for collecting reliable and representative information had not been devised in Pareto's day; nor could they have been used, if available, to study the historical societies from which Pareto draws most of his material. But these considerations cannot influence our judgment of the adequacy of his data. We cannot regard as satisfactory an inductive survey which takes no steps to ensure that its data accurately represent the area under investigation.

From the outset Pareto emphasizes that the complexity of its subject-matter presents a major barrier to successful conceptualization and theory formulation in sociology. He attempts to overcome this difficulty in the first place by excluding from consideration whole classes of factors. For example, in the study of any one society, the impact of other societies is dismissed from consideration. The number of variables to be treated is further reduced by Pareto's policy of constructing his conceptual scheme in as general terms as possible. These tactics do, of course, provide one answer to the problem of complexity. But they can be adopted only at the cost of making concepts so broad that their empirical coverage is vague and scientific rigour put in jeopardy. Thus although some of Pareto's concepts are formulated clearly, they are usually supplemented by 'residual' or negatively defined concepts. For instance, whereas logical action is defined with care, non-logical action refers to all action other than logical action. Similarly, the non-governing élite is composed of all those who do not belong to the ruling élite. Such residual definitions, although simplifying the analysis of a complex social world, are inherently ambiguous.[25]

Even when Pareto tries to make *detailed* conceptual distinctions, as in his typology of residues, he seems unable to provide clear empirical referents. For instance, he includes fashion as an example of conduct arising primarily from residues of sociability. He offers no evidence to vindicate this classification apart from the unsupported statement that fashion is produced as people imitate each other and that imitation is one aspect of the social instinct.[26] We could claim just as convincingly, as long as we remain at the level of verbal assertion rather than empirical demonstration, that fashion should be included under combinations or sexual residues. For fashion may well channel unsatisfied sexual needs and it certainly involves the innovations by which residues of combinations are generally distinguished. The fact is that Pareto offers no unambiguous criteria for distinguishing between these categories of residues. Each class is so broadly defined that any one action can always be included under several headings.

In actual analysis Pareto avoids the difficulties of using his intricate yet imprecise system of classifications by considering only the two categories of combinations and persistence of aggregates. If the six classes of residues had clear empirical referents, then this reduction to two would leave noticeable gaps in Pareto's coverage of non-logical action. No such gaps appear in practice because Pareto is easily able to extend his elastic categories to cover effectively all possible human actions. Any act can be seen either as generating change or as promoting stability. If an act is of the former kind it can be seen as a product of residues of combinations; if of the latter type its source can be taken as group aggregates. Pareto stresses repeatedly that the concept 'residue' is central to his scheme and that, in the social world, residues are the most important influence on the general state of society. Yet his detailed classification of residues is ill-defined and the categories overlapping; and in formulating his explanatory generalizations he has simplified to such an extent that he needs to recognize only two types of human conduct.

If the criticisms levelled so far are valid and important we should find that Pareto fails to provide the results which he regards as the final criterion of scientific success. It cannot be denied that Pareto does offer a wide-ranging interpretation of social phenomena. However, this theoretical coverage is achieved, not through the rigour of Paretian theory, but because the scheme is so malleable that it can be moulded to fit and to 'explain' almost any range of facts. Let us examine how this is done.

> The following statement by Pareto has already been cited:
> ... when periods of rapid increase in economic prosperity are more the rule than periods of depression, the governing class gets richer and richer in speculators, who contribute Class I residues to it in powerful dosage.... That change in the composition of the governing class tends to incline a people more and more to economic enterprise....[27]

In this passage Pareto 'explains' some of the increase in economic activity generated during periods of prosperity by supposing that the proportion of combinations residues within the governing élite has also increased. The increase in Class I residues in the élite is seen as an immediate cause of the expansion of economic enterprise. However, the only evidence offered to support the claim that there has been an inflow of such residues is the increased economic activity of the governing class which the inflow of residues is, in fact, supposed to explain. If Pareto's explanation of economic expansion in terms of residues is to be acceptable he must provide some evidence of changes in residues which is *independent* of economic activity.[28]

The unintentional use of tautological statements in place of proper explanations[29] is common in sociology, and we shall meet with further examples in later chapters. It is, therefore, worth expressing this criticism of Pareto's analysis in more general form. If the occurrence of residue X (or any other factor X) is used to explain the presence of action Y, then evidence for the existence of X must be independent of action Y. In Pareto's scheme this requirement is seldom fulfilled. In most cases the *only* evidence offered of the existence of residue X is behaviour Y itself. Thus every instance of Y must logically, not empirically, be accompanied by X. Consequently, the proposition that residue X causes action Y can be neither verified nor falsified. It is independent of the empirical world and hence cannot be used to provide the kind of scientific explanation which Pareto himself advocates.

Owing to his tactics of selection, simplification and abstraction, Pareto creates a conceptual framework which lacks precise empirical content and which, consequently, is particularly liable to generate vacuous interpretations instead of genuine explanations. In view of these fundamental defects, it is not surprising that Pareto's scheme fails to produce the kind of predictions which play such an important role in the validation and modification of the physical sciences. One of the predictions which Pareto puts to the test is that social prosperity will be maximized in societies where residues of Classes I and II are balanced. This proposition is not the kind of rigorous inference by which he would, ideally, have preferred to test his general theory. Instead of an unambiguous deduction from theory, Pareto's theorem is no more than a rough implication of his analysis of the governing élite. Indeed, Pareto's own formulation of the theorem is so vague that it could not be clearly deduced from *any* theoretical premises. He presents it in the following words:

> When residues are functioning in a manner on the whole conducive to social prosperity, the advantage of proper proportions in them will be apparent in the long run.[30]

Pareto gives no clear criteria for judging what are the 'proper proportions' between residues nor any clarification of what constitutes 'social prosperity'. As a result he is free to vary the meaning of these terms with each example, thereby turning the statement effectively into a tautology. Yet the broad meaning of the theorem is clear enough. Pareto is arguing that effective government requires both innovation *and* stability. Any élite which has a great predominance of Class I residues will place too much reliance on change at the expense of stability. It will tend to squander its resources in its headlong drive for development, thereby failing to achieve the maximum level of social benefit. In contrast, a government with too great a bias in favour of group persistences will fail to take advantage of many opportunities for social improvement. Thus social prosperity will be maximized by governments with a more or less equal balance of the two classes of residues.

These are reasonable inferences from Pareto's scheme, and if we accept them the theorem is certainly worth investigating. Pareto attempts to confirm the proposition, despite its vagueness, by showing that Athens and Sparta, among other societies, were prevented from achieving maximum prosperity owing to imbalance of residues. His procedure, however, is peculiar from the outset, for it begins with a denial that empirical evidence is required of the imbalance of residues in these two societies:

> The great predominance of Class II residues in Sparta and of Class I residues in Athens is too obvious to require documentation. But it will be worth while to show in some

detail how these two extremes in proportions kept the two communities from attaining the maximum of prosperity.[31]

Thus Pareto's test of the theorem degenerates into a mere quoting of episodes in which Sparta rebuffed supposedly beneficial innovations and Athens failed to show sufficient stability to maintain her prosperity: it being *assumed* that such aberrations from economic rationality were brought about by imbalance of residues.[32] This example is typical of Pareto's attempts to validate his theory.[33] There is no alternative but to conclude that he does not succeed in supplying convincing confirmation and that, owing to the imprecision of his conceptual scheme, rigorous validation would be possible only after extensive conceptual reformulation.

So far we have seen that the various facets of Pareto's theoretical strategy are uniformly unsuccessful. It seems unlikely, therefore, that Pareto's introduction from mechanics of the notions 'system' and 'equilibrium' will prove to have been fruitful. It is possible that if the theoretical components based upon induction, such as residues and derivations, had been more satisfactory Pareto could have made better use of his borrowed concepts. As it is, the latter remain little more than formalities and their direct role in substantive theory is negligible. Pareto's concern with social equilibrium does lead him to specify mechanisms whereby departures from existing social states can be seen to generate counterbalancing internal forces. But apart from this the notion of equilibrium entails no more than conceptual recognition of the principle that social systems are determined by their elements. Similarly, Pareto uses the term 'social system' mainly as a way of reminding us that all social elements are interdependent. This means in other words that there are no simple, one-way causal relationships in society. Nevertheless, although these physical science concepts do not dominate Pareto's theory, his underlying assumption that social systems and physical systems are homologous does direct attention away from certain distinct and potentially significant features of human societies.

The analysis of physical systems builds up a map of the total system by examination of component units and the relationships between units. In adopting the same perspective, Pareto is led to emphasize those characteristics which the individual brings to society—residues, for example—and to play down the importance of what the system gives to the individual. This is evident in Pareto's analysis of non-logical theories. We have seen that he divides such theories into a constant element, corresponding to individual sentiments, and a variable element which is provided by the individual's group. The variable factor, or derivation, is then dismissed as being largely irrelevant to conduct. Human action is determined mainly by sentiments and little influenced by socially derived beliefs. Of course, Pareto does recognize that sentiments, although existing within individual minds, are sometimes taken over from the social environment. But for Pareto the question of how sentiments current in the group are internalized by new members is of peripheral sociological relevance. It is a problem for psychology and does not require detailed attention by sociologists. He seems to believe that sentiments are on the whole innate and are modified relatively slowly and infrequently by social influences. This view is exemplified in Pareto's analysis of criminality, where, although allowing that 'the general status of sentiments in a community has its effect on crime', he places great emphasis on inborn sentiments:

> The main causes of crimes . . . lies in the prevalence of certain sentiments. *The theory that there are born criminals* merely adds to that that the individual derives his sentiments from heredity. The theory seems to be in part sound, but it *could hardly be accepted as comprehensive:* for the sum of circumstances of time, place and so on, in which the individual has lived, have certainly modified some at least of the sentiments with which he was born. *But as contrasted with the theory of responsibility, so called, which reduces all conduct to logic, the theory of the born criminal looks like truth contrasted with error.*[34]

If sentiments were acquired in the course of social interaction they could be eliminated by social means. But Pareto argues that the only effective way of reducing crime 'is to rid society of its criminals'. Pareto, then, is convinced that many if not most sentiments are introduced into society along with the biological organism; that they are strongly persistent; and that they are the main determinant of the general form of society. This model of society leads Pareto to ignore the importance of the obvious fact that the members of any human society are born into a pre-existing system. In systems like the solar system, membership is constant and the question of how each newcomer is influenced by existing arrangements does not arise. Where system membership is stable it is appropriate to begin by examining each unit and its relations with other units in order to build up a picture of the total system. Where system units are constantly changing it *may* be more suitable to begin with a study of the overall system, followed by an analysis of how new members are moulded by existing relationships. The fruitfulness of this approach cannot be guaranteed, but it does recognize the fact that social systems differ from physical systems in ways which may require significant changes in theoretical model. We shall see that the culture and structure of social systems as such and their influence upon individual action has become a theoretical focus for functional analysis.

V

In this brief appraisal of Pareto's general theory four major defects have been detected. First, its empirical foundation appears to be inadequate. Secondly, its conceptual framework fails to reflect the complex realities of the social world. Thirdly, as a consequence of these conceptual deficiencies, Pareto's attempts at explanation and prediction are unsatisfactory. Fourthly, as a result of preconceptions taken over from the physical sciences, Pareto fails to consider the possible fruitfulness of beginning theoretical construction with analysis of the social system itself, instead of its component units. These defects are closely bound up with the wide sweep of Pareto's theoretical objectives and the empirical complexity with which he must cope. Thus it is the immense variety of human societies as well as their inaccessibility which forces Pareto to rely on a very limited range of evidence; it is the complexity of factors influencing the general state of any society which forces him to broaden, and thereby weaken, his central conceptions; and it is the complexity of social systems which leads him to apply, as a first theoretical approximation, a model developed in the analysis of different types of empirical system. It is feasible that Pareto's inductive-deductive strategy might be more successful if it were applied on a smaller scale to more narrowly defined empirical areas, where the amount and complexity of data would be less. In short, Pareto's strategy, although of possible value in relation to more modest objectives, appears to be unsuitable as a means of building a comprehensive theory of society.

A similar assessment of Pareto's theoretical strategy is reached by Parsons, the first of the two functional theorists to be discussed here. Parsons sums up his estimate of Pareto's theory in these words:

> ... by far the most important attempt so far made to build up a generalized analysis of social systems as a whole in a dynamic analytical system on the model of mechanics [is] that of Pareto. Pareto's attempt undoubtedly put systematic theoretical thinking about social systems on a new level; it is unique in the literature for its comprehensiveness and the sophistication of its understanding of the physical science model. *And yet it must be regarded as a relative failure.*[35]

He goes on to indicate why the scheme must be judged a failure.

First, he suggests, most of the central conceptual distinctions are both arbitrary and empirically indeterminate. Secondly, he argues that although Pareto's analysis

> yields important though rather general empirical insights . . . it has signally failed to work as a direct source of detailed analytical tools in detailed research. What is successfully established is too vague and general. The gaps have to be filled by arbitrary *ad hoc* constructions and classifications or by the introduction of structural categories which are merely tolerated, not systematically developed.[36]

In this appraisal Parsons maintains that Pareto's fundamental mistake is to attempt to construct a general deductive system before having formed a sufficiently complex, systematic and empirically precise conceptual apparatus. In the next chapter we shall examine how Parsons organizes his own theoretical strategy around the task of *systematic conceptualization* of the structure common to all social systems.

3 Structural-functionalism as a theoretical alternative: Parsons

I

Parsons recognizes a greater variety of theoretical systems than does Pareto, and is accordingly able to vary his theoretical strategy more freely. Pareto distinguishes only two types of theory—namely, the scientific and the non-scientific. Consequently, because he is committed to the scientific approach, he has no alternative but to attempt to construct a full-scale 'logico-experimental theory' for sociology. In contrast, Parsons distinguishes four levels or types of theory within the 'scientific' category.[1] The least advanced level, in terms of theoretical adequacy, is that of the *ad hoc classificatory system*. Such a system provides a means of ordering empirical data, but does so in a relatively unsystematic fashion. Its categories tend to be slipshod and to hinder instead of provoking further development. *Categorial systems*, the second level, involve sets of classifications which reflect more accurately and more consistently the relations existing in the 'real world'. Categorial systems differ from *ad hoc* systems in being internally more consistent and in being related to their subject matter in a more specific and detailed manner. *Theoretical systems* are categorial systems plus laws or empirical generalizations which are formulated within the framework of concepts provided by the categorial system. Finally, *empirical-theoretical systems* are theoretical systems in which a wide range of empirical generalizations or, as Parsons sometimes calls them, 'dynamic generalizations', are systematically related in such a way that highly precise empirical predictions can be formulated. Empirical-theoretical systems represent a scientific ideal which is seldom realized. Nevertheless, the long-term goal of theory construction in sociology 'is the possession of a logically complete system of dynamic generalizations which can state all the elements of reciprocal interdependence between all the variables'[2] of the social system. Pareto would have agreed with this statement and with Parsons' further proposal that such 'dynamic analysis' should aim at the formulation of laws designed to explain specific phenomena. But we have seen in our appraisal of Pareto's work that the satisfactory completion of such a theory is difficult. It is not surprising, therefore, that at this point Parsons raises certain difficulties, very similar to those discussed by Pareto, which he sees as facing sociological theory.

In Parsons' view, there are at least two requirements which must be met if an empirical-theoretical or even a theoretical system is to be successfully formulated. First, variables included in such a system must have clear empirical referents. Secondly, in Parsons' own words, they 'must vary only in numerically quantitative value on a continuum'.[3] They must be quantifiable and open to manipulation by means of the differential calculus. Parsons admits that these demands are too stringent for sociology at present and that, if we were to use such criteria in selecting variables for inclusion in our theoretical framework, we would find our theories limited to a very narrow range of demonstrably insignificant factors. So far, then, Parsons' discussion closely resembles that of Pareto. Both men put forward a theoretical ideal based on the kind of mathematical theory found in the advanced sciences; and both men recognize that such a theory is not yet possible in sociology. But at this juncture they begin to adopt different positions. Pareto has either to try to construct, without mathematical techniques, what Parsons would call a 'theoretical system' or to retreat altogether from general sociological theory. Parsons, in contrast, has one further alternative. He can create a general categorial system before moving on to the next theoretical level. Furthermore, this strategy appears to be particularly appropriate because, in focusing on the construction of a satisfactory conceptual apparatus, it may well avoid the kind of conceptual deficiencies we have found in Pareto's scheme. Thus Parsons takes as his initial goal the creation of a categorial system for sociology.

Categorial knowledge consists in '(k)nowing that a variable is significant and having a definite conception of it and its logical distinctions from other variables and other aspects of the empirical system'.[4] Accordingly, the aim in constructing a categorial *system* is to formulate an array of clearly defined and clearly interrelated concepts which represent all or most significant sociological variables. It is probable that Parsons, if forced to reject all prior theory, would have regarded even the construction of a general categorial system as too ambitious. He argues, however, that there has been a marked theoretical convergence among the theorists of Pareto's generation, which is evident particularly in the work of Weber, Durkheim and Pareto himself.[5] Although this convergence went unnoticed by the theorists involved, it is there to provide Parsons' own generation with the basis for a general theoretical orientation. As we have seen in the case of Pareto, this theoretical inheritance tends to be deficient in several respects: acceptable empirical generalizations have not been accumulated; the knowledge of laws is rudimentary; and the supply of established fact is patchy. Yet, argues Parsons, these theorists have broadly defined the limits of our area of study and have presented enough evidence to indicate the most significant elements within it. This argument for the existence of a theoretical convergence in sociology is not entirely convincing. But the validity of Parsons' thesis is not our concern at the moment. We are interested in those basic assumptions which have shaped his broad theoretical strategy. At present we need only note his conviction that sociology has inherited a body of thought which demonstrates, albeit from several different perspectives and terminologies, the major significance of certain sociological variables and his inference that the current task of sociological theory is to clarify and systematize the conceptual implications of this rather general and sometimes idiosyncratic knowledge, as a prelude to the final stage of constructing a fully theoretical system.

Parsons is aware that concepts and empirical data are linked in a complex and intimate fashion, and that by concentrating upon the conceptual level he is in danger of producing a scheme as empirically vacuous as that of Pareto. He argues, however, that although conceptual and empirical analysis are closely related it is *possible* to operate at the conceptual level without at the same time using the concepts to formulate putative laws. This possibility exists, claims Parsons, because the network of interrelated concepts which make up a categorial system is 'logically prior to' the laws which 'state further relations between its elements'.[6] For example, in classical mechanics there are a number of logically interrelated definitions of elements, such as space, time, particle, mass, motion and so on, which constitute the categorial system. These definitions logically precede the laws which provide explanations and predictions. In other words, although laws cannot be formulated without concepts, conceptual schemes can be constructed before any attempt is made to explain or predict. Of course, if the categorial system is to mature into a scientific theoretical system, its concepts require considerable empirical support. But this empirical evidence need not be of a kind which makes possible the formulation of rigorous empirical generalizations; indeed, if the available evidence had this degree of reliability there would be no need to restrict the theoretical scheme to the status of a mere categorial system. Parsons argues, therefore, that if we have insufficient information about sociological laws to provide a theoretical system, but enough empirical and theoretical work to provide a broad framework, there is no reason why we should not proceed with the formulation of a comprehensive scheme of interrelated concepts. Such a policy is not only possible, but would in practice bear conclusive advantages over both speculative theory along Paretian lines and the 'blind empiricism' characteristic of so much sociological research.

In the first place, the pressure for quantification of variables would be reduced. Secondly, conceptual inconsistency could be cleared up at this preliminary stage. Thirdly, the exposure of unexpected conceptual links would generate new areas for empirical research. Fourthly, clear empirical referents could be gradually and systematically defined. And, lastly, a categorial system would provide both a guide for empirical research and a common frame of reference for interpreting and evaluating such research. These, then, are the benefits which, in Parsons' view, will accrue if sociological theory is directed towards the formulation of a categorial scheme rather than a theoretical system.

Parsons' decision to construct a categorial system based on a convergence in recent theory does not remove the danger that the resulting conceptual scheme might be drastically incomplete and provide a misleading picture of complex social reality. He is aware that his categorial system could easily develop those tendencies to over-simplification and over-abstraction which were so prominent a feature of Pareto's work:

> Where . . . breadth of applicability can be attained only
> through extreme simplicity in the relations of variables, only a
> secondary order of scientific significance can be attributed
> to the results. For where only very simple relationships,
> or only those of two or three variables, can be involved in
> a dynamic generalization it must inevitably remain undesirably
> abstract in the sense that in very few cases of concrete
> empirical systems will these relationships and these variables
> be the only or the predominant ones involved. . . .[7]

Some degree of simplification is, of course, unavoidable and indeed valuable. However, Parsons' task is to devise a systematic conceptual representation of *all* the important aspects of concrete systems at a level which does not over-simplify complex reality. This can be done, he suggests, by using structural rather than dynamic categories. The introduction of structural categories is designed 'to simplify the dynamic problems to the point where they are manageable without the possibility of refined mathematical analysis. At the same time the loss, which is very great, is partly compensated by relating all problems explicitly and systematically to the total system. . . . [This] ensures that nothing of vital importance is inadvertently overlooked'.[8] When sociologists have attempted to build up a general picture of the social system by describing the relationships between its elements, they have tended to become lost in a welter of complexity. If, in contrast, we begin with the total structure and attempt to describe its broad, stable features our task is greatly simplified without our having to abandon the goal of providing full conceptual coverage. This strategy is rather like that of describing the anatomical structure of an organism such as the human body before moving on to examine its physiology. Once we are sure that we have a complete description of organs, muscles, bones, etc., we can proceed to dynamic analysis—that is, to the study of how the system operates. Furthermore, we can ensure that our structural description of the social system is complete by centring it around the notion of 'social function'. Use of the concept function here implies that social systems, like biological organisms, are maintained within limits by the contributions of their component units.[9] For example, our descriptions of heart, liver and pancreas can be linked by showing how each organ contributes to the continuance of the same human body. Similarly, the elements of social structure can be interrelated by describing their function—that is, their contribution to maintenance of the system in which they operate. The concept of 'social function' is intended

> to provide criteria of the *importance* of dynamic factors and processes within the system. . . . It is thus the functional reference of all particular conditions and processes *to the state of the total system as a going concern* which provides the logical equivalent to simultaneous equations in a fully developed system of analytical theory. This appears to be *the only way* in which dynamic *inter*dependence of variable factors in a system can be explicitly analysed without the technical tools of mathematics and the operational and empirical prerequisites of their employment.[10]

By organizing our categorial system around the principle that items of social structure can be related through their contribution to the maintenance of one and the same concrete system we gain two advantages: first, we can be sure that, despite the complexity of social relationships, no elements which are essential to the system will be overlooked; and, secondly, we obtain at least a preliminary notion of dynamic interdependence within the social system and in this way prepare for the eventual formulation of a fully developed theoretical system.

The prologue to Pareto's theory has two broad sections. In the first, Pareto describes his theoretical ideal and the methods to be used in its realization. The second section indicates what modifications are needed in theory and method to take account of the special difficulties facing sociology. Pareto's general conclusion is that, given such modifications as the use of cycles of interdependence in place of simultaneous equations, a first approximation to the scientific ideal can be attained, and he goes on to construct what he believes to be such an approximation. Parsons' approach is similar, but his conclusions are more cautious and his theoretical modifications are more extensive. In view of the complexity of sociological data and the evident failure of earlier theorists to formulate a satisfactory general theoretical system, he decides that general theory must, for the time being, be restricted to the conceptual or categorial level. It is possible to concentrate on this level owing to the logical priority of conceptual schemes and because there has been sufficient theoretical convergence in sociology to justify an attempt at conceptual systematization. This theoretical convergence, however, has led toward a theory of 'social action' rather than a structural-functional scheme. The idea of describing social structures in terms of functions is not derived directly from prior sociological theory, although it had been used by Durkheim and by many social anthropologists.[11] It is rather a corollary of Parsons' commitment to categorial analysis and is designed to reduce complexity to manageable levels, while ensuring full conceptual coverage of concrete social systems. Functional analysis in Parsons' scheme duplicates the role of cycles of interdependence in that of Pareto. Where Pareto is forced to follow through complicated and endless causal chains, Parsons uses the technique of tracing the impact of system units upon the total structure. Because Parsons superimposes structural-functionalism on the emergent theory of social action to attain his own theoretical ends we must turn to a consideration of the social action framework before delving further into Parsons' brand of functional analysis.

II

Parsons suggests that the following concepts must be used in the analysis of social action:

1 Actor.
2 Goal.
3 Situation.
4 Orientation.
5 Norm.

Actor refers to an individual person or to a number of persons who are being regarded analytically as one actor. Each actor attempts actively to bring about certain end states or *goals*. In striving for his goals the actor must take into consideration specific *situations* which impose limitations upon his actions and which provide alternative means of achieving his goals. These situations are made up of social objects—for example, other actors—and non-social objects. In order to act in any given situation actors choose from a range of available actions. These choices are partly determined by subjective processes of *orientation* which are themselves guided by internalized *normative* standards—that is, by beliefs about what conduct is proper in the given circumstances.

This conceptual framework can be used to interpret single acts. But acts tend to become interrelated in an organized manner. They come to form *systems* of action. Parsons claims that three kinds of systems of acts can be distinguished:

1 Personality systems.
2 Social systems.
3 Cultural systems.

The acts which make up these three systems are only conceptually distinct. In other words, any one act may belong to all three systems. What distinguishes one system from another is not their content, but the way in which functional analysis is used to order the data. Thus personality systems are distinguished from social systems 'by the differences in the foci around which they are organized. The personality of the individual is organized around the biological unity of the organism.' In contrast, 'the social system is organized around the unity of the interacting group'.[12] The analysis of personality is designed to show how specific types of acts are related to the 'needs' of individual actors, while the analysis of social systems refers the same acts to the 'functional problems' of groups of actors.

Let me give a simple example. A comedian performs before a TV audience. We can regard his performance as a social action: it is undertaken by an actor, in both meanings of the term, who has a goal in view (e.g. audience laughter), a subjective orientation to the situation (e.g. he assumes that certain kinds of material work better on TV), and who is subject to normative standards which are enforced by others and which he probably endorses himself (e.g. no 'blue' jokes). If we are concerned with the personality system, we can relate his actions to the reduction of certain needs—for instance, the need for self-display, the need to divert the hostility of others, the need for money, etc., these need dispositions being located within the individual organism. If, however, we wish to study the social system we must relate the same actions to the functional requisites of the group of actors—that is, to the things which must get done if the group is to persist. Possible examples would be the need for release of tension within the group or the need for members to participate in activities which promote group solidarity. It is clear from this example that the analysis of personality will not be identical with that of the social system. The functional problems of any social system—for example, group solidarity—can always be resolved in a number of different ways and by a variety of personalities. Consequently, although 'personality and social system are very intimately interrelated . . . they are neither identical nor explicable by one another; the social system is not a plurality of personalities.'[13]

In addition to personality systems and social systems, we have cultural systems—that is, systems of meaningful symbols. The role of culture in Parsonian analysis can be clarified by a comparison of Parsons' conception of social action with that of Pareto. For Pareto most social action is non-logical, a by-product of internal impulses and sentiments. Although, as we noted above, his approach cannot be regarded as a theory of human instincts, it does view those psychological states which generate action as largely innate and as inaccessible to *sociological* analysis. With this conception of the sources of social action Pareto cannot allow such a purely social product as culture to play an important role in determining conduct. Beliefs and theories, therefore, are regarded as having little effect on those non-logical actions which make up the majority of human conduct. Scientific theories are, however, rather different, for they provide a reasonably accurate reflection of reality and can be used to guide rational action toward realization of its goals. But Pareto does not discuss rational action in detail and no account is given of where the goals of rational action originate.

Parsons is forced to reject most of this.[14] Developments which have taken place in psychology since Pareto's day have discredited instinct theory. Little evidence has been found that human organisms bear *any* specific and innate behavioural tendencies. It has to be accepted that human beings are born with a limited number of broad physiological needs plus the capacity to *learn* an immense variety of activities.[15] In addition to the findings of psychology, social anthropology has shown that many forms of conduct and belief are restricted to one society or to a limited range of societies and that societies of the same size, geographical location and 'racial' composition often develop markedly different patterns of culture and conduct.[16] In the light of this evidence, Parsons concludes that human beings acquire particular behavioural tendencies as they grow up in specific societies. Only on this assumption can sociological theory be reconciled with the conclusions of psychology and social anthropology. Sociological analysis cannot begin, as Pareto maintains, with statements about the largely innate impulses of individuals. For human beings learn to conform, on the whole, to the patterns of conduct customary in their society. In this sense, patterns of behaviour and related patterns of belief are primarily characteristics of the social system or group. They tend to precede and outlast any particular group member whose actions are thus more a *product* of the group than a determinant of its structure. In Parsons' view the most important aspects of social action which people acquire while living in society are goals and normative standards.

Parsons argues that the conception of human conduct as directed toward the attainment of subjectively envisaged goals emerges from the convergence in sociological theory. He maintains that even Pareto sometimes conceives of non-logical action as goal-oriented. As it has been interpreted above, Pareto's theory of non-logical action does not *emphasize* the idea of subjective goals. However, Pareto's negative definition of non-logical action allows great scope for variation and undoubtedly some aspects of his analysis can be intepreted in this fashion. Furthermore, his treatment of interests and rational action generally is couched explicitly in terms of actors adapting means in order to attain goals. When these strands in Pareto's thought are aligned with Weber's version of social action,[17] Parsons' argument that social action should be treated as goal-oriented seems reasonably well-founded in preceding theory. None the less, Parsons' conception remains very different from that of Pareto. In Parsons' scheme the notion of goal-directed behaviour is in no way restricted to rational conduct, but extended to cover virtually all social activities. In order to apply his conception of social action in this general fashion, Parsons has to answer two questions. He must, firstly, give an account of the origins of individuals' goals. Pareto avoids this problem by regarding goals as irrelevant to non-logical action and by failing to develop his analysis of logical actions. Secondly, Parsons must explain how actors come to choose one means rather than another in pursuing their goals. Once again Pareto avoids the question; this time by including the rational adjustment of means to ends as part of his definition of logical action and by viewing non-logical acts as the mere expression of impulses. Parsons resolves both these difficulties in a similar manner. Goals are seen as being provided by society and learned or acquired by individual actors. Likewise, all societies provide standards by which to judge the propriety of goals and the suitability of means used to achieve them. Pareto misses the importance of standards or norms by classifying theories either as scientific or as unscientific. Parsons argues that there is a class of theories to which scientific criteria are irrelevant:

Theories, or elements of them, may not only be *un*scientific, they may be *non*scientific, in that they involve entities or considerations which fall altogether outside the range of scientific competence. The 'more extended knowledge' of Pareto's observer does not suffice to arrive at a judgment of their validity; they are unverifiable, not 'wrong'.[18]

These non-scientific or normative theories tell us what we ought to do, how we ought to behave. They inform us which ends we should seek and how we should strive to achieve them. They form an important part of the culture of all societies; and as they come to be internalized by new members of society they provide the goals and standards by which action is guided. Thus where Pareto regards social action largely as a by-product of psychological factors outside the scope of sociological analysis, Parsons reverses the perspective, viewing the actions of individuals more as a by-product of the group or social system. Pareto's conception of human nature is sufficiently concrete for him to derive his sociology from certain psychological propositions, which he takes as given. In contrast, Parsons' image of human nature is highly general, placing most stress on the capacity of the human organism to learn. No substantive sociological conclusions can be derived from such a general propensity and Parsons is forced to focus his sociological analysis on the culture and structure of the human group and the manner in which the behavioural tendencies of the plastic organism are moulded by the social environment.

Parsons maintains that we begin life with certain viscerogenic needs, such as the need for food, which can be satisfied in a variety of ways. These initial needs lead us to react positively to those events which satisfy our needs and negatively to those which cause us deprivation. This tendency to react positively and negatively Parsons calls 'cathectivity'. As we learn to associate need-reduction, on the one hand, and deprivation, on the other hand, with certain patterns of behaviour and with certain persons we become positively and negatively cathected to an increasing range of social and non-social objects. Many of the 'objects' to which we are positively cathected are made available to us only if we behave in certain specified ways. In other words, the occurrence of rewarding experiences depends on conformity to the expectations of others. Gradually we learn to distinguish acceptable behaviour from that which is unacceptable. And gradually, through the frequent association of conformity with reward and non-conformity with deprivation or punishment, we come to adopt as our own the definitions of correct behaviour current in our group. The 'internalization' of the expectations of others is the source of our own morality.

A THEORETICAL ALTERNATIVE: PARSONS

Because the human organism is essentially plastic, it is continuously involved in making selections from alternative courses of action. In any given situation an actor must select his goals along with the strategy he will adopt to attain them. According to Parsons, each of these choices has three aspects or modes:[19]

1. Cognition: the actor needs to perceive his situation, to know the world around him.
2. Cathectivity: he gives positive and negative value to perceived objects depending on their relation to his need-dispositions.
3. Evaluation: the actor must compare alternative actions and come to some overall judgment of suitability.

It is possible, in principle, that the decisions resulting from these processes of cognition, cathectivity and evaluation are totally random. But if this were so, neither human personality nor human society would display organization or continuity. For Parsons this conclusion is unthinkable. It must be accepted, he claims, that the social and psychological sciences—for example, economics—have demonstrated that human activity is orderly,[20] even though the nature of this order has not yet been fully disclosed. Human conduct is systematic rather than haphazard at the level of both social systems and personality systems. This coherence exists mainly because *ready-made solutions* to most problems involving choice among alternatives are not only provided by all societies, but also internalized by most members of any given society. Every society has three cultural systems, corresponding to the three aspects of each individual choice:

1. System of ideas and beliefs (cognition).
2. System of expressive symbols (cathectivity).
3. System of values (evaluation).

Ideas and beliefs provide orderly solutions to cognitive problems. Expressive symbols guide the individual in his attempts to express emotions and generally in matters of taste as opposed to those of morality. Internalized value-orientations help solve difficulties of evaluation. These cultural systems, and particularly the system of values, provide the basic stability or consistency which permeates both social and personality systems. Cultural systems bring order into the social system partly because they are internalized by the individual actor, thereby causing him to act in a consistent fashion, and partly because the ensuing actions are further moulded by the allocation of reward and punishment into conformity with the internalized expectations of others. Each social system is, therefore, stable and coherent to the extent that its participants endorse the requirements of one and the same cultural system.

Parsons' argument so far, as presented here, can be roughly summarized as follows. General sociological theory must be devoted to the construction of a categorial system or framework of related concepts which, by making both theoretical and empirical research more systematic and cumulative, will pave the way for the emergence of a fully theoretical system. Although this conceptual framework will be organized around the principle of functional analysis, it must also build upon the theory of social action incipient in much theoretical work of the preceding generation. The notion of social action implies that social conduct is directed toward the attainment of goals and that actors make a series of choices from alternative courses of action. These choices are not fully determined by biological factors. The human organism, in being exposed to the cultural system of its particular society, comes to internalize certain goals, beliefs and standards which, in conjunction with the social and non-social environment, determine actual conduct. Cultural systems themselves have a strong tendency toward 'consistency of pattern'.[21] This coherence of cultural systems is important because culture, and particularly its evaluational aspect, is the basic source of continuity within social systems. Thus the interdependence of cultural and social systems must be constantly borne in mind during the categorial analysis of the social system.

III

One of Pareto's basic assumptions is that the elements which he studies are interrelated in a complex yet systematic manner. Parsons argues similarly that, although 'social action' is a fundamental sociological concept, the discipline's main concern is not the simple isolated act, but those involved networks of actions which make up human society in all its complexity. 'Instead of single isolated unit acts it is necessary to think in terms of complicated webbed chains of means-end relationships'.[22] These systems of actions emerge out of the interplay between a number of actors. Thus social systems are composed of complex networks of *inter*actions involving a plurality of actors. The analysis of such systems is sociology's central task. Parsons suggests, however, that we should simplify our problems as much as possible by beginning with the least complicated type of social system.

The simplest social system is one made up of two actors, ego and alter (me and some other). When ego interacts with a non-social object there is only one set of expectations involved. Ego expects the object to react in certain specified ways, but the object has no expectations as to how ego will act or how ego ought to act. Non-social action, therefore, consists in a relatively simple choice among alternative ends and alternative means within a fairly predictable situation. When, however, ego interacts with another actor there are sets of expectations on both sides. 'It is the fact that expectations operate on both sides of the relation between a given actor and the object of his orientation which distinguishes social interaction from interaction to non-social objects.'[23] Thus in social interaction ego's behaviour is guided not just by alter's actions, but also by ego's expectations of how alter will react to his (ego's) actions. Because ego enters into social relationships in order to reduce certain needs, alter's responses operate as sanctions for ego. In so far as alter reacts in a way which helps ego achieve his goals and reduce his needs alter's actions constitute rewards. In so far as alter reacts in a way which will prevent ego from achieving his goals, his actions deprive ego of possible rewards. Consequently, if ego wishes to realize his goals he will be led to select those actions which conform to alter's expectations, thereby stimulating alter to reciprocate by conforming to his (ego's) expectations. Similarly, alter will guide his actions in terms of his conception of ego's expectations. As long as both actors have a fairly accurate notion of the other's expectations their interaction will produce a balanced conformity to expectations leading to reasonable gratification on both sides. Parsons argues, however, that this kind of successful articulation of expectations can occur only if both ego and alter share certain standards or values.

If any two actors are to predict accurately how their partner will react during social interaction, they will need to share at least some standards whereby selections from alternative courses of action are made. Unless ego himself endorses those rules which alter uses in choosing his acts, ego will never succeed in presenting the 'correct' responses to alter nor in inducing alter to conform to his own expectations. The partners in a relation which involved no shared rules would continuously misinterpret the other's intentions and only by chance would the participants attain their goals. The relationship would be totally unstable and would in no sense comprise a social *system* which has, by definition, coherence and continuity over time. Social systems composed of two actors must, therefore, involve shared rules or standards. As we have seen, the cultural system provides just those standards of cognition, expression and evaluation which are required in any enduring social relationship. Individuals who have been exposed to the same cultural system will have internalized similar expectations of how their fellow-men should and will behave. Only when actors share expectations in this manner can social relationships achieve that degree of stability and continuity which distinguishes a social system from sporadic social interaction. Thus a cultural system and its internalization by individual actors are necessary features of any social system. Of the three kinds of cultural system, the evaluative is the most fundamental because it provides the criteria for integrating and judging both cognitive and cathectic standards. Thus shared value-orientations provide the basic stabilizing aspect of simple social systems; and if shared values are required to maintain simple social relationships involving only two actors, even more clearly are they necessary for the persistence of large-scale systems in which tendencies toward discontinuity and fragmentation are likely to be much more pronounced.

Parsons himself makes no systematic attempt to furnish empirical evidence supporting his contention that shared values play an important role within social systems. He prefers to work at the conceptual level and to show that the *conception* of a system composed of networks of social actions necessarily implies the existence of shared values. His argument is summarized in the following words:

> Selections are of course always actions of individuals, but these selections cannot be inter-individually random in a social system. Indeed, one of the most important functional imperatives of the maintenance of social systems is that the value-orientations of the different actors in the same social system must be integrated in some measure in a *common* system. All on-going social systems do actually show a tendency toward a general system of common cultural orientations. The sharing of value-orientations is especially crucial, although consensus with respect to systems of ideas and expressive symbols are also very important determinants of stability in the social system.[24]

Parsons refers here in passing to the factual basis for his assertion when he mentions that shared cultural orientations are found in all societies. But his line of reasoning is far from inductive. His argument can be paraphrased as follows: In studying social action we are concerned with actors making selections from a range of possible activities. These selections depend very largely on the subjective orientations of actors. Where these orientations operate according to unrelated principles there will be no stability or continuity among the resulting congeries of social actions. But we are interested solely in social *systems*—that is, with those networks of interactions which *do* show stability and continuity. Within such relatively stable systems actors' orientations must, to some degree, be guided by principles which are held in common, for, as long as we accept the action frame of reference, shared standards furnish the only possible source of stability in social relationships. Consequently, if stable relationships are the distinguishing characteristics of social systems, the latter must always imply the existence of shared standards and, in particular, of shared values. The occurrence of shared value-orientations is thus a functional imperative of the maintenance of social systems. In other words, without shared values no social system can persist.

The train of reasoning outlined above is entirely consistent with Parsons' stated theoretical policy. First, it is devoted to linking together certain concepts in a systematic fashion. Secondly, it starts from the action frame of reference and, thirdly, it attempts to extend this framework by means of functional analysis. In this instance, functional analysis is used to show that shared values fulfil an essential function or requirement in all social systems. We shall now turn to Parsons' description of complex social systems, where the notion of functional prerequisite or functional imperative becomes of decisive importance.

Parsons' treatment of complex social systems, unlike that of Pareto, does not focus on their dynamics. His aim is to describe the *structure* of such systems. The term 'structure' refers, for Parsons, to patterns of social interaction. Accordingly, he formulates his concepts by extending the paradigm which depicts balanced interaction between two actors. In the two-actor situation each actor endorses certain social expectations which, because they are expressions of his values, he regards as legitimate. If both actors have the same values, their pattern of interaction tends to be stable and the relationship accepted as legitimate by both participants. Parsons suggests that complex social systems which persist over time can be seen as extensive networks of such stable and legitimate social expectations. Relatively enduring and legitimized expectations which are widely recognized throughout a system are called 'roles'. Social roles and their constituent expectations are attached to specific positions. Thus any actor occupying a given position will be subject to the same range of legitimate expectations. Because roles are made up of legitimate expectations—in other words, rights and obligations —they can never exist in isolation. Roles, therefore, are always found in clusters; for example, the role-position of grandmother implies the existence of such complementary role-positions as grandfather, father, mother and so on. Such clusters of stable role-positions, focused around societal values, are called 'institutions'. And networks of institutions make up the structure of any complex social system. Parsons formally defines an institution as 'a complex of institutionalized role integrates which is of structural significance in the social system in question'.[25] Taken in isolation, this definition may appear tautologous, for an *institution* is defined as a complex of institutionalized roles. The definition is not vacuous, however, because 'institutionalization' is itself defined elsewhere as the process whereby patterns of interaction become relatively stable and legitimated by shared values. Thus an institution is a structurally important and stable cluster of roles which express certain common values. This definition embodies several of Parsons' central conceptions. In the first place, institutions are seen as complex patterns of standardized social action. Secondly, these patterns are regarded as expressions of shared cultural orientations. At the same time the definition is couched in functional terms, for the reference to 'structural significance' indicates that an institution must make some signal contribution to fulfilling the functional imperatives of its social system.

In addition to the concepts of role-position and institution, Parsons refers to norms, values and collectivities in his analysis of complex systems. Social institutions are clearly distinguished from collectivities. A collectivity is composed of a number of concrete role-performers whose interaction is governed by norms and shared values. Institutions, in contrast, are made up of *patterned social expectations* and can be studied without direct reference to the concrete actors who hold these expectations. Any 'collectivity may be the focus of a whole series of institutions. Thus the institutions of marriage and parenthood are both constitutive of a particular family as a collectivity.'[26] Both institutions and collectivities, however, are stabilized by the same values and norms. A norm is a specific legitimized expectation attached to a specific role. Thus norms tend to be complementary. Values are more general standards which tend to be shared and to provide legitimation for a variety of norms and roles.

The major units of analysis in the study of complex social systems are, then, role-positions, norms, values, institutions and collectivities. When such complex systems are more or less self-sufficient, they are called 'societies'. Clearly this self-sufficiency is a matter of degree. However, Parsons regards the United States as a society— that is, as being able to maintain its structure of institutions, values and so on without outside help. In contrast, the social system of the Catholic Church is not a society because it is 'primarily a culturally oriented social system, [and] is not itself capable of meeting very many of the functional exigencies of a society, especially the political and economic needs.'[27] Although Parsons' scheme is applicable to social systems of all kinds and levels of complexity, he is specially concerned with societies, the study of which must proceed, he suggests, according to three related principles. The first principle is that of examining how the societal structure and its sub-systems become differentiated in relation to the functional requirements of the system. The second principle centres around the specification of normative culture; and the third around the segmentation of collectivities. These principles plus the concepts presented above provide a framework which, in Parsons' estimation, can be used to describe the structure of any social system.

Any given society can be viewed as a single collectivity. However, the greater the number of persons involved in the collectivity the more difficult it is for them to communicate and, generally, to integrate their actions. Consequently, large societal collectivities necessarily split into smaller and more manageable segments, each segment being itself a collectivity. Thus '*segmentation of collectivities*' refers to the tendency for societies as they increase in size to generate internal sub-collectivities. Segmentation is a separate phenomenon from that of functional differentiation. For example, nineteenth-century China was more highly segmented than nineteenth-century England, but its most numerous type of collectivity, in this case the stem family, performed a wide range of functions. In contrast, although segmentation in England at that time was relatively less prevalent, separation of functions was much more highly developed. Segmentation resembles functional differentiation, however, in giving rise to further problems of integration. 'The more units there are, the less likely they will be just "naturally" to co-ordinate their activities in ways compatible with the smooth functioning of the system as a whole.'[28] An effective level of integration is achieved, nevertheless, through the *specification of normative culture*. Normative culture is necessary for the maintenance of system stability, as we have seen, at each social level. However, the values or principles for selection among alternative actions and alternative expectations which are shared by all the members of a society are very general in nature. If they are to guide action within the sub-collectivities of society they must become increasingly *specific*. Thus each type of collectivity within society develops norms which are particularized versions of the societal values and which tend to be appropriate to its contribution to maintenance of the larger system. This leads us to the third and 'master principle' for the analysis of social systems —namely, that of relating the structural differentiation of the system to its functional exigencies.

The functional imperatives of any action system, and therefore of any social system, are four in number.

1 Goal attainment.
2 Adaptation.
3 Pattern maintenance.
4 Integration.

Although Parsons' formulation of these imperatives was stimulated by Bales' experiments with small groups,[29] the categories are closely related to the basic action framework. The connection between the functional imperatives and the conception of social action is self-evident in the case of goal attainment. In a similar fashion the system requirement of adaptation corresponds to the actor's need to come to terms with an external situation; while the imperatives of 'pattern maintenance' and 'integration' continue the fundamental concern with how coherence and continuity are maintained in social relationships.

All social systems, like actors, must be thought of as directed toward the attainment of a goal or goals. Because we are here concerned with complex systems, we can assume that a system oriented toward one goal is a limiting case and that, in most instances, systems 'strive for' many goals. As a consequence of the plurality of goals, we can also assume that they are arranged in some hierarchy of relative urgency. In most societies a distinct sub-system exists which is devoted to judging the relative importance of various societal goals as well as formulating and implementing policies for their attainment. This sub-system is made up of what are usually called 'political institutions'. In striving for various goals, social systems will be faced with the problem of allocating scarce resources in a way which facilitates goal attainment. This is the functional imperative of adaptation. On the whole it is the economy which produces and distributes goods and services in a manner which makes possible the realization of the system's goals. Within complex systems the use of scarce resources tends to become governed by some form of monetary exchange which can be used as a rough criterion for distinguishing the adaptive sub-system.

The third functional imperative is that of pattern maintenance. This concept recognizes the tendency of social systems to maintain their structural patterns and cultural values. In the same way that shared values are seen as necessary if individual actors are to achieve satisfaction in the course of social interaction, so some degree of stability is thought to be required in any system if its goals are to be realized. We saw that in the two-actor situation any acts on the part of ego which deviated from established patterns produced negative reactions from alter, who himself suffered deprivation as a consequence of ego's deviance. Thus established patterns of interaction are maintained in part by the system of rewards and punishments, which are themselves legitimated by widely accepted values. This factor is supplemented by ego's internalization of values and norms in a way which diminishes deviance by making ego *want* to act in the manner expected by others and by causing him feelings of guilt when he does depart from established practices.

Parsons' assertion that pattern maintenance is an integral aspect of all social systems is similar to Pareto's claim that social systems tend to maintain states of equilibrium and, indeed, Parsons himself often uses the term 'equilibrium'. For both Pareto and Parsons the conception of equilibrium is another way of referring to the fact that the elements of the social system tend to be interrelated in a way which contributes to the maintenance of the existing system. But Parsons goes further than Pareto in attempting to show precisely how the social system develops mechanisms which resist forces impinging upon it. For Pareto the basic mechanism maintaining social control is the circulation of élites. Parsons, in contrast, although by no means denying the importance of political factors, stresses the socialization of the young child within the family. For Parsons social control is due as much to internalized values as to external constraints. In the same way that the first two imperatives were fulfilled by political and economic institutions respectively, so the function of pattern maintenance is closely associated with kinship, educational and religious institutions and with group rituals of all kinds.

The last of the functional requisites, that of integration, is also related to the maintenance of social equilibrium. The need for integration arises out of Parsons' image of society as segmented and differentiated into a complex network of sub-systems. Each of the sub-systems discussed so far is conceived as being at least partly independent of the remainder and as organized in a manner which facilitates its own internal equilibrium. The functional imperative of integration requires that rights and duties—that is, role-expectations—be allocated to the sub-systems so as to reconcile their internal dynamics with the effective operation of the total system. Given that each sub-system is partially autonomous, it is necessary, if the society is to persist, that some control be exercised over the relationships between sub-systems. In highly differentiated societies this need is fulfilled in large measure by the system of legal norms and the roles associated with the application and maintenance of the legal system.

Let me briefly summarize what has been stated about complex social systems. These systems are composed of large numbers of concrete actors who interact in pursuance of goals which have become embedded in their personalities during the course of 'socialization' or social learning. These actors belong to collectivities which are organized around certain shared values. Collectivities vary in size from the small family group to the total society. As most actors belong to many collectivities, membership in any one seldom exhausts the whole range of an individual's social action. Thus, individuals act out certain specific and fairly clearly defined roles within each collectivity. Social roles also constitute the central component of institutions. Although sociology is mainly concerned with the analysis of institutional patterns, concrete actors and collectivities are important units in the scheme, not least because they provide the 'organic base' through which roles, institutions and so on are realized.

Social systems are segmented into various kinds of collectivities. Within any one society all collectivities of the same type will be structurally similar and functionally equivalent. All collectivities, however, are multi-functional. Thus, if we are to pursue a functional analysis of social structures we must concentrate upon the way in which roles, norms and institutions become differentiated in response to system 'needs'. This kind of study directs our attention away from collectivities as such, because any collectivity will feature a variety of institutions each of which may fulfil divergent societal functions. The basic assumption in this type of functional analysis is that societal structures become differentiated in a way which resolves the four functional imperatives. Within any given social system, the sub-systems of goal attainment, adaptation, pattern maintenance and integration can be analytically separated. Each of the sub-systems must be regarded as a boundary-maintaining system in its own right and, therefore, as subject to the same four exigencies. For example, economic institutions satisfy the requirement of adaptation within society—that is, the allocation of scarce resources. However, within the economic sub-system there must exist differentiation of roles according to the same four functional imperatives. Consequently, the adaptive sub-system of a society will itself contain four sub-systems—namely, those of goal attainment, adaptation, pattern maintenance and integration. Similarly, the adaptive sub-system of the adaptive sub-system will contain four sub-systems, and so on. It is at this point that Parsons' highly abstract scheme begins to give some indication of being applicable in the analysis of actual social behaviour. The framework of related concepts which constitutes Parsons' categorial system is not an end in itself, and sooner or later, as progress is made toward the formulation of a theoretical system, clear empirical referents will have to be supplied through the examination of empirical data. This empirical reference is possible, however, only when the concepts discussed so far are combined with a further set of categories—namely, the *pattern variables*. The pattern variables provide a means whereby such notions as cultural system, role-expectation, adaptive sub-system and so on, can be linked, at least in principle with empirical material. They are a means of describing in specific instances the content of these general conceptions.

The basic frame of reference of the theory of social action depends upon the notion of an actor selecting, in any one situation, among a variety of possible actions:

> The objects of the situation do not interact with the cognizing and cathecting organism in such a fashion as to determine automatically the meaning of the situation. Rather, the actor must make a series of choices before the situation will have a determinate meaning. Specifically, we maintain, the actor must make five specific dichotomous choices before any situation will have a determinate meaning.[30]

Any actor, in order to act, must resolve five dilemmas of choice. His eventual action can be described in terms of the *pattern* produced by these five aspects of his choice. The five dichotomies are as follows:

1 Affectivity—Affective neutrality: 'In the first place, the actor must choose whether to accept gratification from the immediately cognized and cathected object or to evaluate such gratification in terms of its consequences for other aspects of the action system.'[31] The actor must choose *either* to seek immediate gratification *or* to exercise self-restraint in the light of wider considerations.

2 Self-orientation—Collectivity-orientation: 'In the second place, if the actor decides to evaluate [that is, to consider the wider implications of his choice] he must choose whether to give primacy to the moral standards of the social or sub-system.'[32] The actor must choose *either* to give primacy to self-interest *or* to the moral standards of a group to which he belongs.

3 Universalism—Particularism: 'In the third place, whether or not he decides to grant primacy to such moral standards, he must choose whether cognitive or appreciative standards are to be dominant. . . .'[33] The actor must choose *either* to regard objects and persons as coming under some general principle *or* to consider them solely with respect to their particular relationship to the actor.

4 Ascription—Achievement: '[S]ocial objects as relevant to a given choice situation are either quality complexes or performance complexes, depending on how the actor chooses to see them. . . .'[34] The actor must choose either to treat objects and persons on the basis of their perceived qualities *or* in the light of their performances.

5 Diffuseness—Specificity: '[S]ocial objects are either functionally diffuse (so that the actor grants them every feasible demand) or functionally specific (so that the actor grants them only specifically defined demands).'[35] The actor must choose *either* to respond to selected aspects of social objects *or* to respond without distinction to all possible aspects.

Although the pattern variables have been presented here in relation to the individual actor, they are regarded by Parsons as permeating social life at all levels. He specifies four levels at which they operate. To begin with, they constitute five explicit or implicit choices which all actors resolve in the course of each social action. Secondly, as habits of choice, they form aspects of personality systems. Thirdly, at the level of collectivities and institutions, pattern variables can be used to classify role definitions. And, fourthly, the variables serve to describe value standards. Parsons regards this last level as the most important. Pattern variables do indeed, he argues, characterize unit acts. They can, therefore, be used to portray actual behaviour. But, he suggests, sociology is concerned with acts only in so far as they display systematic interrelationships—that is, in so far as they constitute social systems. If we accept that such systems depend on the existence of shared cultural orientations, then we must use the pattern variables primarily to describe cultural systems and, in particular, value systems. Thus in practice the pattern variables are categories for classifying value standards. In describing any specific social system, we should begin by cataloguing its central value system, its network of shared values, in terms of pattern variables. Having done this, we should continue by showing how these values are actualized within various types of collectivity and, more significantly, how they are functionally differentiated within the four main sub-systems of society. In this way we can construct a description of the structure of any society which is organized in functional terms and which pays proper attention to the dominant role of shared values. This structural functional approach remains, however, essentially static. In his later work Parsons has tried to introduce a dynamic element into his analysis by considering the processes of exchange which link together the various components of social structure.

IV

Parsons places great stress on society's highly complex pattern of internal differentiation. Yet at the same time he draws attention to society's systemic character—that is, to the *interdependence* among its components. Furthermore, this interdependence is seen as being strong enough to produce a powerful tendency toward maintenance of existing relationships. Thus while the units of social systems are sufficiently distinct and separate to fulfil different functions, they are nevertheless interrelated so as to maintain the complex total system in a state approaching equilibrium. Parsons tries to account for the persistence of cohesion within such differentiated systems by stressing the *functional* character of social differentiation and the existence of shared values. It is still necessary, however, to examine the relations which obtain between sub-systems and to show exactly how they work to perpetuate relatively coherent and stable societies. Parsons resolves this problem by showing how functional relationships are maintained by a series of boundary exchanges, or balanced inputs and outputs, among the four sub-systems.

It is worth noting that Parsons' action framework itself contains an implicit conception of social exchange. This becomes evident if we compare Parsons' notion of social interdependence with that of Pareto. Pareto accepts that there is a complicated interdependence between sociological variables. But his conception of interdependence can be applied as well to billiard balls as to human interaction. In Pareto's scheme there is little conception of actors proffering valued actions in order to elicit rewarding responses. For Pareto, social interdependence emerges on the whole from the conjunction of actors impelled by constant internal drives. Social exchange, in contrast, requires a more complex model in which social units vary their responses, depending upon the actual and expected responses of the other participants. Whereas Pareto never adopts this latter model, Parsons' basic paradigm, that of two actors engaged in complementary interaction, is clearly couched in terms of social exchange rather than mere interdependence. Parsons' actors are explicitly conceived as exchanging rewards and punishments with the intention of influencing the actions of their partners and maximizing their own gratification. Theorists other than Parsons might well have built up from this paradigm an image of society as a network of social transactions with actors and collectivities bent on reducing costs and increasing profits. In this sense Parsonian theory has always contained an underlying element of social exchange. Nevertheless, there have been two cogent reasons why Parsons has failed to develop extensively and systematically the notion of exchange implicit in his action framework. First, the exchange of rewards and punishments has been viewed from the outset as a *learning* mechanism. Exchange is thus perceived primarily as the means whereby tendencies to act are acquired. As such it has no implications for the substance of social action, which must, in consequence, be taken as a derivative of the cultural system. Because the learning mechanisms do not influence the content of social conduct, great emphasis is placed upon *what* is learnt—that is, upon the society's pre-existing cultural system. According to this view, exchange, although essential to social life as a mechanism of social learning and social control, cannot be regarded as a central theoretical conception. In the second place, Parsons is strongly committed, on the basis of prior theoretical considerations, to organizing his structural analysis around the principle of functional requirements.

Functional analysis is for him the only viable alternative to the equations of physical science. Given this presumption, it is not possible to conceive that the notion of exchange could be used to organize and link sociological analysis at all levels of complexity. The role of organizing principle is already filled and new notions, such as that of social exchange, must fill a theoretically subordinate position.[36] Nevertheless, in addition to his implicit adherence at the two-actor level to the use of an exchange framework, Parsons is driven to introduce the concept of exchange explicitly into his portrayal of how society's sub-systems are interrelated.

There are really two problems of interdependence facing Parsons. In the first place, there are the relations between organism, personality, social system and cultural system. Secondly, there is the interdependence between the four sub-systems of society. Although the former series of interrelationships was investigated intensively during his earlier work, Parsons has since reformulated his analysis explicitly in exchange terms. The basic innovation is that each of these levels is seen as providing inputs or resources for the other levels. These resources are processed into 'products' which can operate effectively to maintain social equilibrium. For example, the input of the personality system is motivation. Motivation is a resource for society because it is the underlying capacity which enables individuals to take up social roles. However, the motives brought by each actor to society must be moulded before he can play the wide range of differentiated roles which will be expected of him as a mature adult. This processing of motivation takes place as society responds to each input with a corresponding output. Thus the 'primary output to the personality system, analytically speaking, is goal gratification (and, of course, its negative, deprivation)'.[37] Parsons applies this kind of input-output analysis generally to the relations between organism, personality, social system and culture. For example, the 'basic input from the organism is that plasticity which, through appropriate learning processes, can be built into patterns of purposive response'.[38] Despite the new phraseology, Parsons is offering no more than a restatement of his original theses. And, as Parsons himself admits, his treatment is neither complete nor entirely satisfactory. It is important here, none the less, as an indication that Parsons' brand of functionalism has led increasingly towards the use of the concept of social exchange.

The second problem of interdependence is that between the four sub-systems of society. Parsons' treatment of this question is complicated and, once again, far from complete. He is, however, totally committed to analysis in terms of exchange. We will examine two sets of sub-system exchanges—namely, that between the pattern-maintenance and adaptive systems and that between the goal-attainment and integrative systems. These will suffice to show at least the general character of Parsons' exchange analysis.

In Parsons' view the adaptive sub-system can be regarded as being more or less identical with the economy. He tends to speak, therefore, of the economy as a relatively independent system facing its own internal problems of goal-attainment, adaptation, pattern-maintenance and integration. The central goal of the economic system is that of providing goods and services for consumption throughout society. The extent to which this goal can be realized depends in part on resources or inputs originating in other sub-systems. In responding to these inputs, the economy provides outputs which constitute resources for the other sub-systems in their striving for goal-attainment. Because each system is relatively autonomous and because its outputs depend not only upon resources supplied externally but also upon its internal functioning, there is seldom if ever a perfect articulation between inputs and outputs. For example, the preferences of consumers often fail to coincide with what is actually produced by the economy. However, Parsons argues that if society is functionally differentiated—and this remains for him a central theoretical presupposition—there must be some matching of inputs with outputs. This matching is possible because the outputs of any given sub-system are not disseminated indiscriminately throughout society, but are always directed toward a specific and appropriate sub-system. Thus in the case under discussion the output of consumer goods passes from the economy to the family or household, which must, in Parsonian terminology, be regarded as the pattern maintenance sub-system of society:

> But what is the household or family? In sociological terms, the family . . . is not simply a 'random sample' of the non-economic parts of the social structure. It is specifically located in the pattern maintenance sub-system of the society. It follows that the output of the economy over its goal-attainment boundary goes *primarily* to some branch of the pattern-maintenance sub-system, at least in the modern industrial type of society.[39]

Matching the output of goods and services from the economy is the output of labour services which passes from the household into the economy. For completion of this exchange, two separate sets of transactions are required. On the one hand, labour is exchanged for wages, while, at the same time, goods and services are purchased quite separately. There are therefore two sets of exchanges taking place between the adaptive and the pattern-maintenance systems: wages in return for labour and goods and services for consumer expenditures. Because there is a double exchange there exist two markets—namely, the labour market and the commodity market. These markets serve as mechanisms of control. They provide institutionalized settings in which divergent demands and offers, or inputs and outputs, can be balanced. In the case of economic markets this regulation of exchange is facilitated by the use of money. Money acts as a common denominator which is accepted by actors in both systems and which enables them to express their expectations, intentions and values. However, despite the existence of money and exchange markets, in highly differentiated societies the possibility of disequilibrium is always present. For instance, although 'any individual household or firm is under pressure to balance its monetary outgo with its monetary income or face the consequences of default or indebtedness',[40] firms do go bankrupt and families do sometimes starve. Similarly, at the level of the societal sub-system imbalance frequently develops. That which occurs in the interchange between household and economy takes the form of economic inflation and deflation. Thus when households refrain from spending on consumer goods what they have received for labour services, a cumulative deflationary spiral tends to develop which reduces the rate of exchange between the two systems to a lower level of equilibrium. Economics has convincingly demonstrated that such disruptive forces, which can originate at any point in the double exchange between household and economy, generate inflationary as well as deflationary movements.

Parsons' analysis of social exchange between the adaptive and the pattern-maintenance sub-systems has four main features. First, there are two sets of exchanges. Secondly, these exchanges take place within institutionalized settings or markets. Thirdly, they utilize a specific medium of exchange. And, lastly, they are subject to disruptive forces capable of generating inflationary and deflationary spirals. This framework provides, in Parsons' view, a paradigm which 'is capable of generalization to other cases involving quite different content. For example, a double interchange also operates in the electoral process in presidential elections in the United States.'[41] In this case the exchange is said to be between political parties, on the one hand, and members of the voting public, on the other hand. In terms of societal sub-systems, we can regard this as an interchange between the goal-attainment system or polity and that of integration. The basic transaction involved is the exchange of political support for effective decisions. However, as the paradigm indicates, two series of exchanges are required before the bargain is complete. In the first place, the presidential election provides an institutionalized market which controls the acceptance, by political parties, of a broad responsibility for political leadership in return for general political support by the public. Although the various sections of the public give their support to a particular party in the hope that its eventual governmental decisions will be to their advantage, the party makes few specific commitments to its supporters. This situation corresponds to the exchange in which households provide firms with labour without receiving any specific commitment that the firm will produce the particular commodities they might want. In the same way that the businessman rewards his employees with general purchasing power, in the form of wages, so the politician offers his supporters a general acceptance of the responsibility for meeting their political demands. Nevertheless, there is another series of exchanges in which *demands* upon government are met by *binding decisions*. The market which controls this interchange is equivalent to the market for consumer goods in our previous example. It is a little more difficult to identify, but is at least partly evident in those pressure-group politics which occur behind the scenes and through which many demands are made known and many decisions made effective.

Parsons makes a reasonable case for the existence of a double exchange and a dual market structure across the boundary between the systems of integration and goal-attainment. But if the economic-exchange paradigm is applicable in full, he must also demonstrate the existence of inflationary-deflationary spirals and a distinctive medium of political exchange. Political deflation can arise, Parsons suggests, from either of two sources. In the first place, the public can reduce the level of their demands on the polity or, secondly, party leadership can fail to maintain its output of decisions. In both cases there will be a cumulative effect. A reduction in demands reduces decisions; and a reduction in decisions will lower political support and thereby acceptance of political responsibility. Thus a decrease in the rate of exchange at one point in the network will tend to reduce the general level of political activity. Similarly, political inflation has two possible sources. It can occur when demands come to exceed the polity's capacity for generating binding decisions or when commitments by political leaders exceed the limits of their support. In the same way that economic inflation and deflation are accompanied by changes in the amount of money in circulation and in its value, so political spirals involve changes in the quantity and value of power. Parsons suggests that power is the political equivalent of money. Money is a symbolic medium whereby actors communicate economic obligations. Similarly, power is a medium by means of which political obligations are passed on. The analogue between power and money is difficult to follow as long as we think of the substantive properties of money. But if we conceive of both money and power as symbolic representations of obligations, the resemblance becomes more acceptable. Both wages and the income from consumer expenditure can be thought of in terms of generalized obligations which have still to be cashed in. Likewise, the corresponding factors in the political paradigm—namely, responsibility for leadership and potential political demands—can be perceived in terms of obligations and measured, rather crudely, it is true, by reference to political power. Parsons admits that the resemblance between power and money is far from complete. Nevertheless, in his opinion, the similarity is sufficiently close to allow him to claim that the double-exchange paradigm has been applied successfully to both economic and political transactions.

We shall not follow through Parsons' attempts, which are as yet incomplete, to interpret within the double-exchange framework all boundary exchanges between the four societal sub-systems. We need only note that the paradigm is to be regarded in principle as applicable to the whole range of possible interrelations at this level. Moreover, Parsons indicates that the exchange paradigm may be used to describe a variety of other social contexts. He illustrates this suggestion with an example taken from the sphere of education. The units entering into exchange are no longer societal sub-systems. They are instead 'either individual or aggregated groups of teachers and pupils'.[42] Parsons' vagueness about the unit of analysis implies that we may conceive of them at almost any level of complexity without finding the double-exchange paradigm to be inappropriate. Parsons takes a school class as his particular example, suggesting that pupils exchange *performances* for *grades* and other expressions of approval, while teachers provide *opportunities for learning* in response to *readiness to learn*. Undoubtedly this treatment of the teacher-pupil relationship is superficial as it stands. Thus Parsons makes no attempt to delineate the exchange markets, and although he maintains that there is a medium of exchange he does not bother even to give it a name. But we need not emphasize these defects which are perhaps to be expected in an illustrative example. It is much more important for us to note the general theoretical position towards which Parsons appears to be moving—namely, that the dynamics whereby social structures are maintained, and sometimes changed, as in the case of inflationary-deflationary spirals, can be conceived at all levels within a framework built around the notion of social exchange.

V

Parsons' theoretical work is devoted to constructing a categorial system which will lead eventually to the formulation of a theory without the kind of conceptual deficiencies which we have seen to be characteristic of Pareto's scheme. He is aware that this policy of concentrating upon the logical interrelations of concepts carries its own dangers. In particular, he needs to ensure that his conceptual framework includes all significant sociological elements without sacrificing detailed empirical relevance. The only way of doing this, he argues, is to combine structural-functional analysis with the social action framework. The work of previous social action theorists provides a fundamental conceptual apparatus based on firm empirical foundations. Elaboration of this conceptual scheme along structural-functional lines will permit the necessary simplification while making certain that the final categorial system is comprehensive.

Logical extension of the action framework furnishes Parsons with a paradigm of simple social interaction in which the complementarity of expectations is emphasized. This analysis of two actors interchanging rewards and punishments so as to maximize personal satisfaction undoubtedly contains a strong element of social exchange. However, Parsons does not use the concept of exchange as his point of departure when extending the paradigm to cope with complex social systems. This is partly because he regards exchange as a mere learning mechanism and in part because he is already committed to organizing his scheme around the concepts of structure and function. In Parsons' view, actors engage in exchange in order to achieve goals which they have acquired from their surrounding culture. Thus he develops his scheme by combining a strong emphasis on culture with the functional analysis of social systems.

The social system is regarded as a level of analysis distinct from the personality and the cultural system in being focused around the functional problems of the group. The main constituents of the social system are roles and institutions plus the shared values from which roles and institutions are largely derived. There are several ways of investigating the social system—for example, by reference to its collectivities. The most fruitful analytical device, however, is to view it as composed of four main sub-systems, each of which centres on the solution of a functional imperative for the total system. Although it is possible to describe the internal structure of these sub-systems in functional terms, study of their interrelations requires the explicit introduction of exchange analysis.

The double-exchange paradigm is used to supplement structural analysis of the social system by supplying an account of its dynamics. In so far as the advanced sciences are concerned primarily with the dynamics of their systems, the introduction of exchange analysis appears to involve a definite move toward theoretical maturity. On some occasions Parsons himself seems to agree that exchange analysis is likely to hasten the arrival of a fully theoretical system in sociology. Nevertheless, he seldom, if ever, claims for his scheme the status of a fully theoretical system. Consequently it is difficult to decide what criteria to use in assessing its theoretical adequacy. We must, however, try to resolve this problem in the next chapter.

4 An assessment of Parsons' scheme

I

We shall find in this chapter that there are certain special difficulties facing us as we try to estimate the value of Parsons' theoretical work. Pareto makes this task of evaluation relatively easy by attempting to provide clear and generally accepted criteria for judging his theoretical achievement. Success is to be equated with the drafting of well-documented empirical generalizations and the subsequent generation of explanatory and predictive propositions. If such results are not forthcoming the theory is to be condemned as a failure. We have already seen that Pareto does in fact deduce from his theory certain empirical generalizations: for example, the proposition that social prosperity will be maximized in societies where residues of Classes I and II are balanced. We have also noted how, having arrived at such theoretical inferences, he verifies them to his own satisfaction by comparing the propositions with factual data. Yet it is evident from our appraisal of Pareto's scheme that, even when the theorist under discussion is committed to relatively clear standards of achievement, difficulties of evaluation can still arise. In Pareto's case different views as to what constitutes a satisfactory explanation or prediction can produce radically divergent judgments of theoretical adequacy. Thus whereas Pareto seems to have regarded his own attempts at explanation and prediction as reasonably acceptable, most sociologists today would regard his methods of validation as insufficiently stringent.[1] Nevertheless, despite certain difficulties of interpretation, the criteria adopted by Pareto—namely, the capacity to formulate explanatory and predictive propositions—remain the most usual and least ambiguous tests of scientific adequacy. It is specially unfortunate, therefore, that iu evaluating Parsons' controversial scheme we are unable to use Pareto's tactics.

The method of testing used by Pareto is applicable only to logico-deductive systems. Parsons, however, is not attempting to construct a full theoretical or empirical-theoretical system. Time and again Parsons himself clearly states that his theoretical goals are more modest: thus in *The Social System* he writes that the 'subject of this volume is the exposition of a conceptual scheme';[2] similarly, in *Theories of Society* he offers merely 'an outline of the main conceptual resources of current sociological theory'.[3] Parsons does occasionally view his scheme as something more than a conceptual framework but never as a mature theoretical system. In a fairly recent statement he appears to regard his scheme as undergoing a transition from the categorial to the fully theoretical stage of development:

> Notwithstanding some statements which I have made on occasion, my present considered opinion is that, though it has moved in that direction, my approach is not yet a logico-deductive system, but rather a temporal and historical series of contributions toward the development of such a system. Above all I would reject the rigid alternative: either a fully integrated deductive system or a congeries of unrelated conceptualizations and generalizations.[4]

As long as Parsons' theory is not intended as a complete deductive system, we cannot judge it solely or even primarily in terms of its production of predictive and explanatory propositions. However, once we abandon these criteria we are faced with two distinct critical perspectives. In the first place, we can take Parsons' overall strategy, that of prefacing fully theoretical work in sociology with the construction of a categorial system, as given and examine the adequacy of his scheme as a body of categorial knowledge. Or, secondly, we can argue that his theoretical strategy is itself misguided and unlikely to facilitate the development, by which alone it can finally be justified, of a full theoretical system. The first of these perspectives will be adopted later in this chapter. For the moment let us consider the second line of thought.

Parsons' theoretical strategy stresses that an extensive conceptual preparation is required before the formulation of a general logico-deductive system is possible in sociology. This preparation will, in Parsons' view, take the form of the systematic elaboration of certain basic theoretical notions. The early stages of theoretical development will be devoted to the definition of a number of related concepts, and only gradually will there be any move towards formulating empirical generalizations. Nevertheless, this remains the *eventual* goal; and consequently it is essential that, during the preliminary stage, conceptual analysis retains clear links with empirical data. In particular it is imperative that the initial conceptual framework, from which all subsequent developments spring, should itself be well grounded upon factual data. For extensive elaboration of a set of empirically irrelevant concepts would lead toward conceptual formalism rather than theoretical adequacy. When we examined Pareto's *opus* we found his theoretical notions related to empirical material in two ways. On the one hand, an attempt is made to validate theoretical inferences by reference to available facts. As we have just noted, these tactics are denied the theorist who, like Parsons, is confined to categorial knowledge. But Pareto also attempts to base his initial theoretical conceptions upon a comprehensive survey of social facts. Because such facts are not easily accessible, Pareto is forced to limit his inductive survey to one important class of social facts, that of non-logical theories. It was pointed out in the previous chapter that theories are an unreliable source of information about actual sentiments or behaviour. Parsons must have been aware of this defect in Pareto's research strategy. He must also have been aware that, for any theorist concerned primarily with conceptual systematization, the inductive base is of paramount importance. It is surprising, therefore, that Parsons himself adopts very similar tactics to those of Pareto in trying to establish the factual basis for his own theoretical framework. Parsons' inductive survey, if it can be called that, is confined to certain theories put forward by the preceding generation of sociological theorists. Thus in his first major study, *The Structure of Social Action*, he tries to demonstrate the suitability for sociological theory of the action frame of reference by means of an intensive examination of the work of Pareto, Weber, Durkheim and the economist Marshall. He stresses, however, that the theories of these men are to be regarded as empirical material:

> This study has attempted throughout to be an *empirical* monograph. It has been concerned with facts and the understanding of facts. . . . That the phenomena with which the study has been concerned happen to be the theories that certain writers have held about other phenomena does not alter matters.[5]

Parsons argues that the fact of theoretical convergence is not a chance event, and that it cannot be explained by reference to an interchange of ideas or a common intellectual inheritance. In his view, the 'one major factor in the emergence of the voluntaristic theory of action lies in correct observation of the empirical facts of social life'[6] by the theorists concerned. But this thesis is not entirely convincing. As we have already noted in the case of Pareto, and as will become increasingly evident in the course of this study, the conceptions of sociological theory tend to be excessively imprecise and incapable of unambiguous empirical reference. It is therefore relatively easy to show some kind of 'theoretical convergence' among virtually any group of theorists simply because their theoretical notions are open to a variety of interpretations. This is particularly true when the supposed convergence operates at a high level of abstraction. Furthermore, as long as theoretical ideas bear no rigorous relationship to the facts, it is possible to show the existence of a genuine conceptual or theoretical overlap without necessarily implying, as Parsons presumes, the existence of corresponding empirical regularities among social facts. Even if we accept that there has been a convergence at the conceptual level, this convergence could well be accompanied by quite dissimilar empirical observations.

Parsons' argument would apply only if sociological theory during Pareto's era had reached a level of sophistication where rigorous operational definitions[7] of major concepts were widespread. Theoretical convergence in any other circumstances is an unreliable index of empirical uniformities; and, as a sociological theorist, Parsons' long-term concern must be with the facts of social life rather than with the supposed facts of convergence at the theoretical level. It is upon the adequacy of the link between his theoretical conceptions and such *social* facts that the scientific value of his work must ultimately be judged. In taking sociological theories as the initial empirical foundation for his own work, Parsons' access to the indispensable data of social life is second-hand and therefore suspect. Thus, even if the kind of data used by Pareto's generation had been completely satisfactory, Parsons could not claim to have established a firm empirical basis for his action frame of reference. As it is, the empirical deficiencies which lead us to be wary of Pareto's speculations, and to a lesser degree those of Weber and Durkheim,[8] are passed on automatically to Parsonian theory. Of course, if Parsons had proceeded to provide convincing empirical documentation as he extended his original framework, the force of these reservations would have been lessened. In contrast, however, our doubts are strengthened because his actual policy has been to elaborate almost indefinitely upon a number of basic conceptions on the assumption that the initial inductive foundation was sound. Given that the social facts provided by Pareto and his peers are open to criticism and that Parsons' use of this data is based on unjustifiable presumptions, continuous elaboration of the original conceptual framework at a high level of abstraction appears extremely unlikely to maintain that clear empirical reference essential to any scientific theory. There seem to be reasonable grounds for doubting, therefore, whether Parsons' inductive use of factual material is likely to bring forth a satisfactory theoretical system. These doubts are strengthened when we examine Parsons' attempt to justify his method of preparing the way for a mature sociological theory.

Parsons defends his strategy of conceptual elaboration by arguing that concepts are 'logically prior to' the network of substantive propositions which make up a fully developed theory, and are therefore open to separate analysis.[9] He suggests that this logical priority is clearly perceptible in classical physics, which can provide a model for the development of sociological theory. It is not clear, however, that the logical priority of concepts has any necessary implications for research strategy. A theoretical strategy is a means of attaining a satisfactory theoretical system; and there is no necessary connection between the methods by which it is constructed and its logical structure when finally complete. It seems reasonable to suggest, therefore, that instead of guiding the construction of sociological theory by the *logical structure of established theories*, we should refer to the *actual research strategy of a comparatively new and developing discipline*. The following statement by a group of eminent solid state physicists gives some indication of the nature of their discipline and its theoretical strategy:

> Solid state physics is concerned with the elucidation of observed properties of solids in terms of atoms, of electrons, and of the interaction between these constituents. At present, we think that our understanding of these constituents and their interaction is, in principle, adequate to account for all of the observed properties of solids. We do not believe that major new concepts are needed in solid state physics.... Nevertheless... because of the complexity of the many particle aspects... it has proved quite impossible to provide a description of solids that contains all of these features simultaneously. For this reason, solid state physics must resort to the use of physical 'models'. Such models focus attention on those aspects of the situation that are thought to dominate the phenomenon to be described, and disregard other aspects believed to play no essential role. The construction of successful models requires a considerable facility for abstraction. *Often the required insight is obtained only after examination of relevant experimental data. Much of solid state physics is therefore descriptive and explanatory after the fact*, rather than predictive.[10]

This quotation is useful because it demonstrates certain resemblances between the Parsonian categorial system and an expanding scientific discipline, such as solid state physics. In the first place, neither Parsonian theory nor solid state theory has reached the stage where rigorous predictions can be formulated. Secondly, both theories face problems of complexity which can only be resolved by a marked degree of theoretical simplification. And, thirdly, in both instances the major variables are believed to have been identified. Yet despite these similarities there is a marked discrepancy in the two approaches to empirical data. In solid state physics not only are all theoretical developments subject to precise empirical test, but most theoretical insights grow out of the consideration of experimental data; although, of course, these empirical findings themselves depend closely upon prior theoretical notions. The picture that emerges is of an intimate and complex interplay in solid state physics between theoretical conceptions, on the one hand, and controlled observations, on the other hand. And it is precisely this interdependence which is minimized by Parsons' theoretical strategy. If Parsons had chosen to base his strategy on a developing scientific theory like that of solid state physics rather than that of classical mechanics, his whole approach to theory construction would have been radically altered. Of course, once solid state theory has become relatively complete and stable, like that of classical mechanics today, it will be possible to argue that its concepts logically precede its empirical generalizations. But this statement, however valid, will in no way represent the research strategy by which the theory was built up; nor will it necessarily offer any useful guide for disciplines as yet theoretically immature.

The considerable degree of truth in Parsons' argument that the basic conceptions of classical scientific theory tend to form a logically closed system cannot be denied. As a consequence of continual validation, theoretical propositions do take on the form of tautologies; and concepts gradually become defined in terms of each other so as to constitute a logically closed system. This point is amplified in the following statement by the philosopher and historian of science, N. R. Hanson, about the role of the law of gravitation in classical mechanics:

> ... from Newton to Hertz (1894), '$F = \gamma (Mm)/r^2$' had important uses as a principle of inference within axiomatic mechanics, was often set out in texts as a definition, and was sometimes a principle of instrument construction. Finally, it was invoked ... sometimes as an empirical truth whose contradictory was consistent but psychologically inconceivable. ....[11]

On the whole, sociologists stress the empirical character of scientific propositions, thereby ignoring their status as axioms, definitions and so on. Parsons' recognition that certain basic concepts and propositions come to form a logically complete nucleus within the most fully developed theories is a notable exception. But Parsons largely neglects the fact that this kind of logical interrelationship occurs only after long exposure to the possibility of modification in the light of empirical evidence. Logical closure is the *end-product* of a protracted process of induction and deduction, of verification and falsification. To strive for conceptual closure as a prelude to systematic empirical documentation reverses the development usually found in physical science and seems more likely to produce conceptual formalism than satisfactory theory.

The strategy of constructing an elaborate categorial system, although it frees Parsons from the rigorous demands facing genuine theory, is itself open to criticism. First, despite his attempt to provide an inductive basis for his conceptual framework, Parsons is unable to establish that the concepts are fully justified by the empirical evidence or that the evidence is reliable. Secondly, instead of trying to remedy any possible deficiencies in the empirical foundation of his initial concepts, Parsons adopts the contrasting procedure of elaborating these concepts at a high level of abstraction and with sparse empirical support. Finally, his attempt to justify his strategy by reference to the logical structure of established scientific theories is unsatisfactory. Examination of the research strategy used in physical science indicates that Parsons' approach involves a radical departure from the usual scientific methods, a departure which is calculated to exaggerate any tendencies which his scheme may have toward conceptual formalism.

These arguments provide grounds for reasonable doubt about the correctness of Parsons' theoretical strategy. But they remain inconclusive. They establish at best that the odds are against Parsons' long-term theoretical success, but not that he has definitely failed. To decide upon this latter point we must estimate the adequacy of Parsons' scheme *as a categorial system*. If, despite the peculiar research strategy, Parsonian theory actually constitutes a reasonably good categorial system, then there is a fair chance that it may lead in due course to good theory. We must, therefore, before reaching any final judgment, examine the worth of Parsons' framework as a system of categorial knowledge.

II

Parsons defines a categorial system as an orderly network of concepts 'which is formed to fit the subject-matter'.[12] No special difficulties are faced in judging how well ordered is Parsonian theory. But precisely how we are to demonstrate that a conceptual framework *fits the subject-matter* is much less clear. Pareto holds that any particular set of observations can be expressed in terms of a wide variety of conceptual schemes and that, as a result, the only acceptable method of choosing between competing schemes is by reference to their capacity to generate testable propositions. Unfortunately, Parsons, although rejecting Pareto's approach, does not commit himself to any specific alternative and we are left with no clear guide as to how the link between highly abstract concepts and empirical material is to be made. We are not told how to check that concepts *do* fit the facts. Nevertheless, if the relations between concepts in a categorial system are to correspond accurately with the relations existing in the 'real' world the conceptual framework *must* be given unambiguous empirical referents. For if we cannot specify the empirical content of a conceptual scheme we will be unable to establish that there is any correspondence between concepts and social reality. Thus clarity of empirical reference must be one of the criteria by which we estimate the value of Parsonian theory. It is fortunate, therefore, that Parsons does apply his conceptual framework to the analysis of specific empirical areas and, in so doing, shows the extent to which his scheme can be used to express factual data. One of the areas which Parsons investigates most systematically is that of social stratification. Accordingly, whenever the empirical relevance of the Parsonian scheme is questioned in this chapter reference will be made to his analysis of stratification and in particular to the paper entitled 'A Revised Analytical Approach to the Theory of Social Stratification'[13]. The 'theory' of stratification can be used in this way because it is not an independent theory, but a reorganized statement, with special attention to social ranking, of the broader scheme. As Parsons himself writes:

> ... the theory of stratification is not an independent body of concepts and generalizations which are only loosely connected with other parts of general sociological theory; it is general sociological theory pulled together with reference to a certain fundamental aspect of social systems.[14]

In the attempt to specify general theory in this fashion, conceptual inconsistencies tend to be revealed and any lack of clear empirical reference brought to light. It will, therefore, be possible to substantiate certain criticisms of the total framework by reference to the more restricted, but empirically documented, study of social ranking.

In addition to displaying systematic organization and clarity of empirical reference, fully elaborated categorial systems should resemble incipient theories. They should, for example, provide unexpected insights into empirical relationships as well as offering empirical generalizations of various degrees of adequacy. This last statement must not be misunderstood. Categorial knowledge is primarily conceptual and Parsons' main concern is conceptual clarification. However, the construction of a categorial system is essentially a transitional stage which is expected in time to engender a fully developed theoretical system. Thus in the mature categorial system, and after thirty years of development, we can safely regard Parsons' scheme as nearing maturity, conceptual analysis will have been combined with the formulation of empirical generalizations at various levels of abstraction. Parsons endorses this interpretation in a fairly recent statement:

> The conceptual scheme has, in my opinion, now reached a stage of development where the principal difficulty is not in deriving generalized hypotheses, but in stating them at the level of generality and in the system-reference which is most meaningful for the purposes in hand; the complexity of the scheme is such that this presents so very formidable a problem. . . .[15]

Although the formulation of empirical generalizations is not sufficiently advanced in Parsonian theory to allow us to use it as the major criterion of theoretical adequacy, some reference to empirical generalizations must be included in our attempt to judge the scheme's worth as a categorial system.

In general, then, the ideal categorial system is a consistent series of interrelated concepts which have clear empirical content and which have been used to prepare for the transition to the final stage of theoretical development. Parsons, however, adds one further requirement. He intends his scheme to give exhaustive coverage of relevant data. For example, although as a sociologist Parsons' main concern is with the social system, he finds it necessary in order to make his framework comprehensive, to deal with the empirically related but analytically distinct systems of personality and culture in great detail. In addition, functional analysis is introduced specifically to ensure that no significant phenomena are omitted from the conceptual scheme. This factor must be included in our frame of reference for evaluating Parsons' categorial system. We shall, therefore, inspect in turn the systematic character of Parsonian theory, its empirical content, its level of theoretical maturity, its capacity to generate unexpected insights and, finally, its comprehensiveness.

III

The Parsonian scheme ranges methodically from the unit act to the structure of complex social systems. Beginning with a statement of the terms necessary to study the individual actor and the isolated act, Parsons tries to show what additional conceptions are required to examine large aggregates of actors and complex networks of acts. In this way, by a process of gradual conceptual elaboration, he is led to introduce such interrelated notions as the paramount value system, the functional imperatives and the specification of normative culture. It is clear, therefore, that Parsons' scheme is systematic in the sense that it consists of a series of principles and concepts which are related in an orderly fashion to certain basic assumptions about the nature of social life. The logic of particular conceptual extensions can, of course, be challenged. Nevertheless, even if we condemn, for example, the pattern variables as inconsistent and incomplete, we can hardly deny that orderly conceptual interrelations predominate in the Parsonian system. Furthermore, there can be no doubt that in general this kind of well-organized theoretical articulation is necessary in any theoretical system. However, certain reservations are required in relation to Parsons' scheme. For instance, if, as has already been suggested, Parsons' attempt to provide an inductive basis for his initial frame of reference is unsatisfactory, the product of any systematic extension of this framework will itself be suspect. Thus the systematic development of fundamental presumptions is insufficient to guarantee theoretical adequacy. But more important than this is the fact that it gives rise to a definite inconsistency in Parsons' use of the notion of social exchange.

In Chapter 3 it was noted that Parsons' analysis of simple interaction, although proposed as an extension of the action framework, is as much an analysis of social exchange as of social action. The important role which social exchange plays within the Parsonian scheme remained implicit, however, until Parsons began to describe the interrelations between the sub-systems of complex social structures in terms of the double-exchange paradigm. This paradigm, although originally derived from the transactions obtaining between household and economy, has subsequently been applied to a variety of social situations. At present, therefore, Parsons' scheme is inconsistent because it includes a paradigm of two-actor interaction which is couched in terms of social action, yet which has a strong underlying conception of social exchange, while at the same time it includes an explicit exchange model which has been used at all levels of social interaction, thereby to some extent duplicating the original paradigm. If the categorial system is to regain its consistency, some reformulation of the paradigm of simple interaction explicitly in terms of exchange appears to be required. In itself this conceptual modification would change the content of Parsons' scheme very little. It would, however, draw attention to the fact that the conception of social exchange is today as central to Parsonian theory as those of social structure, social function and paramount value system.

IV

Having reviewed the consistency of Parsons' categorial system, I shall now examine the clarity of its empirical referents. This problem can best be approached by concentration on a study in which the theorist intends to give his theoretical conceptions 'concrete empirical content'.[16] As noted above, I have chosen to consider the analysis of social stratification. Parsons opens his analysis by delineating certain implications of the concept of social action. According to the action frame of reference, actors become engaged in a complex series of choices as they strive to achieve their goals. Each act of choice involves selection from a range of possible actions on the basis of a valuation, either implicit or explicit, of the various components which make up the social situation. Those aspects of the situation which the actor regards as likely to help him attain his goals are valued highly, while those which are seen as impeding his gratification are accorded little or no value. It is, of course, possible that in any given instance all aspects of a situation will be valued equally. But in practice, and especially in complex systems, social objects are seen by the individual actor as being more or less favourable to realization of his aims and, consequently, as ranking either high or low in his order of preference. Social selection, then, entails evaluation, and evaluation, in turn, involves social ranking. In this sense, Parsons argues, the notion of social ranking or social stratification is inherent in the action frame of reference. Furthermore, he suggests, we know from the general theory of action that evaluation and selection in complex social systems are guided by shared values. Thus social ranking, being a by-product of processes of selection and evaluation, must also be regarded as an expression of common values. As a result of this line of reasoning, Parsons concludes that the main sphere of interest in the empirical analysis of stratification is 'the ranking of units in a social system in accordance with the standards of the common value system'.[17]

Having established this essential conceptual link between his theoretical framework and the phenomenon of stratification, Parsons puts forward his central principle for the analysis of stratification in complex systems. He argues that the units of social systems—that is, status-role complexes—will be ranked according to the degree to which they express the central value system. This proposition is simply a logical extension of the prior discussion of ranking in relation to individual actors. Its rationale is as follows: In the first place, we know from general theory that shared values are required for the continuance of any complex social system. We also know that social ranking is an expression of such commonly held values. In any ongoing system, therefore, most actors will rank the components of their social world according to the same or very similar standards; and those roles which most fully embody these standards will accordingly be given highest rank generally within the system. Furthermore, these highly ranked roles, because they express the central value system most completely, will tend to make the greatest functional contribution to maintenance of the existing system. The resulting principle, that highest rank will accrue to those roles which are most functionally significant and which most fully actualize shared values, constitutes Parsons' major theoretical guide for the analysis of stratification in complex social structures. He attempts to demonstrate its empirical relevance by using it in a brief illustrative analysis of social ranking in the United States.

The American paramount value system can be classified, Parsons suggests, largely in terms of the pattern variables of universalism and achievement. These values are institutionalized to varying degrees within the four societal sub-systems, being approached most fully in the adaptive sub-system. As a result, adaptive or economic roles receive highest rank in American society. The rank order of the other sub-systems depends on their relative contribution to the fulfilment of these central values within the economy. Parsons argues that in the United States the adaptive sub-system is followed in rank by those of pattern maintenance, integration and goal-attainment, in that order. This first application of the guiding principle gives us what Parsons regards as a broadly accurate overview of the hierarchy of sub-systems within American society. Economic roles come at the top; educational roles somewhat further down, political roles toward the bottom and so on. Within each sub-system, however, roles are ranked according to their contribution to the functional requirements of the sub-system rather than their direct fulfilment of societal values. For example, within the American adaptive sub-system, roles concerned with attainment of sub-system goals tend to rank higher than those concerned with sub-system adaptation. This is so because goal attainment within the economy is more 'strategic', as Parsons puts it, for the functioning of the sub-system than adaptation. To provide empirical support for these assertions, Parsons makes a number of statements purporting to present the facts of American social ranking. Thus he claims that in the United States occupational roles, which he identifies with the adaptive system, do have in general the high prestige that we would expect on the basis of the rank ordering of societal sub-systems. In addition, *within* the economic system, roles which are functionally strategic, such as that of managing director, although concerned with goal-attainment rather than adaptation, receive highest rank of all. This brief résumé of the central thesis in Parsons' analysis of stratification does great injustice to the complexity of the actual study. It does, none the less, provide us with sufficient background to raise the question of the empirical referents of Parsonian theory in relation to the study of social ranking.

In the appraisal of Pareto's work we saw that, despite his emphatic concern with establishing unambiguous empirical referents for his concepts, he experiences great practical difficulty in attaining this goal. Parsons similarly, although distinguishing categorial from *ad hoc* analysis in terms of its more accurate and orderly representation of empirical reality, finds it far from easy to specify precisely what are the empirical referents of his categorial scheme. This conceptual indeterminacy is clearly perceptible in his treatment of social stratification. Although it is undoubtedly true that Parsons succeeds in using his categorial apparatus to make certain statements about stratification, there is a considerable gap between the theoretical statements proposed and the empirical statements offered in confirmation. Take, for example, the argument that the rank awarded to any particular position within the adaptive sub-system will depend on its strategic contribution to the overall function of that sub-system. Parsons' nearest approach to an empirical application of this thesis is the following proposition:

> Broadly we may say that in the occupational system . . . status [prestige] is a function of the individual's productive 'contribution' to the functions of the [economic] organizations concerned. . . .[18]

The first use here of the term 'function' is in the quasi-mathematical sense of 'varies with' and seems to indicate an attempt at formulating an empirical generalization. In more precise theoretical language, this generalization would be phrased as follows: the social rank of status-role complexes within the adaptive sub-system varies in direct proportion to their productive contribution to that sub-system. This is the only proposition which can be directly derived from Parsons' theoretical treatment of social stratification. Parsons does give this statement concrete empirical content, but not without introducing considerable elasticity into his terms. In the first place, when examining the empirical evidence, he replaces 'rank within the adaptive sub-system', with 'occupational status'. There is, of course, no doubt that the economic or occupational system is to some extent coterminous with Parsons' adaptive sub-system. However, even Parsons is forced to admit that 'some of what are defined as occupational roles are not primarily in the adaptive sub-system'.[19]

For example, scientists, teachers and clerics are placed in the pattern-maintenance sub-system of American society, while the roles of government official and politician are located within the integrative and goal-attainment boundaries. These examples alone are sufficient to undermine the correspondence between the theoretical proposition quoted above and the empirical evidence cited in corroboration; and undoubtedly there are many more instances where the adaptive and occupational systems fail to coincide. Yet Parsons dismisses such divergences as being of minor significance and makes no attempt to estimate even roughly the extent of the separation between his theoretical conceptions and the empirical material. He proposes that rank within the adaptive system is directly proportional to contribution to the goals of that system. But the only index offered of 'rank within the adaptive system' is 'occupational status', which is, as we have just seen, to some unknown degree inaccurate. The relevant *conceptual* distinction is, of course, perfectly clear: adaptive roles are those which allocate scarce resources for the total society. But Parsons fails to specify criteria which can be used to supply the concept with clear empirical content.

Similar difficulties apply to the second term in the proposition, that of 'strategic contribution to the goals of the adaptive sub-system'. In order to show that highly ranked roles do in fact make a strategic contribution, it is necessary to provide an index whereby the contribution of a role can be discerned independently of its rank. Parsons fails to do this. Instead, he selects for attention certain high-status economic roles and then asserts, without empirical support, that their productive contribution is 'strategic'. To distinguish the adaptive contribution of a variety of economic roles would be an immensely complicated task, if it could be done at all. Yet until it has been done we can in no way demonstrate that the productive contribution of, say, a director is greater than that of a department manager; we can only assume it. Once again Parsons' meaning is clearly articulated at the conceptual level: the functional contribution of a role refers to those of its consequences which facilitate system goal-attainment. But when we face concrete examples we find that the empirical situation is too complex for us to distinguish the contribution of one role from that of another and that the theorist simply makes no attempt to resolve this problem.

It cannot be claimed that this single example of conceptual imprecision gives sufficient grounds for condemning the whole Parsonian scheme. Yet the generalization selected for study cannot be dismissed as trivial, for it involves an attempt to specify such central theoretical notions as 'functional contribution', 'adaptive sub-system' and 'functional differentiation of roles'. Parsons' inability to eliminate ambiguities when using such crucial concepts in a study designed to demonstrate their empirical content must raise serious doubts about their *general* utility. And these doubts are strengthened when we note that other critics have made similar judgments of the conceptual adequacy of various of Parsons' theoretical terms and principles.[20] Black examines, for example, Parsons' basic assumption that all human action is directed towards goals. He suggests that the meaning of this claim is inherently indeterminate. If we restrict the principle to actions involving only explicit goals, it is relatively clear, but, argues Black, demonstrably false. This is so because many actions give no indication of being directed toward any overt end. On the other hand, if we interpret the principle to cover both explicit and implicit goals, as does Parsons, it becomes indefinitely malleable and applicable to all actions without the need for or the possibility of supporting evidence. Having reviewed several of Parsons' more general assumptions, Black concludes as follows:

> I have been suggesting that Parsons' principles are close to the level of proverbial wisdom. Now, it is characteristic of proverbs, and one reason for their use as a substitute for precise thought, that they embody ambiguities making them indefinitely adaptable to almost any circumstances. ('Look before you leap.' Of course. But then it all depends on what you recognize as the 'leap' and what is to count as 'looking'.) I want to argue that Parsons' principles manifest the same peculiarity. . . . I suspect an endemic *ambiguity of scope* in Parsons' use of his key terms. . . .[21]

Despite Parsons' introduction of categorial analysis specifically to eliminate those conceptual inadequacies which we found to be characteristic of Pareto's scheme, Parsonian theory itself is free neither from definite inconsistencies nor from marked ambiguities of empirical reference both at the general and at the more particular levels.

If these criticisms of conceptual inadequacy are unfounded, we would surely find that Parsons, during the development toward theoretical maturity, has succeeded in formulating satisfactory empirical generalizations. On the other hand, if Parsonian concepts *are* inherently ambiguous, we are likely to find that the attempt to construct verifiable empirical generalizations is regularly avoided. It can be shown that in most cases Parsons adopts the latter policy. Consider, for instance, the assertion that in any given society the sub-system which most directly institutionalizes the paramount value system will have highest rank. At first sight this appears to be a definite empirical generalization. Assuming that we can give empirical content to such terms as 'societal sub-system' and 'paramount value system', then Parsons is postulating a relationship between empirical entities. The theorist, however, prefers to give his statement a different logical status. He suggests that it is 'not an empirical generalization about rank ordering, but only a set of categories in terms of which the empirical problem can be approached'.[22] This interpretation is undoubtedly in accord with Parsons' explicit theoretical strategy and does show a concern on his part to avoid claiming too high a status for his ideas. But this theoretical reticence has the disadvantage of making his statement untestable in principle. A similar unwillingness to allow his generalizations to be subjected to rigorous scrutiny is found in Parsons' treatment of the statement that the rank of economic roles varies according to their productive contribution. Having put forward this generalization, he goes on to note that there are 'innumerable' factors which prevent its operation in practice and that such 'factors are of the greatest importance for detailed empirical analysis, but are secondary from the point of view of the broad characterization of our stratification system'.[23] Parsons states clearly that the theory of stratification does include empirical generalizations; and there is good reason to believe, from the manner of its formulation, that the proposition under discussion is intended as such a generalization. Yet the looseness of its terms plus the indefinite qualifications placed upon its empirical operation make any comparison with factual data impracticable. Once again, although in a different way from the previous example, Parsons removes his generalization from critical appraisal.

To concentrate, however, on one or two statements taken in isolation is perhaps a misleading procedure. All empirical generalizations are idealized statements which come into effect fully only when other factors are held constant. Parsons could argue, therefore, quite justifiably that the rationale behind his complex scheme is precisely to account for, in due course, the whole range of 'other factors' which influence the operation of any one generalization and that such qualifying clauses are for this reason unavoidable. The difficulty with this argument is that it can be used to defend any and every discrepancy between theoretical propositions and factual data. Furthermore, Parsons appears to have gone beyond this argument to a position where he admits not only that he cannot provide the kind of empirical specification which his theory ultimately requires but also that this task is not his responsibility:

> ... a general theory should not be expected to give directly the answers of empirical use to the problems of operational criteria in particular situations. There must be many sets of such criteria for the many different kinds of uses and it is my

opinion ... that it is too big a task for the same person to be the kind of theorist I have attempted to be and at the same time to supply the answers to the relevant operational questions over any very large part of the range for which the scheme is relevant.[24]

At best such an argument is acceptable only as long as the theorist states clearly in which 'part of the range for which the scheme is relevant' he will attempt to supply operational criteria. In its present general form, this contention can be used to avoid *any* direct confrontation with the problem of empirical specification.

Parsons' categorial system appears to consist of a series of concepts, principles and loose generalizations which, in the author's view, provide a broadly appropriate model of social systems in general. It has been argued above that Parsons' attempts to provide empirical content for this model are unsuccessful largely because his conceptual apparatus is ambiguous at all levels of abstraction. Although these conceptual difficulties do not entirely prevent the formulation of low-level empirical generalizations, the latter tend to be safeguarded by so many qualifications that any form of testing is impossible. Moreover, Parsons admits not only that much of his scheme has not been operationalized, but also that the task is beyond him. Thus we must accept that, in relation to most sociological specialties, he has no intention of providing empirical specification and that where the attempt has been made the results have been far from satisfactory.

Despite Parsons' admission that his own efforts will never bring into being a full empirical-theoretical system, he argues occasionally that the relatively recent development of exchange analysis does promise to bridge the gap between categorial knowledge and a rigorous theoretical system:

... the general theory of action ... has taken a turn which may prove to be a harbinger of quantifications closer to the level of generalized theoretical significance than before. This is the statement ... of the equilibrium conditions of systems in terms of the balances of inputs and outputs in relatively clearly defined categories over the boundaries of the system. In a logical sense, this is an inherently quantitative approach. ...[25]

There are good reasons for expecting the explicit introduction of exchange analysis to facilitate the transition to theoretical maturity. In the first place, investigation of processes of exchange seems more likely than the description of social structures to generate generalizations expressing dynamic relations between variables. Secondly, in the use of such notions as inflation and deflation, profit and loss, exchange analysis appears to entail a move towards measurement; and quantification, as we have seen, tends to be regarded by sociological theorists as a necessary feature of theoretical maturity. Despite these reasonable expectations, however, the propositions which Parsons puts forward in connection with his analysis of social exchange suffer from the usual defect of ambiguity as well as, in many cases, excessive complexity. Consider the following example:

> The generalization is that, when the structure of the larger system is undergoing a relatively continuous process of change in the direction of increasing differentiation, the mechanisms involved in this change will, under circumstances, operate to dichotomize the population of units receiving the primary 'real' output of the focal system of reference and to produce an orderly alternation of relative predominance of the two nearly equal parts.[26]

No analysis of this generalization will be offered here. The proposition, with its whole series of built-in qualifications, speaks effectively for itself. It is *possible*, of course, that such assertions do bring nearer 'quantifications closer to the level of generalized theoretical significance than before'. Nevertheless, it appears more reasonable to suggest that the level of conceptual clarity in this case is no more satisfactory than that associated with Parsonian structural-functional analysis. If this is so, we must conclude that the exchange paradigm, although still an interesting theoretical innovation, does little to remedy the basic conceptual inadequacies of the Parsonian categorial system.

V

We have concluded so far that the Parsonian scheme is not entirely consistent, that its empirical content is obscure, and that its shift towards theoretical maturity, although undeniable in the sense that an increasing variety of generalizations have gradually accumulated, adds nothing to the scheme's explanatory or predictive capacity. Nevertheless, the charges levelled above against Parsons' work are of a general character, and we may still find that, despite such defects, it has provided a framework for research capable of generating unexpected sociological insights. Parsons explicitly offers as one justification for the paper on stratification such 'specific insights about the dynamics of the system . . . which would either not be possible at all, or would be far more vacillating and uncertain if the same empirical problems were approached in a more *ad hoc* or common sense way'.[27] With this claim in mind, let us inspect the conclusions produced by the application of Parsonian theory to the analysis of stratification in the United States. These can be stated simply as follows:

1. In America nuclear families are the main units of social ranking.
2. A family's rank depends primarily upon the husband's occupational role.
3. The class structure contains three main strata.
4. Social mobility is high.
5. Ethnic factors do influence the American stratification system but not centrally.

In the course of his study Parsons gives no indication as to which of these findings he regards as unexpected insights. It is difficult to imagine that he would have thought any of these conclusions to be unexpected or that he would regard them as less vacillating because restated in his own terminology. For these findings, apart from proposition 5 which is highly questionable, are the commonplaces of any American textbook on stratification.[28] Nevertheless, these are the central empirical conclusions of the study. Clearly, we cannot accept results of this kind, even if unambiguously derived from the Parsonian scheme in relation to a number of special areas of study, as vindicating Parsons' elaborate system.

VI

Structural-functional analysis is adopted by Parsons because it promises to combine an acceptable level of conceptual simplification with comprehensive coverage of sociological data. We have just concluded that Parsons' scheme of structural concepts does not avoid inconsistency or ambiguity in its attempt to simplify 'social reality'. We must now, finally, examine whether the organization of Parsons' framework around the notion of social function has successfully ensured the inclusion of all significant social phenomena. Of course, the content of any theoretical system will itself largely determine which classes of facts are to be regarded as significant. For this reason, theoretical schemes tend to be self-validating in the sense that any data not included in the theory are seen *ipso facto* as insignificant. This difficulty will be exacerbated when, as in the case of Parsonian theory, the empirical content of the scheme is indeterminate and the concepts themselves open to divergent interpretations. Under these conditions we will be unlikely to reach any firm conclusion as to whether the framework provides complete conceptual coverage of the relevant empirical systems. Bearing in mind these difficulties, let us examine a charge frequently levelled at Parsons' work and at functionalism in general—namely, that it has a static bias.[29] In the context of our present discussion we are particularly concerned to discover whether Parsons' use of functional analysis, instead of furthering conceptual completeness, tends to exclude from consideration those factors which generate structural change in societies.

As Parsons has often stated, one of the central substantive problems which his theory is intended to resolve is that of social order. Parsonian theory is intended as a preliminary answer to the fundamental question: How do orderly social relationships persist? This theme emerges with great clarity in *The Structure of Social Action*, where Parsons surveys the work of his predecessors. But it is not simply inherited from those theorists whom Parsons regards as the main forerunners of the social action framework. For example, Weber's central interest was the dynamics of the transition to capitalist society. Similarly Pareto's general theory was as much a theory of social change as of social order. Even Durkheim retained a lifelong conviction that the science of society was necessarily a science of social development.[30] Undoubtedly these three sociologists conceived of social change as an *orderly* process. However, to the extent that such a distinction can be made in relation to their work, the problem of change had priority over that of social order. Thus the construction of a general theoretical scheme which takes as its point of departure the question of order and stability in society is Parsons' personal contribution to sociology. This is the element which he selects out of prior theory. Given Parsons' unique concern with the problem of social order, it is reasonable to expect that Parsonian theory will experience *special* difficulties in dealing with social change.

In Parsons' paradigm of simple interaction the concern with stable relationships is already evident. When he argues that, if social interaction is to persist, shared values are essential, he appears to be excluding from consideration social relationships which are unstable and which do not persist. But this is not the intention. The paradigm of balanced conformity describes an 'ideal' situation and provides a point of reference from which unstable relationships can be perceived more clearly. None the less, Parsons does stress the theoretical importance of those factors which foster stable interaction. In addition, he clearly presumes that the elaboration of this particular paradigm is likely to lead to a more accurate notion of social life in general. The validity of this latter assumption can be judged only by reference to the results of Parsonian analysis, and these results are not entirely satisfactory. There is, therefore, no obvious reason why we should not start from a conception which assumes social interaction to be inherently unstable and dynamic. We will find when we examine exchange theory that this basic perspective produces a rather different kind of theory as well as a different view of social change.

There is, then, a tendency within the social action framework for social instability to be regarded as a subordinate phenomenon. This aspect of Parsonian theory is further emphasized by the functional analysis of complex systems which, as we have seen, are credited with strong homeostatic[31] tendencies. This concern with the phenomenon and mechanisms of system-maintenance pervades Parsonian functional analysis. In the first place, two of the four functional imperatives, which are presumed to be resolved in all ongoing social systems, operate to maintain and integrate the existing structure. No functional imperative dealing with structural change is included, despite the fact that social systems, almost without exception, do more or less gradually alter their structure. Furthermore, the Parsonian perspective endows all societies with a network of values and other rules which are widely endorsed, which regulate behaviour and which ensure a considerable degree of social stability. In virtually every analysis—for example, in the study of stratification—Parsons takes this central value system as given. When social change *is* examined, attention is usually confined to the processes by which normative culture becomes specified to meet functional requirements. Thirdly, even the analysis of exchange processes is introduced initially as a means of showing how the subsystems of society work together to perpetuate social equilibrium. Thus Parsons' scheme is designed primarily to provide a conceptual apparatus by means of which stable social structures can be described. Somewhat subordinate to this goal is the analysis of those processes whereby social structures are maintained and, in certain circumstances, gradually modified in the course of the specification of normative culture. Parsons defends this approach by the argument that clear structural conceptions are a prerequisite for the successful investigation of change and development:

> The problem of systematizing the morphology of living—
> i.e. biological, psychological, social, and cultural—systems
> is intrinsically easier to solve than that of their dynamics. . . .
> Dynamic analysis must, in our theoretical scheme, be referred
> to morphological premises or else be subject to complete loss
> of orientation. . . . Science is not a photographic reproduction
> of reality, but is a highly selective mode of organizing man's
> orientation to reality—however philosophers define the latter.
> The scientifically specific component of this organization

depends on ability to establish reference-points structurally stable enough to justify *simplification* of dynamic problems prerequisite to logically manageable analysis.[32]

In this quotation Parsons admits that structural-functional analysis has a static bias. However, he defends this bias on the grounds that it is necessary because societies, like biological organisms, have structures which must be accurately described before the course of change can be mapped. The validity of this argument depends upon there being certain resemblances between biological organisms and social systems. If the existence of these parallels between the two kinds of system is shown to be doubtful, it may be necessary to adopt in sociology a distinct approach to the problems of structural maintenance and structural change.

There are several reasons why it is possible to divorce the study of *biological* structures and their functioning from the study of structural development. In the first place, biological organisms have clearly identifiable structures which, through systematic comparison of numerous examples, can be classified into various types of 'normal' structure. Secondly, the mechanisms whereby structures are maintained can be precisely determined and the conditions of structural dissolution stated with some certainty. Thirdly, structural types change very slowly, largely through the selective impact of environmental factors. Given these conditions, it is reasonable to postulate a built-in tendency toward structural maintenance within biological organisms and to organize analysis around the contribution which each structural unit makes to perpetuating the total structure. It is also possible to deal separately with the problem of structural development—that is, with the way in which relatively small and infrequent structural variations are either maintained or eliminated in accordance with environmental influences. However, because social systems differ from biological organisms in several relevant respects, it is much less reasonable in sociology to use such a predominantly homeostatic model or to make such a clear separation between structural-functional and developmental analysis. First, in sociology there are seldom more than a few examples of any one type of structure. It is, therefore, impossible to demonstrate by means of extensive comparison which structures are 'normal'. Secondly, we can only vaguely indicate the control mechanisms which are said to maintain social systems in a state of equilibrium. And, thirdly, it has proved impossible to specify just what is being maintained within systems where the 'normal' structure is itself undergoing constant, sometimes radical and often violent change. This last point, that continuous though variable change is a permanent feature of many social systems, is probably the most important.

Sociologists are now generally agreed that selective evolution along Darwinian lines does not account for this kind of social development. Parsons himself accepts that there are powerful internal or endogenous sources of structural development quite unlike the 'chance' structural variations found among biological organisms. It is reasonable to suggest, therefore, that a different model is required in sociology. The sociological model, instead of concentrating upon the sources of system-maintenance, will need to combine an account of homeostatic mechanisms with a consistent treatment of structurally generated change. If this argument is accepted, then any scheme which, like Parsons' structural-functional analysis, places overwhelming emphasis on the basic identity of approach needed to study biological and social systems will be guilty of an unjustifiable static bias.

Almost from the outset Parsonian theory has been charged with having a static bias.[33] But as Parsons has further extended the scheme in recent years, undoubtedly taking such criticisms into account, the defect has to some extent been remedied. At the conceptual level, Parsons can now claim to deal with several types of structural change. He considers those structural changes which are brought about by variation in a society's social environment; he examines the ways in which faulty socialization leads to deviance from established normative patterns and, in the long run, to alterations in role-expectations; and he surveys the processes whereby normative culture becomes functionally specified.[34] There is, however, one important feature of Parsons' treatment of dynamic problems which should not be overlooked—namely, that social change and development have come to be conceived increasingly in terms of social exchange. Thus the criticism that Parsonian *structural-functionalism* is ill-equipped to deal with dynamic phenomena is strengthened when we consider that Parsons has managed to include such phenomena within the scheme only by the introduction of exchange analysis.

Parsons first uses exchange analysis in his examination of how the functionally differentiated societal sub-systems combine to maintain the wider-spread system. Thus the *dynamic* aspects even of structural-functional equilibrium analysis are couched in terms of exchange. But, in addition to conceptualizing in this manner the processes whereby the existing structure is maintained, Parsons comes to perceive that the interchange between sub-systems is the basic internal source of structural change:

> *The most general, commonly used term for an endogenous tendency to change is 'strain'.* Strain here refers to a condition in the *relation* between two or more structured units (i.e. sub-systems of the system) that constitutes a tendency or

pressure toward changing that relation to one incompatible with the equilibrium of the relevant part of the system. If the strain becomes great enough, the mechanisms of control will not be able to maintain that conformity to relevant normative expectations necessary to avoid the breakdown of the structure. *A strain is a tendency to disequilibrium in the input-output balance between two or more units of the system.*[35]

In so far as each sub-system faces its own functional problems as well as the demands of other sub-systems, actual outputs will seldom correspond perfectly with the requirements of other sub-systems. Although there will be negative responses from receiving sub-systems which reduce the production of inappropriate outputs, only infrequently will these outputs be entirely eliminated. It is this asymmetry in exchange relationships which gives the more recent formulations of Parsonian theory the potential for an extensive examination of endogenous structural change. But, as we have noted above, this examination is far from complete. Furthermore, although this approach holds some promise of enabling Parsons to deal more fully with the dynamics of social systems, and thereby to complete the conceptual coverage of his categorial system, it must be recognized that it entails use of theoretical conceptions of exchange which are by no means inherently linked with either the structural-functional or the action framework. It seems reasonable to conclude, therefore, that structural-functional analysis alone does exclude from consideration certain aspects of structural change and development. Before reaching any final conclusion, however, let us inspect Parsons' treatment of dynamic problems in the study of stratification. By reviewing this attempted specification of the general theoretical scheme, we shall obtain a clearer idea of the practical limitations of Parsons' structural-functional scheme when it is not supplemented by exchange analysis.

The most obvious gap in Parsons' coverage of dynamic phenomena is occasioned by his failure to deal systematically with radical social disturbances and particularly with those accompanied by violence. This omission is not surprising, because it is precisely these phenomena which most clearly distinguish social from biological systems. Traditionally, sociologists have conceived of this kind of social change as linked with the stratification system. There is a whole body of literature, much of it Marxian in inspiration, which views social inequality as both potentially and actually a source of societal disruption and revolution. If the style of argument by which Parsons attempted to substantiate the social action framework were adopted here, it would be possible to maintain that this massive theoretical agreement about the dynamic effect of social hierarchies must represent with some accuracy certain empirical regularities.[36] In addition, we could show that this consensus is not solely a Marxian assumption. Even Pareto, who was in many respects extremely hostile to the Marxist view, regarded group conflict and open violence, not only as ever-present facets of societal change and development, but also as associated with the unequal distribution of power, prestige and material goods. We do not wish to argue this kind of thesis as strongly as Parsons in *The Structure of Social Action*. The intention here is, by referring to the conclusion offered by this other perspective on social stratification, merely to highlight the peculiarly static character of Parsons' study.

For Parsons social stratification is an aspect of social structure 'of primarily integrative significance'.[37] This basic theoretical assumption alone does not commit Parsons irrevocably to minimizing its dynamic consequences. For social ranking, if it is 'to function in a positively integrative way, must be a genuine expression of the institutionalized system of values'.[38] This formulation does leave room for situations where there is only minimal convergence on values or where social ranking fails to embody the paramount values. In these circumstances we would envisage the possibility of open conflict and social change being fostered by the system of social ranking and by the accompanying unequal distribution of possessions. But in practice these possibilities are ignored. Parsons simply assumes that certain values are widely shared and that social ranking is closely aligned with these values. Indeed, it would appear that Parsons *must* assume the existence of a value consensus, for if there is no central value system it becomes impossible to determine which sub-system most fully expresses these values, and the whole analysis falls apart. Thus in his theoretical analysis of stratification he is forced to assume that there are shared values which remain constant and which guide social ranking throughout the total society. Once this assumption has been made, a dynamic analysis is no longer feasible, and Parsons himself admits his inability to deal with the dynamic aspects of his problem:

> After . . . 'spelling out' the paramount value system in each of the primary functional contexts of system process, we can then approach the problem of analysing the differentiation of roles in the system. It should be remembered that *we are dealing with this on a purely descriptive structural level*. We are aware that the number of units belonging to a system for example is itself a function of system-process over time, and from the dynamic point of view should not be assumed, but for present purposes we will ignore this.[39]

AN ASSESSMENT OF PARSONS' SCHEME

When Parsons turns to the investigation of American society, these theoretical assumptions determine his empirical conclusions. The possibility that various groups in the United States have essentially different values or that social ranking is far from being a 'genuine expression' of paramount values are never considered. Given this perspective, the central conclusion is inevitably that differences in class, prestige and ethnic background will tend to become increasingly institutionalized and thereby lose much of their potential for generating structural change. It is this perspective which leads Parsons to state, for example, that the importance of ethnic ranking in the United States 'would, in the normal course of development in our type of society, be expected to decrease'. In the light of subsequent events, this analysis does seem to have underestimated the strong link within American society between social ranking, and the unequal distribution of social facilities, on the one hand, and violent social change on the other.[40]

VII

In the previous section it was suggested that Parsons' structural-functional framework systematically exaggerates the tendencies toward stability and structural maintenance displayed by social systems and that, in consequence, various kinds of structural change are either excluded from consideration or regarded unjustifiably as subordinate phenomena. This static bias was seen to operate, not only at the conceptual level, but also in empirical studies where dynamic problems would be expected to be prominent. Parsons' attempts to reduce this conceptual deficiency by introducing the double-exchange paradigm. It is at least possible that, by increasing his reference to social exchange, Parsons may be able in due course to offer relatively complete conceptual coverage of the sources of endogenous structural change. But conceptual bias was only of the criticisms levelled at Parsonian theory. It was also suggested that Parsons' categorial system is conceptually inconsistent and that the remedy seems to lie in systematic integration of the double-exchange paradigm into the total scheme. At present the exchange paradigm is not consistently linked to the remainder of the conceptual framework. This is so largely because it does not emerge directly from the elaboration of the original frame of reference, but rather constitutes a new theoretical principle intended to supplement structural-functional analysis. Parsons is particularly hopeful that exchange analysis will facilitate conceptualization of dynamic processes within the social system. In addition, however, he sometimes argues that exchange analysis is a major breakthrough in the direction of theoretical maturity, because it brings quantification nearer and consequently entails that high degree of conceptual precision without which quantification is inconceivable.

We have seen that this level of theoretical attainment is neither achieved nor even consistently claimed by Parsons, whose most reasoned appraisal of the status of his scheme leads to the broad conclusion that it is somewhere between a generalized conceptual framework and a general theory. In Parsons' view the most important task at this stage of theoretical development is that of specifying his principles and generalizations in such a way that they become amenable to rigorous comparison with concrete data. Although he recognizes the necessity for such specification, Parsons argues that, owing to the complexity of the social system and the corresponding complexity of any general sociological system, much of this work must be left to others. But if this is the case, Parsons must offer to others some demonstration that eventual theoretical success is probable or at least possible. Pareto would have maintained at this point that only by results can any convincing demonstration of theoretical potential be made. And, indeed, it is difficult to envisage any other way of settling this question. Unfortunately, Parsons presents very little in the way of positive results. Although his writings cover a wide range of topics, the conclusions proffered bring to light few empirical relationships.[41] Thus the only result that can be volunteered is that the scheme corresponds in some general fashion with the relations existing in the real world. But this claim is insupportable if, as has been argued above, Parsons signally fails to provide clear links between his theoretical conceptions and empirical data. In the long run it may be possible to remove the conceptual inconsistencies in the Parsonian categorial system and to include all data regarded as significant by the sociological community. But while generalizations are untestable and concepts without clear empirical referents, conceptual consistency and comprehensiveness are too easily achieved. Conceptual closure is valuable only when unambiguous links are established between theory and fact in such a manner that the ordered relationships within the theoretical scheme are known to represent the relationships among empirical phenomena. As long as empirical clarity is not forthcoming Parsons' scheme must remain primarily a gigantic exercise in conceptual formalism.

Our confidence in the cogency of this central criticism of Parsonian theory is strengthened when we recall the implications of Parsons' theoretical strategy. For the biggest danger facing any theorist who elaborates systematically and at a highly general level upon suspect empirical foundations is without doubt that of conceptual formalism—that is, the formulation of an extensive series of concepts which lack detailed specification. The charge of conceptual formalism entails a damning verdict upon a scheme *intended specifically to resolve conceptual problems as a preparation for the construction of a genuine scientific theory.* It is this conceptual failure, on the part of Parsons as well as earlier theorists, such as Pareto, which provokes Merton to advocate a significant change in theoretical strategy. Merton's reaction against over-ambitious strategies is clearly expressed in the following quotation:

> To concentrate entirely on the master conceptual scheme for deriving all subsidiary theories is to run the risk of producing twentieth-century sociological equivalents of the large philosophical systems of the past, with all their varied suggestiveness, all their architectonic splendour and all their scientific sterility.
>
> Men allocate their scant resources somehow, whether they know it or not, and this allocation reflects their workaday policies. This holds as much for the men concerned with the production of sociological theory as for the men concerned with the production of plumbing supplies. These observations, elicited by Parsons' paper on the position of sociological theory, are intended to bring out one such policy decision faced by the men who practice sociological theory. Which shall have the greater share of our immediate energies and resources: the search for confirmed theories of the middle range or the search for all-inclusive conceptual schemes? I believe . . . that for some time to come it is the theories of the middle range which hold the largest promise. . . .[42]

In the next chapter I shall examine Merton's attempt to combine a 'middle-range strategy' with the use of a functional theoretical perspective.

5 A second functional alternative: Merton

I

Merton follows both Pareto and Parsons in accepting that sociology should strive for a comprehensive theory which, in his own words, is 'adequate to encompass vast ranges of precisely observed details of social behaviour and fruitful enough to direct the attention of thousands of research workers to pertinent problems of empirical research'.[1] He differs from them, however, in his estimation of how much preparatory work is required before theorists should concern themselves directly with this task and, consequently, is led to adopt a radically different approach to the construction of general theory. In Pareto's view, the best way of building a general theory is to attempt a crude but recognizable deductive system which can be tested and gradually modified to meet, in due course, even the most demanding criteria of scientific adequacy. Although adopting certain of Pareto's substantive conceptions, Parsons rejects this broad theoretical strategy, arguing that systematic conceptual reformulation is required in sociology before a comprehensive and empirically relevant logico-deductive system can be successfully composed. Merton's policy more closely resembles that of Parsons in its assumption that construction of a complete general theory must be preceded by certain preliminary operations. He is particularly concerned, however, to ensure that this preparatory work should not be overambitious. In Merton's view, general theoretical schemes, at the present stage of development, offer merely 'orientations toward data, suggesting types of variables which need somehow to be taken into account, rather than clear, verifiable statements of relationships between specified variables'.[2] We have seen that the criticism implied in this statement applies to Parsons and to Pareto. It is precisely this lack of attention to the detailed specification of general theory, this inability to provide clear propositions unambiguously relevant to concrete social systems, which vitiates the work of both theorists. Merton's theoretical strategy, in contrast, is designed to avoid just this defect. Merton argues that clarity of empirical reference can be attained only if we lower the level of theoretical abstraction. This can best be done, he suggests, if we shift our attention from the construction of one master theory to the formulation of numerous sub-theories or theories of the middle range.

Parsons and Merton agree that their theoretical inheritance, exemplified in this study by the work of Pareto, is in many respects unsatisfactory. Parsons argues, however, that there has been sufficient theoretical convergence among a number of reasonably adequate sociological theories to provide a firm basis for the formulation of a comprehensive theoretical framework. Merton does not deny that there has been a convergence or that further development of this conceptual legacy may prove fruitful in the long run. But he maintains that few broad theoretical perspectives have survived detailed application; and in his view this is the acid test of theoretical adequacy. Consequently, as there can be no conclusive demonstration in advance that these general perspectives will ever achieve the kind of precision required, and as we know from past experience that such precision is seldom realized in practice, we will be more assured of eventual success if we formulate middle-range theories— that is 'theories intermediate to the minor working hypotheses evolved in abundance during the day-to-day routines of research, and [to] the all-inclusive speculations. . . .'[3] The major advantage of these modest theoretical conceptions is that their empirical relevance can be unambiguously demonstrated from the beginning, before any attempt is made to codify them into a more comprehensive system. As a result, the main problem facing general theory, that of empirical specification, will be resolved from the outset. However, despite this emphasis on the merits of middle-range theory, Merton does not exclude general theory entirely from his scheme.

> . . . I believe . . . that for some time to come, it is theories of the middle-range which hold the largest promise, *provided that*, underlying this modest search for social uniformities, there is an enduring and pervasive concern with *consolidating* the special theories into a more general set of concepts and mutually consistent propositions.[4]

Given that both special and general theories are needed in sociology, the basic strategical problem becomes that of allocating our limited resources most productively. We must, therefore, ask such questions as: Will we more quickly attain our long-term goal by concentrating upon general schemes in the hope that less comprehensive but more concrete theories can be extracted? Or would we arrive at a mature theoretical system with less expenditure of time and effort if we were to reverse the procedure and establish first a series of special theories? Merton is convinced that the second approach will prove to be a more profitable theoretical investment, not only because general theory has, as yet, failed to satisfy accepted criteria of theoretical or conceptual adequacy, but also because it fails to foster that close relationship between theory and research without which theoretical speculation becomes scientifically irrelevant. Although the question of the connection between theory and research has been raised in earlier chapters, it requires further discussion here, in view of its relatively detailed examination by Merton.

All general theories are based upon some kind of survey of empirical material. Merton argues, however, that once the broad outlines of a general theoretical scheme have crystallized, empirical research tends to be given but one role—namely, that of testing the validity of propositions inferred from the theory. As we have seen, Pareto adheres strictly to this policy, as, for example, in his hypothesis about the relationship between residues and social prosperity. Parsons' approach differs only in being more cautious. Instead of deducing propositions to be tested, he remains satisfied with showing that his conceptions can be given empirical content within limited areas, like that of stratification. For both theorists, after the initial empirical survey, theory tends to determine the course of empirical research. The findings of such research can, of course, in principle, be used to modify or reject prior theory as well as to confirm it. But as long as we operate at the level of general theory systematic theoretical reformulation is easily avoided. The gap which separates general theoretical propositions from factual data, when combined with conceptual imprecision, makes it only too easy for even the most scrupulous theorist to conclude that his theoretical inferences have been broadly verified. Merton maintains that the middle-range strategy reduces difficulties of this kind by making possible an interplay between theory and research which is more varied and which engenders more concrete and rigorous theoretical conceptions:

> ... empirical research goes far beyond the passive role of verifying and testing theory: it does more than confirm or refute hypotheses. Research plays an active role: it performs at least four major functions which help shape the development of theory. It *initiates*, it *reformulates*, it *deflects*, and it *clarifies* theory.[5]

Empirical research does, ideally, test and thereby verify or falsify theoretical propositions. In this way the direction of research is determined by theoretical preconceptions. However, the process can and should be a reciprocal one in which research feeds back upon theory and leads to its improvement. In the first place, empirical research can reveal unanticipated and previously unobserved phenomena which require theoretical treatment. Secondly, phenomena which are consistently noted by the observer, but which have been theoretically neglected, call for elaboration of existing theory. Thirdly, the emergence of new research techniques produces new types of data which exert pressure for theoretical reformulation. These pressures for reformulation are more easily met at the middle-range level, where theoretical commitment is relatively specific. New or previously unobserved data are more likely to be ignored at the level of systematic general theory, because initially minor conceptual revisions will tend to have far-reaching implications for the whole interlocking scheme. But perhaps the most significant advantage of working at the middle-range level arises from the fact that the inherent vagueness of many theoretical concepts becomes evident only when they are *used* in the actual process of research. Merton argues that the limited notions of middle-range theory are more readily available for such use than the more abstract conceptions of general theory. He does not disagree with Parsons' contention that much theoretical work must be devoted to conceptual systematization and clarification. But, he points out, this task is most effectively pursued when conceptualization and empirical research are undertaken jointly:

> . . . the clarification of concepts, commonly considered a province peculiar to the theorist, is a frequent result of empirical research. Research sensitive to its own needs cannot easily escape this pressure for conceptual clarification. *For a basic requirement of research is that the concepts, the variables, be defined with sufficient clarity to enable the research to proceed,* a requirement easily and unwittingly not met in the kind of discursive exposition which is often miscalled sociological theory.[6]

From Merton's perspective, conceptual elaboration which is divorced from direct and continuous contact with empirical research is almost certain to end in theoretical formalism.

Despite the identity of their long-term theoretical aims and despite their agreement over the inadequacy of prior general theory, Parsons and Merton differ considerably in their assessment of the appropriate theoretical strategy for sociology. Compared with Pareto, Parsons' immediate theoretical aims have always been modest, although their realization has involved him in more complex theoretical work. But Merton has retreated even further than Parsons from immediate commitment to general theory. Nevertheless, the two latter theorists share at least one major theoretical conviction. They agree, not only that certain preparatory work must be undertaken before a general logico-deductive system can be framed in sociology, but also that these preliminary operations must adopt the functional viewpoint. However, the contrasting strategies of the two theorists lead them to use this approach in markedly different ways.

II

Merton's theoretical strategy is designed to produce numerous special theories at various levels of abstraction below that of fully general theory. Because this approach is incompatible with the use of an overall theoretical framework, Merton is unable to furnish any consistent link between these middle-range theories through the application of a set of prior substantive conceptions. Yet he is reluctant to create a congeries of theories which are connected only haphazardly, for this would undoubtedly increase the difficulties which will unavoidably arise when, at some future date, attempts are made to reconcile these special theories within a comprehensive theoretical scheme. Merton resolves this problem in two ways. First, he takes many of the substantive concepts used in his various special theories from the writings of a restricted range of theorists, in particular from Durkheim and Weber.[7] In this way he establishes a degree of conceptual continuity among his own theories as well as forging conceptual links with other theorists, such as Parsons, who have drawn upon the same sources. Secondly, and more significantly, he uses the same *functional method* to guide each of his analyses. Where functional analysis provides for Parsons a way of organizing the structural concepts of an incipient general theory, it constitutes for Merton a method by means of which the empirical data involved in a series of specialized and partly independent theories can be systematically gathered and interpreted.

Merton's ploy of replacing speculative theory with a form of small-scale functionalism, which he first proposed during the 1940s, was not a new device. For it had been used some decades earlier in social anthropology, where functional analysis had been adopted as a substitute for the speculations of evolutionary theory. It is not surprising, therefore, to find that Merton turns to anthropology when searching for an appropriate analytical perspective. Evolutionary anthropology had suffered from two major defects. In the first place, because pre-literate societies could supply no documentary evidence of their historical development, the application of evolutionary theory had to remain highly speculative. Secondly, what evidence there was indicated that many of these societies had changed very little over long periods of time, except when exposed to external social influences. Thus critics of evolutionary anthropology argued that when the societies under study appear highly stable and when they provide no historical record, genetic accounts of social structure[8] are unverifiable and therefore worthless. These difficulties within anthropology were resolved by abandonment of the evolutionary approach in favour of structural-functional analysis, which attempted to explain any one aspect of society by its connection with other aspects of the same society at the same point in time.[9] Associated with this change in theoretical perspective was a change in research method whereby anthropology came to rely for its data on intensive field research. Thus, like Merton, functional anthropologists placed great emphasis on the collection of reliable evidence. But anthropological functionalism was more than a method of gathering data. Although the need for relatively limited and well-documented studies was stressed, anthropological functionalism retained certain guiding notions about the nature of human societies.[10] Merton derives his own brand of functional method from a critical review of some of these theoretical assumptions.

Merton maintains that social anthropologists often made use of three assumptions which may well have been fruitful in the study of relatively simple, stable and cohesive societies, but which are in principle 'unnecessary to the functional orientation',[11] and which may prove to be a particular hindrance in the application of functional analysis to more complex societies. These assumptions are as follows: that *all items* within any one society contribute to the maintenance of that society; that all items help maintain the *whole social structure*; and that existing social or cultural forms are *indispensable* for the persistence of the society under study. Merton calls these three theoretical presumptions respectively the postulate of universal functionalism, the postulate of the functional unity of society, and the postulate of functional indispensability. He suggests, not that these postulates have been universally accepted in anthropology, but that they have appeared frequently in anthropological literature. His concern is not to establish the inadequacy of anthropological theory, but to demonstrate that careful scrutiny of these recurrent assumptions will lead to significant improvements in functional analysis.

The postulate of functional indispensability contains, in Merton's view, two distinct assertions. The first of these is that 'there are certain *functions* which are indispensable in the sense that, unless they are performed, the society (or group or individual) will not persist'.[12] The second is that in any particular instance only *certain cultural or social forms* can fulfil these functions. The former statement can itself be intepreted in two ways. On the one hand, it can be argued that certain *general functions* must be performed in all societies or social systems. It is precisely in this sense that Parsons, for example, uses the term 'functional requisites'. On the other hand, it is possible to maintain that within any specific group or society *particular functions* must be performed. In accordance with his middle-range strategy, Merton tends to emphasize the second of these interpretations. But, even when the notion of functional requisite is given this restricted meaning, Merton is dubious of its value for functional analysis. The basic defect of the concept is that it adds virtually nothing to our knowledge of any given society. Thus to argue that items A, B, and C are functional requisites for society X is to do little more than redescribe certain activities that are observed to take place within society X. To maintain, for instance, that mechanisms for the transmission of given values are essential for the persistence of a particular society adds nothing that can be clearly demonstrated to the statement that the transmission of these values at present helps to hold that society together. Although Merton is sceptical about the notion of functional requisites, which he regards as 'one of the cloudiest and empirically most debatable concepts in functional theory',[13] he does not insist on rejecting it from the functional framework. He is willing to accept that it may be possible on occasion to supply useful indices of those requirements which must be fulfilled if a given society is to persist. However, the second aspect of the postulate of indispensability—that is, the indispensability of specific items—must in his view be totally repudiated.

The tendency to assume that particular social items are indispensable often becomes evident when attempts are made to provide functional explanations. Such explanations have the following underlying logic:[14]

1   If system S is to persist, function F must be fulfilled (indispensability of functions).
2   *Only* item I can fulfil functional requirement F (indispensability of items).
3   System S is maintaining itself.
4   Therefore, I must be part of S.

When the indispensability of functions is combined with the indispensability of items, functional analysis can provide a *logically* adequate explanation of the occurrence of item I within system S. But Merton objects in principle to the use of statements like No. 2, above. To assert that a specific item is the only possible means of fulfilling a given function, he argues, is unacceptable on both empirical and theoretical grounds. It is, in the first place, contrary to fact, in that all functional requisites mentioned in the literature can be shown to have been satisfied in a variety of different ways within different societies. For example, the transmission of values, which is often cited as a functional requisite, has been performed by families of various types, by a great variety of school systems, and by many different combinations of educational and kinship networks. Difficulties of a theoretical nature also arise unless we accept that 'the same function may be diversely fulfilled by alternative items'.[15] These difficulties are particularly evident in relation to the question of social change. If we assume that each specific item of standardized thought and behaviour within a given society is essential to the persistence of that society, we are either unable to envisage any possibility of structural change or we are left with a tautology to the effect that: because any change in the existing structure will, by definition, alter that structure, each structural component is indispensable for the persistence of the total structure. In Merton's view, therefore, the postulate of indispensability must be replaced by three related conceptions. He retains provisionally the idea of *functional requisite*. The concept is to be used, however, only in so far as it can be given clear empirical content in relation to specific societies, groups or individuals. Secondly, he introduces the notion of *functional alternative*. This concept draws the analyst's attention to that *range* of items which might cater for any given functional requirement. Finally, if we are to give a convincing account of how particular items are selected from the range of functional alternatives, we must examine how the structural context limits the variety of attainable solutions to functional problems. Merton adopts, therefore, a notion of *structural constraint*.

In general, then, Merton argues that the question of functional variation should be left empirically open. Instead of assuming indispensability in advance, he suggests that we should use a conceptual apparatus which gives full recognition to the range of potential empirical variety. Only in this way can functional analysis be reconciled with Merton's stress upon conceptual clarity and empirical relevance. It is worth noting, however, that in his critique of the postulate of indispensability Merton has implicitly repudiated the functional explanatory scheme formalized above. This question of the capacity of functional analysis to furnish explanations is important, and we shall return to it later.

Merton's objection to the postulate of the functional unity of society is based on much the same grounds as his opposition to the postulate of indispensability. Whether or not a particular item contributes functionally to the total society is seen by Merton as a matter for empirical determination; it should not be decided by theoretical axiom, but by an investigation of the facts. We must, of course, assume that the constituents of any ongoing society do operate in a general way to maintain that society. Nevertheless, it is still possible that items contribute differently, even negatively, to various groups within society. Especially in complex societies, the impact of any given item may be positive for certain groups and negative for others; and, furthermore, actual objective consequences may be quite different from intended consequences. Merton suggests that these empirical possibilities must be recognized conceptually and that, consequently, we cannot accept the definition of function used by the anthropologists. Radcliffe-Brown expresses in the following manner the anthropological conception of function against which Merton is rebelling:

> The function of a particular social usage is the contribution it makes to the total social life as the functioning of the total social system. Such a view implies that a social system ... has a certain kind of unity which we may speak of as a functional unity. We may define it as a condition in which all parts of the social system work together with a sufficient degree of harmony or internal consistency, i.e. without producing persistent conflicts which can neither be resolved nor regulated.[16]

Built into this definition is the notion of social usages making a positive contribution to society. Although Radcliffe-Brown himself proposed this conception only tentatively, it did guide his research and direct his attention towards the positive consequences of social phenomena. Merton, however, replaces it with a series of conceptual distinctions which embody a wider range of empirical possibilities. *Social function* refers to the observable objective consequences of a repeated social event. When consequences are negative, when they reduce the level of satisfaction of individual needs or group requirements, the term *dysfunction* is to be used.[17] Consequences which are intended are *manifest functions* while those which are unintended are *latent functions*. This latter distinction is important for Merton, for, in his view, it is in the study of latent rather than the more obvious manifest functions that sociologists can make their most significant contributions to social analysis. Functional analysis is, then, for Merton the study of how social items have 'diverse consequences, functional and dysfunctional', manifest and latent, 'for individuals, for sub-groups, and for the more inclusive social structure and culture'.[18] It is potentially a more complex undertaking than Radcliffe-Brown's search for the positive contribution made by social usages to the total social system.

Finally, there is the postulate of universal functionalism. Merton maintains that this can be no more assumed than the other two postulates. Thus it has already been suggested that some social usages may have negative consequences for certain groups and beneficial effects for others. It is also possible that some items have no observable consequences at all. The functional perspective indicates, in Merton's view, that items *may* have functions, but not that they *must* have them. He therefore suggests that we replace the postulate of universal functionalism with:

> the provisional assumption that persisting cultural forms have a *net balance of functional consequences* either for the society considered as a unit or for sub-groups sufficiently powerful to retain these forms intact, by means of direct coercion or indirect persuasion. This formulation at once avoids the tendency of functional analysis to concentrate on positive functions and directs the attention of the research worker to other types of consequences as well.[19]

This directive is worth quoting, not only because it emphasizes the importance of identifying the mechanisms whereby functional and dysfunctional consequences are passed from one element of the social structure to another, but also because it introduces, in the reference to coercion and persuasion, an implicit notion of exchange or social reciprocity. This implication becomes more clearly evident when Merton puts his paradigm for functional analysis into use, and we shall discuss it further when we examine the paradigm in that connection.

In the course of this critique of some of the major postulates occurring in anthropological functionalism, Merton introduces the conceptual apparatus which makes up his paradigm for functional analysis. The next step is to arrange these conceptions in a systematic framework within which to pursue the formulation of middle range theories. Merton's arrangement is straightforward and can be summarized as follows:

1 Identify precisely those items within the area under study which have observable consequences for surrounding units.
2 Specify the purposes, the intentions, of the actors involved.
3 Distinguish between manifest and latent functions, and between functions and dysfunctions.
4 Note which units are affected by the objective consequences of the items being investigated.
5 If possible, identify the needs of individuals concerned and the functional requirements of groups.
6 Specify the mechanisms by which functions are mediated.

7 Examine possible functional alternatives and the limitations imposed by the structural context.
8 Investigate sources of structural change, especially in relation to dysfunctions.
9 Validate the analysis, if possible, by means of systematic comparison with similar social situations.

Unlike the anthropological model, this paradigm contains virtually no concrete assumptions about the character of human societies. Within the anthropologists' framework, pre-literate societies were seen as highly integrated and stable communities, all or most aspects of which contributed significantly and perhaps irreplaceably to maintenance of the existing structure. Merton's substantive assumptions are, by contrast, much more tenuous. From his perspective, persisting social usages *can* be functional; but they can also be dysfunctional. Similarly, their consequences *can* be those intended by the actors involved; but they can also be unintended. And, although functions *can* be related to society as a whole, they can also be linked to the requirements of sub-groups and even to those of individuals. Thus Merton himself postulates only that the constituents of any society will be interdependent to some unspecified extent; and that this interdependence operates to prevent complete dissolution of the group. Compared with the basic theoretical conceptions of either Pareto or Parsons, these postulates appear excessively weak. But perhaps we should ask no more from an analyst who wishes, at present, to avoid general theory. Merton replaces the kind of broad notions which furnish a guiding model for these two theorists as well as for the anthropologists with a method for formulating theories, a method whose central principle is that sociological analysis should concentrate on functions or objective consequences rather than causes. There can be no doubt that by applying this paradigm in a number of special areas Merton has become a seminal figure in many branches of modern sociology. Nevertheless, this approach does have its defects. In order to discuss these we must examine the paradigm in use.

III

Merton's study of *Social Structure and Anomie* is an attempt to use the paradigm for functional analysis to investigate the phenomenon of social deviance.[20] This study shows that despite important theoretical differences, Merton's approach resembles that of Parsons in several ways. First, there is the rejection of that psychologistic perspective which was such a central feature of Pareto's sociology. Pareto, for example, saw crime, perhaps the most obvious form of social deviance, simply as the typical behaviour of persons characterized by certain internal and largely innate propensities.[21] Merton argues that functional analysis is strongly opposed to this kind of interpretation:

> ... functional analysis conceives of the social structure as active, as producing fresh motivations which cannot be predicted on the basis of knowledge about man's native drives. ... The functional approach therefore abandons the position, held by various individualist theories, that different rates of deviant behaviour in diverse groups and social strata are the accidental result of varying proportions of pathological personalities found in these groups and strata. It attempts instead to determine how the social and cultural structure generates pressure for socially deviant behaviour upon people variously located in that structure.[22]

Functional analysis, in this context, is concerned with culture, with social structure and with the impact of these influences upon individual action. Like Parsons, Merton has come to think of personality, culture and social structure as analytically distinct levels of conceptualization. These three levels are, of course, interdependent. But Merton, as well as Parsons, regards cultural values as extremely important, not only because they prescribe which goals are to be sought within specific groups, but also because they define which means are legitimate. Merton assumes that in any given society the rules concerning the adoption of goals and means will be effectively internalized by the great majority of members. Thus, in true Parsonian fashion he states that it is 'only because behaviour is typically oriented toward the basic values of the society that we may speak of a human aggregate as comprising a society'.[23] Both Merton and Parsons, then, postulate that there is a close resemblance between the normative system, the social structure and actual behaviour. But Merton emphasizes more strongly than Parsons that resemblance is not identity. In *Social Structure and Anomie* Merton tries to show how a particular kind of discrepancy between cultural values and social structure can generate behavioural responses which depart significantly from culturally defined expectations.

The main thesis put forward in this study of Merton's is that 'when a system of cultural values extols, virtually above all else, certain *common* success-goals *for the population at large* while the social structure rigorously restricts or completely closes access to approved modes of reaching these goals *for a considerable part of the same population*, [then] deviant behaviour ensues on a large scale'.[24] In order to examine the types of nonconformity which might arise in such a situation, Merton assumes that those individuals involved can either accept or reject goals and/or means. Given this assumption, five responses are *logically* possible. Merton tabulates them in the following manner, using (+) to indicate acceptance and (−) to indicate rejection:

	Success-Goal	Means
Conformity	+	+
Innovation	+	−
Ritualism	−	+
Retreatism	−	−
Rebellion	±	±

It is presumed, as we have seen, that in any stable society most members will continue to strive for prescribed goals and to use legitimate channels. They will conform. However, for certain groups and categories of persons the divergence between prescribed goals and actual opportunities will be so great that they will be driven to adopt one of the four deviant responses. Which deviant adaptation is adopted by specific actors will vary with their position in the social structure.

Although in Merton's view this typology of deviant responses will apply to any situation where there is a dissociation between socially prescribed goals and available opportunities, he attempts to give it specific empirical content by using it to study the consequences of the overwhelming emphasis on the goal of monetary success in American society. Convincing evidence is produced to show that 'Americans are bombarded on every side' by exhortations proclaiming the importance of the success-goal; that a sizeable proportion of them have internalized this culturally prescribed aspiration; and that there are marked social differences in access to the legitimate avenues for achieving success. Merton also suggests that the tendency towards deviant behaviour is accentuated in the U.S. by the relatively weak cultural stress on use of proper means. In America, he argues, success is recognized almost independently of how it is attained and the barriers inhibiting nonconformity are correspondingly weakened. The evidence produced to support this latter assertion is far from adequate.[25] Nevertheless, his analysis to some extent justifies the claim that middle range theories facilitate precise conceptual formulation and the use of unambiguous empirical evidence. For example, one well-defined goal is singled out for attention and empirically documented, while reference is made to research which establishes the existence in America of differential class access to such avenues to success as formal education. Unfortunately, this clarity of empirical reference is not maintained uniformly throughout the analysis.

Merton's analytical scheme in *Social Structure and Anomie* is very simple. It includes one major goal, an unspecified range of ways in which this goal may be achieved, plus four deviant adaptations for those actors who are prevented by the realities of the social structure from attaining culturally prescribed aspirations. But in applying this middle range framework to American society Merton experiences great difficulty in reconciling the simplicity of his scheme with the actual complexities of American culture and social structure. In the first place, he is forced to ignore the existence of alternative goals which may be used by many groups as substitutes for monetary success. Secondly, Merton pays little attention to the possibility that the success-goal may be regularly reinterpreted by actors in various social positions in ways in which make attainment possible. Thirdly, no allowance is made for variations in the definition of 'legitimate means' held within different sections of society. For instance, robbery and theft may well be regarded as legitimate ways of becoming successful within certain lower-class communities. Thus members of such groups who strive to achieve success by use of criminal means will be conforming rather than innovating. Of course, the criminal community as a whole may be seen as deviant by other groups in society. But the adaptations of individual criminals (and Merton's classification is a typology of *individual responses*) cannot automatically be regarded as deviant. Merton's analysis stresses the importance of structural diversity within American society, but fails to recognize that there may be an accompanying *cultural diversity*. As soon as we admit that the success-goal may be systematically reinterpreted, that it must compete with alternative and perhaps more easily achieved goals, and that there may be structured differences of opinion as to which means are legitimate, Merton's analysis of goals and means begins to look unduly simplistic. And as was noted in previous chapters, when relatively simple theoretical schemes are applied to a complex reality conceptions tend to become imprecise and the relations between fact and theory only vaguely specified.[26]

The consequences of using an extremely simple and selective scheme to investigate the complexities of American society can be clearly seen if we examine more closely Merton's typology of adaptations and his attempts to locate these adaptations within the social structure. Merton suggests that innovation, which is more or less equivalent to property crime, occurs most frequently among the 'lower strata'. This is reasonable, for it is among the lower classes that the legitimate avenues to success are least accessible and the official crime rate most high.[27] The attempt to link ritualism with the lower middle class is, however, less convincing. Ritualism, which entails virtual abandonment of the success goal, accompanied by compulsive conformity to instrumental norms, is said to be located most frequently in this class because, although actual chances of success are small, 'parents typically exert continuous pressure upon children to abide by the normal mandates of the society . . .'.[28] In this interpretation, lack of opportunities account for the supposed tendency among the lower middle class to abandon the success-goal, while effective socialization explains the continued commitment to prescribed means. But the argument is inconsistent. On the one hand, Merton argues that in America much more stress is laid on the need to succeed than on the use of legitimate channels. Yet, on the other hand, he argues that lower-middle-class patterns of socialization, although effective enough to produce compulsive use of prescribed means, will frequently allow total abandonment of the success-goal. Even if we were to accept this argument, we would still be left with two adaptations—namely, retreatism and rebellion—which are not placed at all in relation to the social structure. Merton simply fails to specify in which groups or categories of persons these responses will occur most frequently. He does mention that within the category of retreatism 'fall some of the adaptive activities of psychotics, autists, pariahs, outcasts, vagrants, vagabonds, tramps, chronic drunkards and drug addicts'.[29] But no clear account is given of the social and psychological mechanisms by which this adaptation is produced. These defects would be less serious if Merton were to succeed in supplying clear empirical content for the adaptations. Unfortunately, the typology itself is far from unambiguous.

The adaptation of rebellion furnishes a good example of the imprecision of Merton's typology. Theoretically, the term refers to rejection of the success-goal and to its replacement with some other value. Merton, however, tends to use the term with its normal 'revolutionary' connotation: 'When rebellion becomes endemic in a substantial part of the society, it provides a potential for revolution which reshapes both the normative and the social structure.'[30] Within the limits of Merton's analysis, the concept of rebellion should be linked to just one goal and to role-behaviour directly associated with that goal. It cannot be generalized to cover revolutionary groups without extending in a much more complex fashion Merton's analysis of American society. Yet the theorist himself tends to forget this. This kind of inconsistency is possible because nowhere does Merton supply clear empirical denotation for the concept of rebellion, or for the other deviant adaptations. They are all used in a loose manner, which enables Merton to vary their empirical content almost at will. For a further example we can refer to Merton's attempt to counter a criticism put forward by Cohen. Cohen argues that Merton's analysis does not account for the 'non-utilitarian' or destructive character of much delinquent behaviour.[31]

Merton replies that his typology not only includes irrational behaviour, but actually implies the existence of destructive criminal tendencies:

> ... this theory does *not* maintain that the resulting deviant behaviour is rationally calculated and utilitarian. Instead, it centers on the *acute* pressures created by the discrepancy between culturally induced goals and socially structured opportunities. The responses to these pressures with the consequent strains upon individuals subject to them may involve a considerable degree of frustration and of non-rational or of irrational behaviour ... it would appear that 'wholesale negativism' can be construed, without enlarging the theory to incorporate new *ad hoc* variables, as a sustained repudiation of the authorities which exemplify the contradiction between legitimized aspirations and socially restricted opportunities.[32]

In the initial formulation innovation appears to cover solely those acts where new means are introduced to bring about improved chances of monetary success in response to limitations on the use of legitimate channels. In the light of Cohen's finding that much delinquency is totally negative and non-acquisitive, Merton appears to argue that the concept of innovation covers not only illegitimate *acquisition*, but also illegitimate *destruction* of property as well as generally negative behaviour. However, Merton does not actually specify *which* category covers these destructive acts. He simply asserts that non-utilitarian behaviour is implicit somewhere within the typology of adaptations. It is possible, therefore, that destructive delinquency is to be included under retreatism rather than innovation. This is quite feasible. Destructive delinquency could be regarded as a rejection of both the means and the success-goal, accompanied by intense frustration, which is expressed through aggression against alien groups and against alien property. There seems to be no clear and convincing reason for placing it in one category rather than another. Furthermore, whichever category we choose, destructive delinquency will be classified with behaviour which appears to be quite dissimilar. If we regard it as innovation, then, theoretically, it is identical with 'rational' property crime. If we regard it as retreatism, it is theoretically equivalent to drug-addiction and vagrancy. The very fact that such behaviour can plausibly be included in several categories, each of which has diverse content, must lead us to conclude that Merton's typology, as currently formulated, is imprecise. It signally fails to achieve that level of precise empirical content which is proposed as the major advantage of operating at the level of middle-range theory.

The main benefit of the middle-range strategy is supposedly that it deals with relatively simple problems where correspondingly simple and rigorous theoretical schemes can be applied. In Merton's study of the success-goal in America, however, an inappropriately simple analytical scheme is used to study an unmanageably complex body of data. As a result, the cultural and structural diversity of American society is treated in a crude fashion and the empirical content of the typology of deviant responses left indeterminate. Merton himself admits that the analysis in *Social Structure and Anomie* is far from theoretically mature. He seems to regard his analysis in a manner similar to that adopted by Pareto and Parsons in relation to their more general theoretical schemes—namely, as an initial formulation to be further specified, modified and developed:

> This essay on the structural sources of deviant behaviour *remains but a prelude*. It has not included a detailed treatment of the structural elements which predispose toward one rather than another of the alternative responses open to individuals living in an imbalanced social structure; it has largely neglected but not denied the relevance of the social-psychological processes determining the specific incidence of these responses; it has only briefly considered the social functions fulfilled by deviant behaviour; it has not put the explanatory power of the analytical scheme to full empirical test by determining group variations in deviant and conformist behaviour; it has only touched upon rebellious behaviour which seeks to refashion the social framework.[33]

Although Merton recognizes in this paragraph most of the charges levelled against him above, their importance is not thereby reduced. Merton's admissions merely support the argument being made here that middle-range theory does not resolve the problems of empirical documentation and conceptual clarity. We are offered in *Social Structure and Anomie* a theoretical prelude, but this is hardly what we had been led to expect would be the result of adopting the middle-range strategy. Of course, it can be argued that the limited scope of the study makes possible a closer link with empirical research and consequently makes more likely a rapid and detailed theoretical specification. This thesis, however, is a mere repetition of the argument originally proposed by Merton in support of the middle-range strategy. It remains an assumption rather than a demonstrated principle in relation to the analysis of the success-goal in America. Nevertheless, although Merton's scheme cannot yet be regarded as a rigorous deductive system, it must be recognized that his analysis has stimulated empirical research which has been, in several instances, both clear and well-documented. Yet much of this research has achieved its relatively convincing level of clarity and empirical content only by lowering still further the level of abstraction. A good example occurs in Blau's investigation of a government employment agency.[34] Within one section of this agency Blau finds evidence of 'ritualistic over-conformity', not in relation to bureaucratic rules generally, but with regard to a particular regulation. This rigid conformity is explained as a response to fear of censure by superiors. Blau's analysis differs from Merton's mainly with respect to its restricted scope and its unambiguous empirical content. In the first place, Blau deals with only one adaptation—namely, ritualism. Secondly, only one rule and its associated goal are examined. Thirdly, the ritualistic adaptation is clearly located within the bureaucratic structure. Fourthly, the behavioural response is described in detail and is clearly identical for all those involved. And, fifthly, the social psychological processes which generate the adaptation are indicated. There can be no doubt, of course, that Merton's study of social structure and anomie has been more fruitful than Blau's limited examination of one case of fearful over-conformity, in the sense that it has provoked much more research. Nevertheless, it is only in studies of particular small groups and the adaptations of their individual members that versions of Merton's simple analytical scheme have been given the kind of precise empirical content which the middle-range strategy is designed to foster. The most important implication of this fact appears to be that if sociological analysis is to attain the kind of operational rigour favoured by Merton, it must reduce the level of abstraction further than Merton has been willing to do and must depart even further from a general theoretical strategy.

There exists in sociology, and perhaps in all would-be sciences, a problem of reconciling general statements which appear to be theoretically significant with the kind of conceptual precision necessary for empirical validation. Merton's strategy is adopted in large measure because it promises to reduce the gap between theoretical conceptions and available factual material. But Merton's so-called theories fail to bridge this gap. In fact, these middle-range analyses are no more theories, in the fullest sense of the word, than the schemes of Parsons or Pareto. They are not precise logico-deductive systems with limited empirical scope, but fairly well-documented, though loose, explanation sketches or theoretical outlines. Merton is himself aware of the difficulty of reconciling theoretical formulation with empirical data, not only in principle, but also in relation to his own analyses; and, despite his middle-range strategy, he states explicitly that ideas which appear to be theoretically significant must not be abandoned merely for lack of empirical support. In his own words: 'A premature insistence on precision at all costs may sterilize imaginative hypotheses. ... In the search for precision, care must be taken to see that significant problems are not thus inadvertently blotted from view.'[35] The gap between fact and theory is perhaps reduced by Merton's strategy, but it is by no means eliminated. Analyses such as that in *Social Structure and Anomie* are valuable, not because they provide rigorous middle-range theories, but because they offer a series of imaginative hypotheses which retain reasonable promise of further empirical and theoretical specification.

IV

Merton requires genuine sociological theories to have certain definite characteristics. They must, in particular, 'be sufficiently *precise* to be *determinate*'.[36] But, it has been suggested above, Merton's own theories do not satisfy this criterion—a criterion so basic that failure to comply severely restricts the capacity to fulfil most other theoretical requirements. Explanation for example— that is, the inferring of unambiguous empirical generalizations or particular empirical statements from more general propositions—is impossible without conceptual precision. Conclusive empirical inferences cannot be made from propositions having vague empirical referents. However, although our main topic in this section will be the explanatory power of Merton's middle-range functionalism, I shall disregard the question of conceptual precision and concentrate on the *form* or *type* of explanation offered. The explanatory form used by Merton is problematic because, in the first place, functional explanations tend to be formally distinct from causal explanations and, secondly, because the paradigm for functional analysis makes no explicit provision for explanation of sociological data. If we are to understand how a paradigm which makes no mention of explanation deals with this basic theoretical objective, we must once more examine that paradigm in use.

Merton's paradigm provides a series of steps which should ideally be undertaken in any functional study. First, a certain item (I) which is in some way problematic is identified. Secondly, the motives of those involved in item I are examined, thus enabling the analyst to distinguish the intended consequences of I from those which are unintended or, in Merton's terminology, to distinguish manifest from latent functions. The third step is to note which consequences are positive and which negative, and in relation to which institutions, roles, groups and individual actors. In Merton's terms, functions and dysfunctions, social and psychological functions are delineated. At this point we examine the functional requisites of the system under study and those of its sub-systems, the mechanisms whereby these requirements are met, and, finally, the functional alternatives which are eliminated by structural constraints.

When the empirical material under investigation is complex, it is often impossible to complete all these operations. This is so in *Social Structure and Anomie*, where analysis is confined to steps 1 and 3, and these only in part. In this study Merton identifies first certain cultural and structural items—namely, the success-goal and the unequal distribution of opportunities for achieving success legitimately. These items together constitute a sociological problem which Merton approaches, in accordance with his functional perspective, by focusing on objective consequences—in this instance on the types of individual adaptation. There is no attempt, however, to deal with functional requirements, structural constraints or functional alternatives; and little attention is paid to the mechanisms whereby consequences are produced. Thus this particular study is no more than a partial application of the paradigm for functional analysis. It is perhaps for this reason that the form of explanation used by Merton appears not to be functional in any distinctive sense. The peculiar characteristics of functional explanations, as was noted above,[37] is that items are explained by reference to their contribution either to the total system or to its sub-systems. Items are regarded as explained when it is shown that they contribute to certain necessary prerequisites or end-states, and thereby to the continuance of the system under study. For example, in biology it is possible to explain the existence and nature of the heart by showing what function it fulfils—that is, what necessary contribution it makes to maintaining the body. If Merton were using this type of explanatory procedure in *Social Structure and Anomie*, he would attempt to explain the dissociation between goals and means by reference to its functional consequences. Clearly, he does not do this. He tries to explain, not the dissociation, but the individual adaptations *produced* by this dissociation. If this interpretation is correct, Merton's explanatory scheme is no more functional than that, say, of Pareto. These two theorists differ, in this connection, only over terminology. Where Pareto talks of cause and effect Merton refers to items and their objective consequences. But both of them proceed by attempting to show how certain social facts are directly produced by other aspects of the social system. Whether these social products are called 'effects' or 'objective consequences' does not alter the explanatory logic involved. Thus, with respect to the analysis put forward in *Social Structure and Anomie*, the answer to our initial problem is clear. Merton is able to use his non-explanatory functional paradigm to generate explanations simply by formulating causal explanations in functional terms. If we are to appreciate how this is possible, we must examine the character of genuine functional explanations in greater detail.

Functional explanations have been used most commonly and most successfully in biology. As an example, let us consider the following proposition: 'In living organisms of a certain type, the function of the pancreas is to maintain a steady sugar-level in the blood.' Although such functional statements are frequently used in biology, they can always be restated in non-functional terms. Thus the proposition above becomes: 'In living organisms of a certain type, a necessary *condition* for a steady sugar-level is the presence and activity of the pancreas.' To cite Nagel: 'The difference between a functional and a non-functional formulation is thus one of selective emphasis; *it is quite comparable to the difference between saying that B is the effect of A and saying that A is the condition of B.*'[38] This quotation emphasizes the purely *formal* aspect of functional analysis whereby stress is laid upon consequences rather than causes or necessary conditions. But this formal and reversible feature of functional analysis, which Merton has adopted, is of little importance in itself. It is used in biology only when certain specific assumptions are made about the nature of the system under study. Merton's fundamental error is that of retaining the form of functional analysis while having rejected the substantive assumptions which make it a distinct type of explanatory procedure.

Functional statements are used in biology only when the following assumptions can be made about the organisms being investigated: first, the system must be assumed to be goal-directed—that is, organized to maintain such states of the system as body temperature or the sugar content of the blood. Secondly, these end-states must be clearly described and the range of tolerable variation stated. Thirdly, the mechanisms whereby item I fulfils function F—for example, whereby the pancreas maintains a steady sugar-level in the blood—must be portrayed in detail. This condition is essential to the use of functional statements because it is through statements about these mechanisms that the relation between an item and the end-state which it maintains is explained in causal terms. Fourthly, the description of these mechanisms must include reference to processes whereby changes in the end-state generate *compensating* changes in item I. These are known as negative feedback mechanisms and they are central in maintaining the stability of biological organisms. Thus the statement that the function of the pancreas is to stabilize the sugar-content of the blood is no more than a convenient way of summarizing a complex series of interrelations. On the one hand, it implies that the pancreas, by secreting insulin, controls the blood sugar-level. On the other hand, it implies that the blood sugar-level controls the secretion of insulin. Functional statements of this kind, then, can be made only when there exists a balanced and reciprocal relationship between a structural organ, such as the pancreas, and an end-state of the system. Furthermore, such statements can be used to explain the functioning of the organ in question only when the steady state and the way in which it feeds back upon that organ can be specified. In short, functional statements in biology are used in relation to relatively stable, cohesive systems within which specifiable steady states are maintained by negative feedback mechanisms. Parsons and the functional anthropologists, although usually unable to supply detailed accounts of social feedback networks, use versions of this biological model in their study of social systems.[39] Parsons, for instance, assumes that all social systems must meet the same four functional requirements and that these requirements operate to maintain the existing structure. Merton, however, in his critique of the anthropological postulates, has come to reject the relevance of this model for sociology. For instance, Merton not only fails to include any reference to end-states in his paradigm for functional analysis, but even questions the utility of the weaker notion of functional requirements. His departure from the biological model is also evident in his introduction of the term 'dysfunction', which appears to be incompatible with the functional conditions just outlined. It is difficult to envisage how dysfunctions could be interpreted as working to maintain specified end-states. But perhaps the difference between Merton's variety of functionalism and that used in biology can be most clearly appreciated if we examine Merton's definition of the term 'function'.

For Merton, the term 'function' is equivalent to 'objective consequence'. In biology, however, the terms are used differently, 'objective consequence' having a wider denotion than 'function'. For biologists, objective consequences are functional only when they are linked by some feedback process with an end-state of the system.[40] For example, the pulsing of the heart has at least two objective consequences—namely, the pumping of blood and the creation of those sound patterns which we identify as heart-beats. Only one of these consequences is, however, susceptible to functional analysis. To examine the circulation of blood within a functional framework is meaningful because there are several steady-states involved, interference with which will produce compensating changes in the heart's rate of pumping. Furthermore, reference to the heart's function of maintaining an adequate supply of blood throughout the body can be used to explain changes in the rate at which the heart is pumping, although this explanation will be acceptable only if the mechanisms are specified whereby changes in blood distribution affect the pumping of blood. In contrast to the circulation of blood, the production of 'heart-beats' is not a functional activity. Heart-beats are *mere* objective consequences. They are linked neither with steady-states of the organism nor with feedback processes. And because functional explanations require the specification of steady-states and feedback mechanisms, reference to 'heart-beats' cannot be used to account for the operation of the heart or for changes in its rate of activity. By concentrating on consequences, Merton has retained the *formal* aspect of functional analysis. But he has failed to retain those substantive assumptions which make functional statements explanatory statements and which alone distinguish functionalism from other theoretical perspectives.

Because Merton fails to make a conceptual distinction between functions and objective consequences, his functional analyses fall into two definite types, depending on which kind of consequence is involved. In one type of analysis he examines objective consequences which are analogous to the heart-beats discussed above. These consequences are unconnected with any steady-state or functional imperative. Moreover, as they do not feed back upon their source, no functional explanation of the latter can be attempted. Such an analysis of mere objective consequences is exemplified in *Social Structure and Anomie*. But in certain instances Merton examines functions in a manner more closely resembling that used in biology. Thus functional imperatives are stated, explanations of the initial structural item are attempted, and feedback mechanisms are implied, if not openly described. The analysis of these feedback processes, however, tends to involve strong overtones of social exchange.

As an illustration of how the paradigm for functional analysis should be used, Merton offers a brief analysis of the American political machine. This analysis is more in accordance with the genuine functional model than that in *Social Structure and Anomie*. To be specific, an attempt is made to explain the existence of the political machine by reference to its contributions to the needs of various groups within American society. This kind of functional analysis is clearly different from that used in biology. For example, the end-states of the organic system provide a point of reference quite unlike the needs of sub-groups within the social system. Nevertheless, the analysis is no longer functional in a merely formal sense. Merton begins by identifying the political machine as a recurrent type of social organization, the persistence and operation of which require explanation. The next step is to outline the structural context. Merton suggests that the official political structure in the U.S., which furnishes this context, is organized to prevent concentration of political power. But the resulting dispersal of political control generates certain dysfunctions or functional deficiencies. Owing to the dispersal of power, the legitimate political organizations cannot satisfy the needs of some of the groups involved. The political machine emerges to cater for these needs: '... *the functional deficiencies* of the official structure *generate an alternative* (unofficial) *structure to fulfil existing needs somewhat more effectively.*'[41] Merton identifies several sub-groups whose special needs are met by the political machine. In the first place, the 'deprived classes', faced with an impersonal political bureaucracy, require personalized help through recurrent periods of hardship. This the political machine provides. For the legitimate business community as well as the professional criminals, the political boss acts as a means of control over impersonal market forces. And, finally, the machine serves as an avenue of social mobility for all those groups barred from full use of legitimate channels to success. Merton concludes his analysis with the following statement:

> Without assuming that the foregoing pages exhaust either the range of functions or the range of sub-groups served by the political machine we can see that *it presently fulfils some functions for these diverse sub-groups which are not adequately fulfilled by culturally approved or more conventional structures.*[42]

There are at least two ways of interpreting this analysis. On the one hand, it can be seen as a straightforward description of the consequences or effects of the political machine in American society, very similar in objective to the study of anomie. On the other hand, it can be viewed as a definite attempt *to explain the persistence and character of the political machine by reference to the functional consequences* of that machine. There can, in practice, be little doubt that the second interpretation is correct. Merton *is* trying to provide an explanation of the machine by adumbrating its objective consequences and, in this sense, is offering a distinctly functional analysis. Yet, to show that the political machine supplements the legitimate structure by serving certain classes of unsatisfied needs in no way explains the persistence of the machine. Gouldner makes this point in the following manner:

> ... in so far as the objective of the ... analysis was to provide an explanation of the persistence of the political machine, then the mere establishment of the consequences of the machine for the larger structures in which it is involved provides only a partial and one-sided answer. The explanation is incomplete in so far as the analyst has not

explicitly traced the manner in which the groups or structure whose needs have been satisfied, in turn 'reciprocate' and repay the political machine.[43]

Merton's functional analysis can only provide an explanation of the original item, in this case the political machine, by showing how the item's contributions to the larger structure or to specific units within that structure are returned in such a way that the initial item is maintained. However, this kind of interpretation is more than just a functional analysis. It is also an analysis of social exchange. It appears, therefore, that when Merton attempts to use his functional paradigm to formulate genuinely functional explanations he is led in the direction of exchange analysis.

V

Two main themes run through Merton's work. The first of these centres around middle-range theory, while the second focuses on functional analysis. Merton advocates the formulation of middle-range theories because they foster close contact between theory and empirical research. Such contact is valuable because it is likely to lead to more rigorous empirical specification of theory. Nevertheless, although the conceptual clarity and empirical content of Merton's theories are an improvement on Parsons' achievement, Merton fails to provide a conclusive demonstration of the advantages of the middle-range strategy. Despite having withdrawn from the excessive complexities of general theory, Merton still finds it difficult, if not impossible, to formulate analytical schemes which provide adequate representation of social reality. In *Social Structure and Anomie*, for example, many pressing theoretical questions are left untouched. Furthermore, the areas actually studied are examined through the medium of loose and overlapping concepts. Merton's so-called middle-range theories are not, in fact, theories at all. As he himself admits, they are at best preliminary analyses. The kind of conceptual precision and clarity of empirical content which proper theory requires is found at present in sociology at much lower levels of abstraction than those at which Merton is willing to work. Thus Merton's strategy has not eliminated the gap between theoretical concepts and empirical data. At most this separation has been reduced. Merton's claim that the intimate relationship fostered by the middle-range strategy between theory and research will eventually produce satisfactory general theory remains no more than a reasonable assumption.

The second conception dominating Merton's work is that functional analysis is 'at once the most promising and possibly the least codified of contemporary orientations to problems of sociological intepretation'.[44] Naturally enough, in view of this appraisal, Merton tries to supply the required codification in a manner entirely consistent with his middle-range strategy. In his hands, functionalism becomes a method of analysis rather than a theoretical orientation, and substantive presumptions about the character of social systems are kept to a minimum. Merton arrives at his functional paradigm by examining, and almost totally rejecting, certain postulates which were recurrent in anthropological functionalism. The paradigm which results remains consistently functional *in form*. But Merton appears to see within societies few of the tendencies toward system-maintenance which are prominent features of biological organisms. Accordingly, he reduces the functional perspective to a basic minimum—that is, to the search for objective consequences without presupposition as to their nature. Many of Merton's studies, therefore, amount to no more than an investigation of how one set of social facts has consequences for other social facts. On occasion, however, Merton does offer analyses in which the attempt is made to explain an item by reference to its positive functions. Such studies are functional in more than a merely formal sense, for they include references to such phenomena as functional imperatives and imply the existence of feedback mechanisms. But examination of functional feedback processes requires some notion of reciprocity or exchange between the units inolved. This indication that functional analysis needs to be supplemented by the notion of social exchange is much weaker in Merton's work than in that of Parsons. It is, nevertheless. unquestionably present.

Whilst Merton and Parsons were moving, to varying degrees, toward a theoretical combination of functionalism with exchange analysis, Homans was laying the foundations for his own theory of social exchange. Homans' theory developed in the course of an extended critique of such functionalists as Parsons and Merton. Yet this critique was focused initially, not on theoretical content, not on the substantive superiority of 'exchange' over 'function', but on the inadequacy of the theoretical strategy of functionalists in general and of Parsons in particular:

> What I quarrelled with were [Parsons'] ideas about the characteristics of a theory of any sort and about the relations between theory and investigation. I quarreled both with what he said about theory and with the way he himself practised theory-building. . . . I felt sure that a theory was a set of propositions, each stating a relationship between properties of nature. The named properties constituted a conceptual scheme, but the conceptual scheme by itself was not enough

to constitute the theory, which also had to state the propositions. The propositions were contingent, in the sense that their truth did not follow automatically from postulates assumed *a priori*, as did the truth of the theorems of geometry. Nature, not logic, made a proposition what it was. . . . If these were the characteristics of a theory, the official sociological theorists often seemed to be talking about something else. One sort of statement they were fond of making distressed me particularly. Parsons said: 'A theoretical system in the present sense is a body of logically interdependent generalized concepts of empirical reference'; and Robert Merton echoed him by saying that 'the term sociological theory refers to logically interconnected conceptions which are limited and modest in scope, rather than all-embracing and grandiose'. The two differed in degrees of modesty but agreed in the view of theory as 'logically interdependent concepts'. . . . Parsons seemed to think that both the process of reasoning in a completed theory and the process by which that theory was arrived at worked in the same downward direction. He started with very general considerations and hoped to work downward to the empirical findings. That he started from concepts and not propositions, and so could not work downward deductively, does not concern me now. Downward was the direction in which he thought the construction of a theory proceeded. He was always a little patronizing toward 'mere empirical generalizations' and once complained that 'a great deal of current research is producing facts in a form which cannot be utilized by any current generalized analytical scheme'. So much the worse, I was inclined to think, for the scheme. In keeping with my own idea that good science had been attained by some of the damnedest methods, I could not rule out the chance that Parsons' strategy might someday pay off. But if I had to make a bet, I would bet on the strategy that started with the empirical propositions and worked upward.[45]

To some extent, Homans' criticisms of Parsons and Merton are based on a misunderstanding. Neither of the two functionalists maintains simply that a conceptual scheme *is* a theory, but rather that considerable conceptual preparation is required before a genuine theory can be formulated. Homans differs from the functionalists, not in his conception of theoretical structure, but in his conviction that the proper strategy for sociology is to concentrate exclusively on the formulation of a series of explanatory generalizations. The most effective way, he argues, of preparing the way for a general deductive system is that of gradually constructing such a system by induction, rather as Pareto attempted, though on a less ambitious scale. Homans' theory of social exchange and his repudiation of functional analysis emerge as by-products of his attempt to pursue this policy and to construct inductively, a relatively general deductive system.

6 Functionalism rejected: Homans

I

This chapter has three main objectives. The first is to describe the kind of theory which Homans wishes to construct. The second is to examine his reasons for regarding functionalism as an inadequate framework within which to pursue his theoretical goals. The third is to outline the inductive basis on which he builds his theoretical system. As each of these themes is developed, we shall find Homans continually trying to resolve his theoretical problems by establishing links between sociological theory and psychology. This attempt will be the central concern in the next chapter and will lead into an evaluation of Homans' work.

Homans, like the other theorists studied here, wishes to contribute to the formation of a fairly general and scientific theory of social behaviour. He defines a theory as an explanation of a particular empirical phenomenon or series of phenomena by means of a deductive system.[1] Any such deductive system will have at least three elements. First, there will be propositions describing particular phenomena which are to be explained. Secondly, there will be statements describing phenomena which are used in the explanation, but which are not, for the moment, regarded as problematic. These phenomena and the propositions describing them are called 'the givens'. Finally, there are certain empirical generalizations which, together with the givens, enable the theorist to explain—that is, to deduce the occurrence of the phenomena under investigation. Homans takes an example from Durkheim's analysis of suicide,[2] where a generalization is put forward which can be used in the following way to explain the relatively low incidence of suicide in Spain.[3]

(a) All well-integrated societies and groups have low suicide rates (empirical generalization established by induction).
(b) Spain is a well-integrated society (given).
(c) Therefore, Spain has a low suicide rate (deduction and explanation).

For Homans, then, a theory exists when a proposition describing a phenomenon which we wish to explain can be logically deduced from more general propositions. When Homans says that the propositions from which the deduction is made are more general, he means that 'other phenomena besides the one in question may also be deduced from them under different given conditions'.[4] Durkheim's empirical generalization meets this requirement. For example, if we can establish that Protestant communities are less well integrated than Catholic communities, then, by applying the generalization, we can explain why their suicide rate is higher. Similarly, if we can demonstrate that married men are better integrated into society than unmarried men, we can account for their relatively low suicide rate. Thus, assuming that Durkheim's generalization can be used in this way to generate accurate deductions when combined with a variety of givens, and that reliable and independent evidence of social integration as well as of suicide rates can be provided, Durkheim's schema constitutes for Homans a model sociological theory.

The view adopted by Homans which identifies theory with explanation can be reconciled with various theoretical objectives and research strategies. It could be coupled, for example, with a middle-range strategy like that of Merton. But Homans is unwilling to limit his endeavours in this way. He prefers from the outset to strive for a series of related generalizations covering a more extensive range of social activity. In this respect his approach closely resembles that of Pareto, who also wanted to formulate a general deductive system.[5] And, once again like Pareto, he believes that this general theory should be reached by induction. The first step in constructing a general deductive system, suggests Homans, is to examine particular instances of social activity in search of uniformities. Once regular relationships between sociological variables have been observed, they should be expressed in the form of empirical generalizations. Such generalizations should then be applied to new data. If they fail to express adequately the uniformities there observed, the original generalizations must be appropriately modified. In time a coherent series of generalizations should become available, capable of furnishing a wide range of empirically verifiable deductions. When this deductive system is used to generate propositions which have already been empirically established, it is said to be providing explanations. When it generates propositions for which, as yet, there is no firm evidence, it is said to be predicting. Homans, like Pareto, believes that a general theoretical scheme must ultimately be assessed according to the range and precision of its explanations and predictions.

So far I have proceeded as if Homans thinks of theories as having no more than two levels: the first level being that of statements describing actual observations, some of which are to be explained while others may be taken as given; the second level being that of propositions which express in more general form observed empirical uniformities. This is not strictly accurate. For Homans stresses not only that the generalizations used to explain particular facts can be formulated at various levels of generality, but also that these generalizations can often be deduced in turn from more abstract propositions. Any extensive sociological theory should, therefore, ask the question, Why? at least twice. It should ask why particular social events occur; and it should answer this question, as we have seen, by deducing these events from more general sociological statements plus certain givens. But it should also ask why these generalizations hold true; and it will answer this question in the same way—that is, it will deduce the generalizations from an even more general set of propositions plus certain givens:

> I think it idle to claim that any theory is ever complete. In the first place, the most general propositions in the theory as formulated may themselves be explainable by another, still more general set of propositions. When they are so explained, they are often said to be reduced to the more general set . . . even if at any given time the most general propositions are not reducible, the possibility is always open that at some future time they will be. . . .[6]

In the course of his intellectual development, Homans comes to believe that the empirical generalizations of sociological theory can be reduced to a set of psychological axioms. We shall examine the emergence of this view and its implications in some detail during this chapter and the next.

II

In the previous section we saw that Homans emphasizes the theoretical importance of explaining systematically a wide range of social facts by means of empirical generalizations, which can in turn be explained in psychological terms. From this perspective, structural functionalism can hardly appear to be a promising theoretical approach. In the first place, functionalism has made a firm distinction between the psychological and sociological levels of analysis. This is most evident in Parsons' contention that personality systems and social systems are organized around different functional foci, but is also present, for example, in Merton's rejection of 'individualistic' interpretations of crime. Secondly, functional analysis has been expressly designed to evade the difficulties involved in producing a coherent series of empirical generalizations. It has been adopted into sociology as a way of preparing for, and at the same time *temporarily avoiding*, the task of constructing a fully theoretical system. Furthermore, on those occasions when functional analysis has been used to supply explanations, the results, as we have noted in relation to Merton, have been empirically and logically suspect. It is not surprising, therefore, that Homans finds functionalism an unsuitable framework within which to construct the kind of deductive system he envisages.

In this section we shall examine Homans' response to a particular functional analysis. We shall see that the criticisms he puts forward and the alternative interpretation he proposes express his concern with explanation, with the formulation of precise empirical generalizations, and with the necessity of relating sociological analysis deductively to psychological assumptions. It will become evident that Homans' own theoretical perspective develops, at least partly, out of his attempt to remedy the defects of functionalism.

Lévi-Strauss has provided an analysis of rules of marriage in primitive societies which is criticized by Homans and which serves as the point of departure for Homans' own study in this area.[7] Both Homans and Lévi-Strauss are especially interested in the rules governing cross-cousin marriage. There are, broadly, two types of cross-cousin marriage found in pre-literate communities. In certain tribes young men are required to marry a cousin related to them through the male line—that is, a daughter of their father's sister. This pattern is called patrilateral cross-cousin marriage. In other groups young men are expected to marry a cousin on the mother's side—that is, a daughter of the mother's brother. This pattern is called matrilateral cross-cousin marriage. The analysis offered by Lévi-Strauss of such rules of marriage is a mixture of functionalism and ideas of social exchange. He investigates rules of marriage by showing how they create social exchange, in this case exchange of women, which in turn promotes social solidarity. But in Homans' view Lévi-Strauss goes further than this and tries to explain the existence of the rules in the same way. Marriage rules are said to exist *because* they foster solidarity. As a corollary, it is claimed that those rules which generate greater solidarity will occur in more societies. Homans summarizes his interpretation[8] of Lévi-Strauss's thesis as follows:

> Indeed tribesmen adopt the different rules *in order to* create the exchanges and so the organic solidarity of their societies. Some rules, though, create a higher degree of organic solidarity than others. The more fully each kin-group is dependent, for getting its wives, on all the others, and thus the more 'roundabout' the process of exchange, the greater the organic solidarity of the society. If one rule creates more organic solidarity than another, more tribes will adopt it. . . . [For example] mother's brother's daughter marriage creates a higher degree of organic solidarity than father's sister's daughter marriage, and so more societies will follow the former than the latter rule.[9]

Homans accepts that Lévi-Strauss has pointed out an interesting sociological problem in asking why matrilateral cross-cousin marriage should occur more frequently than the patrilateral form. Nevertheless, he regards the anthropologist's attempt at explanation as totally unsatisfactory. It is true that Lévi-Strauss has formulated several empirical generalizations. One proposition is, for instance, that any form of cross-cousin marriage will increase the level of organic solidarity within the community at large. Another is that matrilateral cross-cousin marriage creates more solidarity than patrilateral cross-cousin marriage. But these generalizations can be used to deduce only the degree of social solidarity within various tribes, not the occurrence of cross-cousin marriage.

If we have two communities similar in all respects, except that one has patrilateral marriage rules and the other matrilateral rules, then, taking the marriage rules as given, we can deduce and thereby explain a greater degree of solidarity in the latter tribe. But we cannot explain thereby the existence of marriage rules or why one group should have matrilateral rather than patrilateral rules of cross-cousin marriage. Homans argues that the typical functionalist concern with consequences has led Lévi-Strauss to construct generalizations in which the original problematic items—that is, rules of cross-cousin marriage—appear as unexplained givens. However, Homans is forced to admit that Lévi-Strauss's generalizations could be used to provide a more adequate account of cross-cousin marriage if they could be combined with one of two further assumptions.[10] In the first place, it could be argued that tribesmen are aware of the relation between cross-cousin marriage and solidarity and that they adopt the former to promote the latter. In Homans' view, however, there is no evidence which enables us to assume that primitives have a knowledge of social relationships which is sufficiently sophisticated to allow them to construct those structures which they know to be cohesive. In the second place, it could be argued that there is an evolutionary mechanism, like that controlling the development of biological species, which gradually eliminates those tribes with low levels of solidarity. This assumption, together with Lévi-Strauss's generalization, would indeed help explain the predominance of matrilateral cross-cousin marriage. But once again, Homans suggests, empirical evidence which alone would make this argument convincing is lacking. For Homans, with his strong commitment to an inductive strategy, the need to introduce these unsubstantiated assumptions is fraught with danger. In particular, it removes us increasingly from the realm of empirical fact to a position where any *ad hoc* hypothesis can be introduced to maintain our original theoretical commitment. Furthermore, argues Homans, there is no point in trying to bolster the functional analysis put forward by Lévi-Strauss, because there exists a perfectly satisfactory alternative.

Homans' alternative interpretation of the predominance of matrilateral cross-cousin marriage begins with the assumption that the form which cross-cousin marriage takes in any society will depend on other features of the social structure, and in particular upon other aspects of the kinship network. Homans knows, from Malinowski's work on the Trobriand Islanders, of a society where patrilateral cross-cousin marriage is associated with a family structure in which authority is vested in the mother's brother.[11] He suggests that it is reasonable to suppose that among the Trobriands young men feel greater affection for their father and their father's kin than for their maternal uncle and his daughters. If it can also be assumed that marriage will follow the ties of sentiment, then the direction of cross-cousin marriage can be regarded as determined by the location of familial authority. This kind of intepretation is supported by data on the Tikopia and on the primitive Germans.

In *Marriage, Authority and Final Causes* Homans and Schneider try to generalize this tentative analysis. They hypothesize that the form of cross-cousin marriage generally will 'be determined by the locus of jural authority over ego and the consequent pattern of interpersonal relations among kinsmen'.[12] More particularly, they postulate that the direction of cross-cousin marriage will vary inversely with the *locus* of familial authority. Thus the patrilateral pattern should occur when authority over ego—that is, the marriageable male—is vested in the mother's brother, while the matrilateral pattern should occur when authority within the conjugal family is vested in the father. Having formulated these propositions, Homans and Schneider test them by means of a cross-cultural survey. They examine all societies for which there is relevant and reliable information. In this way they succeed in demonstrating a 'significant correlation between the *locus* of jural authority over ego and the rule of unilateral cross-cousin marriage'.[13] This correlation is in the expected direction, although they are, of course, unable to produce evidence of a universal relationship.

In Homans' view the analysis in *Marriage, Authority and Final Causes* is preferable in several respects to that offered by Lévi-Strauss. In the first place, it provides a logically satisfactory deductive system for inferring the direction of cross-cousin marriage. For example, if we wish to explain an instance of patrilateral cross-cousin marriage we would use the following deductive system:

(a) In any given society, if the *locus* of authority within the family lies with the mother's brother, then cross-cousin marriage, if it exists, will be patrilateral (generalization established by induction).

(b) In this particular society, the *locus* of authority lies with the mother's brother (given).

(c) Therefore, cross-cousin marriage will be patrilateral (deduction and explanation).

The generalization will not hold true in all cases. Consequently, our deductions will be less than 100 per cent accurate. Nevertheless, this deductive schema will enable us to predict the direction of cross-cousin marriage much more effectively than by flipping a coin.

This, for Homans, is a proper explanatory scheme. It makes possible logical inferences about cross-cousin marriage—that is, about the item which was originally problematic. Thus Homans' scheme avoids the difficulties, faced by Lévi-Strauss and also by Merton, of explaining phenomena by their consequences. Furthermore, as well as predicting the direction of cross-cousin marriage in particular societies, Homans can furnish a perfectly adequate explanation of the overall preponderance of matrilateral cross-cousin marriage. According to Homans and Schneider, the matrilateral pattern occurs more frequently simply because jural authority is more often vested in the father than in the mother's brother. Of course, this interpretation leaves unexplained the predominance of paternal authority. But this incompleteness does not, from Homans' perspective, invalidate his analysis, for any scientific explanation must take certain facts as given. Thus the Homans-Schneider hypothesis accounts not only for the relative frequency of matrilateral cross-cousin marriage, but also, with considerable accuracy, for its occurrence in specific societies. Homans argues accordingly that it is preferable to Lévi-Strauss's generalization because it makes the latter redundant: '. . . if Lévi-Strauss could predict that *more* societies would practise one form [of cross-cousin marriage] than would the other, we could predict *which* societies would practise *which* form, and in this case Lévi-Strauss's proposition appeared to be unnecessary.'[14] Furthermore, the empirical content of Homans' terms are relatively clear. Any attempt to test Lévi-Strauss's thesis would require the construction of an index of 'organic solidarity'. Such an index has not yet been produced. In contrast, there is little disagreement over the location of jural authority within the tribes included in Homans' survey or in later surveys.[15] Thus Homans regards his analysis as an improvement upon that of Lévi-Strauss because it furnishes a clear, testable and tested generalization which generates logically satisfactory explanations and accurate predictions in relation to the direction and frequency of cross-cousin marriage.

Homans and Schneider take one further step in *Marriage, Authority and Final Causes* which is fully in accord with Homans' theoretical strategy. They try to explain the sociological generalization which proposes an inverse relationship between the *locus* of authority and the direction of marriage by examining the psychological sources of the social behaviour involved. They argue that authority discourages intimacy and that young men will interact more frequently with and become emotionally 'closer' to those members of the family who do not exercise authority over them. They also suggest that any particular young man 'would tend to seek as his wife the daughter of the member of the older generation, outside his nuclear family, with whom he had formed the closest attachment, and that that person in turn would have good sentimental reasons for giving the daughter . . .'.[16] This interpretation implies the existence of a psychological generalization which may be expressed crudely, but formally, as follows: For all human beings, other things being equal, subjection to authority in a social relationship generates antipathy while freedom from authority fosters liking. Two further assumptions are made: in the first place, that people tend to marry those whom they like, and, secondly, that marriage rules tend to reflect the existing pattern of sentiments and social relationships. The psychological assumptions made here are not formalized by Homans and Schneider, and there is little attempt to demonstrate their general validity. They are hardly more than common-sense assumptions which enable the analysts to account for their findings in a plausible fashion. In this study Homans takes no more than the first tentative step toward a comprehensive and psychologically based deductive system.

In the first section of this chapter it was noted that Homans' main theoretical preoccupation is with explanation and the formation of logically consistent and empirically adequate deductive systems. These preconceptions underlie Homans' repudiation of functionalism. Parsons' scheme is rejected because it is formed by deduction instead of induction; because, as a result, it is empirically indeterminate;

and because it offers concepts without explanatory propositions. Functional analysis on a smaller scale, as practised by Merton and Lévi-Strauss, is rejected because many of its terms are imprecise and because its tendency to explain social phenomena by reference to their consequences is seen as both logically and empirically unsatisfactory. Homans attempts in *Marriage, Authority and Final Causes* to replace functional analysis with the formulation of 'structural' generalizations—that is, propositions which express the dependence of one social institution on another. In the example discussed above, Homans and Schneider try to show that the direction of cross-cousin marriage depends upon the location of jural authority. Such a generalization is seen as valuable because it can generate deductive explanations of social activities in various primitive communities. In addition, partly because its empirical referents are relatively clear, it is amenable to empirical validation or falsification as well as providing unambiguous predictions. At the same time the sociological generalization can itself be loosely deduced from certain psychological propositions, in this way showing some promise of contributing toward a more general deductive system. The remainder of Homans' writings are devoted to the gradual development of this more general scheme.

III

Homans' main theoretical writings are divided into two parts. The first part, which is presented in *The Human Group*[17] (referred to below as HG), is an attempt to build up inductively a series of empirical generalizations. The second stage, presented in *Social Behaviour: Its Elementary Forms* (referred to below as SB), is an attempt to complete the theoretical scheme by furnishing a number of psychological principles from which the previously constructed generalizations can be derived. The rest of this chapter will be devoted almost exclusively to *HG*. The latter study resembles the analysis of cross-cousin marriage to the extent that in both instances the main objective is the formulation of sociological generalizations. But there is one fundamental difference. In *HG* Homans uses a radically different conceptual apparatus.

In the analysis of cross-cousin marriage, Homans investigates the relationship between particular forms of kinship institution and, in so doing, adopts the kind of structural terms used, not only by Lévi-Strauss, but also by Parsons and Merton. In his more comprehensive work, however, he argues that, although legitimate for certain kinds of study, these complex abstractions are unsuitable for the formulation of universal empirical generalizations. To show what he means

Homans discusses the terms 'status' and 'role'. He argues that when we describe a particular role we blend together a variety of different types of empirical data: 'We do not directly observe *status* and *role*. What we do observe are activities, interactions, evaluations, norms and controls. Status and role are names we give to a complex of many different kinds of observations.'[18] The 'big abstractions' of structural-functionalism vary along several, perhaps partly independent, dimensions. For this reason it is difficult, if not impossible, to express in terms of universal generalizations any regular relationships between the empirical phenomena which they represent. For example, it is the complexity of its empirical referents which makes the Homans-Schneider hypothesis unavoidably a statement of probability rather than a universally valid proposition. Furthermore, because the empirical content of such abstractions tends to be unreliable and ambiguous, they can too easily obscure 'minor' empirical variations. In fact, Homans argues, conceptualization at this level of abstraction may actually prevent us from noticing explanatory uniformities among such component elements as activities and interaction. He decides, therefore, to begin his theoretical induction at a lower level of abstraction, even if this necessitates the use of a more common-sense terminology. In this way he hopes to ensure that his eventual deductive system will have a reliable empirical foundation and will be composed of universally applicable generalizations: 'The great point is to climb down from the big words of social science, at least as far as common-sense observation. Then, if we wish, we can start climbing up again, but this time with a ladder we can depend on.'[19]

In pursuit of conceptual clarity, Homans makes a distinction between first-order and second-order abstractions. A first-order abstraction is a name given to a single class of observations which cannot be further sub-classified. A second-order abstraction is a name referring to several classes of observation combined. Homans' aim is to construct a conceptual scheme composed entirely of first-order abstractions. Such a scheme would have the major advantage of referring unambiguously to given classes of observations. It would accordingly improve the reliability of sociological analyses, facilitate the formulation of empirical generalizations, and foster cumulative theoretical development. His first step is to ask: What kinds of observations do sociologists actually make in the course of their investigations? After an examination of a representative study, he concludes that there are four main classes of observations. These classes he calls activity, interaction, sentiment and norms. The terms are defined as follows:

Activity. This term refers to things people do; it refers 'in the end to movements of the muscles of men, even though the importance of some of the movements, like talk and ceremonies, depends on their symbolic meaning'.[20]

Interaction. Although the terms 'activity' and 'interaction' are closely related, they are, in Homans' view, analytically distinct. He states that when 'we refer to the fact that some unit of activity of one man follows, or, if we like the word better, is stimulated by some unit of activity of another, aside from any question of what these units may be, then we are referring to *interaction*'.[21]

Sentiments. This term covers the entire range of physical and psychological states experienced by human beings. It includes hunger and thirst as well as anxiety, anger, liking, disapproval and so on. Homans is a little worried by the fact that sentiments, unlike activity and interaction, cannot be directly observed. The existence of sentiments must be *inferred* from observable actions and such inferences may be far from reliable. Nevertheless, although 'reliability is the rock on which science is built',[22] Homans believes that sentiments are such an important determinant of social behaviour that the danger of unreliability must be risked.

Norms. Norms are ideals in the minds of members of a group which specify what behaviour is expected in given circumstances. Like sentiments, norms must be inferred rather than directly observed.

The conceptual scheme which Homans constructs is designed primarily to clarify the empirical referents of his proposed generalizations. It is important to note, however, that in trying to achieve this end Homans is led towards a considerable simplification of sociological analysis. First, he rejects second-order abstractions because they are, at present, too complex to be unambiguous. Secondly, he reduces the number of basic categories to four. And, thirdly, as is particularly obvious in the case of sentiments, he makes these concepts as inclusive as is compatible with their being first order abstractions. But the consequences of Homans' search for clarity and simplicity do not end there. For he decides also to abandon the study of complex social structures and to concentrate upon the small human group: 'Perhaps we cannot manage a sociological synthesis that will apply to whole communities and nations, but it is just possible we can manage one that will apply to the small group.'[23] In fact, this is not a separate decision, for Homans' conceptual scheme necessarily limits him to the study of small groups. This is so because one of the basic terms—namely, interaction—can only be applied to face-to-face social behaviour. As his theoretical scheme matures it becomes increasingly evident that Homans' main interest is face-to-face interaction, or, as he calls it, 'elementary social behaviour', rather than the small group as such. 'Small groups are not what we study but where we study it.'[24]

Thus Homans' conceptual framework leads him to concentrate almost exclusively on those interpersonal relations which occur within small groups. But even this restricted range of data is subjected to one further simplification.

Homans suggests that any small group can, for purposes of analysis, be regarded as constituted by two interdependent but distinguishable systems—the external system and the internal system. The external system is not, as the name might suggest, outside the group. It is in fact composed of the patterns of behaviour by means of which the group solves those problems set by its physical, technical and social environment. The external system of a group is the solutions it has evolved to the problems of surviving in an environment. 'We call it external because it is conditioned by the environment; we call it a system because in it the elements of behaviour [that is, activity, interaction, etc.] are mutually dependent.'[25] But, according to Homans, no human group remains at this minimal level of organization. Instead, they elaborate upon the patterns directly conditioned by the environment, and in so doing generate an internal system. This internal system arises out of the external system and reacts back upon it. Homans summarizes the distinction in the following words:

> We shall not go far wrong if ... we think of the external system as group behavior that enables the group to survive in its environment and think of the internal system as group behavior that is an expression of the sentiments towards one another developed by the members of the group in the course of their life together.[26]

The notion of external system has pronounced functional overtones, for it requires us to think of groups as facing problems to which adequate solutions must be, and are, found. But this version of functional requisites has been subjected by Homans to a characteristic theoretical reinterpretation. For functionalists, the question of how functional requirements come to be met is problematic. For Homans it is not. He takes the external system as *given* and examines only its impact on the further structuring of group relations. For example, in his analysis of the Bank Wiring Room which will be examined later in more detail, Homans assumes that the group has a particular physical layout, that it meets the demands of a particular technology, and that its members enter the group with specific motives and needs. He then attempts to show how, with these factors given, the remainder of the group's behaviour emerges. Thus in *HG* the external system can be defined as those aspects of group structure which Homans chooses not to explain. The theorist himself does not fully recognize this until in the course of his later work he is led to revise the notion to make it identical with what we have so far called the givens:

> The kinds of things we have called *givens* ... are the same as what I called in my earlier book the *external system*. I now think this is too pretentious a term and suggests what is not true. If 'system' means that a set of parts are related to one another, the givens sometimes do constitute a system. ... But givens do not always constitute a system. ... If the word *givens* ... [does not] suit the reader's taste, let him try some other phrase like *parameters* or *boundary conditions*, the boundary being the arbitrary and imaginary line dividing elementary social behavior from what, for the purposes in hand, we choose to consider its physical and social environment in time and space.[27]

Owing to this, clearly correct, decision to drop the term external system, I shall not in this study mention it again. I shall instead concentrate increasingly on the givens. However, what needs to be noted here is that, whether we refer to givens or to external system, the concept makes possible further simplification of Homans' analytical task. Not only does he concentrate on elementary social behaviour to the exclusion of more complex social relationships, not only does he choose to study elementary social behaviour by means of a small number of inclusive concepts, but he also allows himself the freedom of drawing an 'arbitrary and imaginary line' between those data he must explain and those he can regard as unproblematic. We have seen earlier, in our study of Pareto's attempt to use similar theoretical tactics, how this policy of selection and simplification can create acute theoretical difficulties. Nevertheless, Homans' approach is a systematic and reasoned response to the defects of structural-functionalism. In the first place, it attempts to lower the level of abstraction even further than does Merton. Secondly, it attempts to combine conceptual precision with the formulation of a series of truly universal propositions which can take their place within a general theory of society. Thirdly, it concentrates on the use of these propositions to produce logically acceptable explanatory systems. Fourthly, by introducing the notion of 'the givens', it recognizes the need for selectivity and builds this requirement into its explanatory logic. And, finally, it bases its explanatory generalizations on a firm inductive foundation. This approach to sociological theory has its own dangers. It is undoubtedly highly selective and may easily lead to undue simplification. Yet if it were to yield a series of clear and precise empirical generalizations, who would doubt that it was a genuine theoretical advance and a reliable basis for subsequent theoretical elaboration?

IV

Homans wishes to ensure that his theory grows out of an impartial and direct examination of available facts. Among the theorists surveyed so far in this study, only Pareto is strongly committed to this kind of approach. But Pareto's facts are taken piecemeal from the whole course of human history. Accordingly, not until he begins to use his theory deductively does Pareto try to demonstrate how the constituents of social life are systematically interrelated. Homans, in contrast, prefers to show inductively that the elements of social behaviour are interdependent and to clarify from the start the nature of the relationships involved. Consequently, unlike Pareto, Homans does not build up his generalizations from separate historical references, but examines instead five case studies, each of which gives a connected body of information about a particular human group or social system.

> If we want to develop a theory of group behavior that will show every element of group life related to every other element in a system, then the material we use must be as connected as the theory. If we are to show connections, there must *be* connections. We must not, in the classical manner, use isolated facts to back up our theory, but related facts.[28]

Homans' procedure is to present a summary version of each case study, which is then reinterpreted in terms of his own conceptual framework. The purpose of each interpretation is to express any observed regularities in the form of empirical generalizations. These generalizations are further substantiated, whenever possible, in relation to the next study, which is also used as the source for additional generalizations. The end-product, it is hoped, will be a series of related propositions which express in one general form the results of observations of many particular groups. I shall now present a number of Homans' hypotheses and give some indication of their empirical basis. In a few cases these propositions have been slightly simplified:

1. If the frequency of interaction between two or more persons increases, the degree of their liking for one another will increase, and vice versa.[29]
2. Persons whose sentiments of liking for one another increase will express these sentiments in increased activity, and vice versa.[30]
3. The more frequently persons interact with one another, the more alike both their activities and their sentiments tend to become, and vice versa.[31]

4   The higher the rank of a person within a group, the more nearly his activities conform to the norms of the group, and vice versa.[32]

5   The higher a person's social rank, the wider will be the range of his interactions.[33]

These propositions are first presented by Homans as generalized statements of empirical regularities observed in the study of the Bank Wiring Room. This study was concerned with a dozen or so men working in one section of a large American corporation. Most of the men were involved in connecting wires to banks of electric terminals and were allocated by management to small soldering units within the Bank Wiring Room. These divisions within the bank wiring section produced definite and unavoidable patterns of interaction which were clearly reflected in the structure of friendship choices. As the men themselves had no control over their location in the room it can safely be assumed that these likes and dislikes did not precede their social interaction within the section. It is, therefore, reasonable to infer that friendship or sentiments of liking grew out of continual interaction. Moreover, it appears that these sentiments, once established, led to further interaction. For example, each friendship clique developed its own games, topics of conversation and patterns of temporary job exchange: 'The interactions between Bank Wiremen were in fact more frequent than the set up of work required. It is not just that favourable sentiments increase as interaction increases, but that these sentiments then boost interaction still further.'[34] It is this kind of evidence, although presented in much greater detail, that Homans tries to summarize in hypothesis No. 1, to the effect that the frequency of interaction and the degree of liking are directly related.

The second proposition postulates that sentiment and activity are mutually dependent. Homans suggests that as people come to like one another, they feel the need to express their sentiments by means of additional activity. In the Bank Wiring Room this need was satisfied most commonly by helping other men complete their work:

> There were few occasions when helping another man was required by the necessities of the work—indeed it was forbidden by the company; yet it took place just the same, and many of the men testified that helping and being helped made them feel better. Everyone took part in helping. . . . In fact it was one of the activities that united the whole group. . . .[35]

Not only do sentiments of liking lead to further activity, but the activity, in turn, promotes more liking. This is so, argues Homans, because all sentiments seek expression in activity which, if it is rewarded with approval, will tend to increase.

The two generalizations discussed so far summarize the tendency observed within the Bank Wiring Room for interaction to produce sentiments of liking which, in turn, generated further activities and interactions in the form of games, job-trading and helping. Homans calls this building up of new sentiments, activities and interactions *group elaboration*. He suggests that it is usually accompanied by *group differentiation*. This latter process is seen clearly in the development of cliques or sub-groups within the Bank Wiring Room. Each clique was characterized internally by higher rates of interaction and by stronger sentiments of liking; at the same time each clique developed distinct patterns of behaviour—for example, its own games, its own topics of conversation, its peculiar controversies and its characteristic level of output. Homans attempts to recognize this process of differentiation within the Bank Wiring Room in generalization No. 3 that the more frequently people interact the more alike their activities and sentiments tend to become.

The fourth proposition is concerned with social ranking. A man's rank is his evaluation relative to other members of his group. In Homans' view this evaluation is an expression of peoples' sentiments. But these sentiments depend upon the existence of standards or norms generally accepted within the group, in terms of which relative judgments can be made. Thus social ranking is seen as a product of sentiments which arise out of a comparison of a man's activities with those of other members of his group in accordance with the group's norms. Having established this, Homans turns to the Bank Wiring Room. He makes no attempt to account for the norms of this group, but, taking the norms as given, he examines the relationship between activities and sentiments of social ranking. He pays particular attention to the norm which requires all members of the Bank Wiring Room to complete around 6,000 soldering connections per day, and shows that highest rank tends to be given to those individuals and cliques which conform most closely to this norm. Further evidence indicates that high rank tends to be associated with conformity to other, less precise norms. Consequently, Homans puts forward the tentative hypothesis that the higher the rank of a person within a group, the more nearly his activities will conform to the norms of the group.

Proposition No. 5 is also a speculative hypothesis about social ranking. Homans postulates that persons of high rank will tend to interact with more group members than will those with low rank. The evidence cited deals with the pattern of job-trading within the Bank Wiring Room. In particular, he notes that, whereas low-ranking soldermen never traded jobs outside their own soldering unit, high-ranking soldermen tended to trade jobs with all three soldering units. Homans admits that the evidence for these hypotheses on social ranking is tenuous. Nevertheless, he believes that we have nothing to lose and perhaps much to gain by formulating these relationships as contingent propositions and testing their applicability to other human groups.

We have not examined all the generalizations put forward by Homans in connection with the Bank Wiring Room, but those we have examined are basic, in the sense that many of his subsequent propositions are merely refinements of them. These propositions and the supporting analysis of the Bank Wiring Room are intended to supply not only a number of related empirical generalizations, but also a preliminary account of certain fundamental processes occurring within the small group. Although any of the four conceptual elements could provide his point of departure, Homans chooses to begin by assuming that a certain pattern of *interaction* has been set in the course of the group's response to its environment. He then argues that interaction, *if it is rewarding*, produces positive sentiments which constitute a kind of social surplus beyond the minimum requirements of the group. This surplus finds expression in new activities, which are inevitably accompanied by further interaction. Thus the social system of the small group elaborates upon itself. Sub-groups emerge and activities come to differ from one sub-group to another. How far these processes of elaboration and differentiation can go Homans does not try to specify. Nevertheless, he accepts that limits to internal development are imposed and that group behaviour tends to become standardized. One aspect of social standardization is, of course, the formation of norms. Norms are a particularly important factor controlling that form of differentiation known as social ranking, while social ranking is important because, among other things, it is closely linked to leadership. In search of propositions about leadership, Homans turns to his next study.

The second case study is that of the Norton Street Gang, an American adult gang observed during the late 1930s. This study is used in the first place to confirm the existing hypotheses. As in the case of the Bank Wiring Room, Homans begins by establishing the patterns of recurrent interaction which mark off the Norton Street Gang from its social environment. It is shown that the members of the gang had lived for some time in the Norton Street neighbourhood and that they had gone to school together and had formed an earlier adolescent gang. In addition to this long record of social interaction, the gang members, being unemployed and living in a poor immigrant area, had little opportunity for interaction outside their peer group. Thus the environment 'tended to throw the members of the gang together and keep them together'.[36] And as they interacted there emerged sentiments of liking. The Nortons were firm friends. Homans suggests that we can, therefore, regard the Norton Street Gang as furnishing further evidence for the generalization that interaction fosters sentiments of liking.

As an expression of their surplus of favourable sentiments, the Nortons carried out many activities as a unit. The most frequent group activity was that of 'hanging around' and talking on streetcorners or in cafeterias. They also played bowls regularly and took part in political campaigns. However, friendship within the group was most clearly expressed in the provision of loans and other favours in time of need. In fact, this activity and its accompanying sentiment acquired normative standing among the Nortons. Homans' second hypothesis, then, that positive sentiments are expressed through activities, and his third that interaction produces similar activities and sentiments, both receive additional support from the Norton Street Gang study. In both the studies examined so far Homans tries to show that regular interaction produces a surplus of sentiments which enables the group to evolve a more elaborate structure. And, as in the case of the Bank Wiring Room, he argues that the behaviour and sentiments of the Nortons became standardized:

> The Nortons fell into a routine, and a rather rigid one at that. At certain hours they hung out on the corner, at others they went to a cafeteria for coffee. It was always the same cafeteria: they always sat down at the same table and at the same seats. On Saturday nights the group went bowling. Anyone who knew the group could tell where it was almost certain to be found at any moment. In elaborating their activities, the Nortons also made them customary.[37]

At this juncture Homans gives a brief indication of how this phenomenon of standardization might be explained. He suggests that, if we assume social interaction to be rewarding, then failure to interact will be a punishment. This will be particularly true of groups like the Nortons where other opportunities for social activity are scant. Group members will, therefore, maximize rewards and minimize deprivations by making their activities regular and predictable, for in this way they will seldom lose contact with the group and will seldom be deprived of highly valued interaction. Homans, however, drops this deductive approach to his material before his explanation is complete and returns to the task of induction.

Homans experiences no difficulty in providing further evidence for hypotheses 4 and 5. For example, he examines conformity to the norm current among the Nortons that members should perform well at bowling and finds that those who achieved higher average scores had consistently higher rank than those with lower scores. Similarly he finds that Doc, the leader, and his lieutenants had a wider range of interaction both within and outside the group. Thus, having established the applicability of the generalizations derived from the Bank Wiring Room, he induces further propositions from the Norton Street Gang study, three of which are listed below:

6   The higher a man's social rank, the larger will be the number of persons that originate interaction for him, either directly or through intermediaries.[38]

7   The higher a man's social rank, the larger will be the number of persons for whom he originates interaction, either directly or through intermediaries.[39]

8   The more nearly equal in social rank a number of men are, the more frequently they will interact with one another.[40]

Because there was no clearly established informal leadership in the Bank Wiring Room, these propositions could not be formulated in that context. Nevertheless, the first two are little more than corollaries of hypothesis No. 5. For if we accept that persons of high rank have a wide range of interaction, either proposition 6 and/or proposition 7 follow almost by definition. Despite this logical connection between his generalizations, Homans puts forward hypotheses 5 and 6 separately because they express empirical regularities observed within the Norton Street Gang, where Doc was the focus of a fairly complex network of communications and interactions. It is suggested that interaction flowed toward the leader because lower-rank members found it rewarding. They originated interaction with Doc because such interaction was highly valued. But interaction is a two-way process. Having been the recipient of social contacts, the leader is required to respond by initiating interaction with his followers. It must be noted, however, that the relation between rank and interaction is mutual. The Nortons valued their interactions with Doc. Yet, in the very act of seeking him out, they substantiated his rank as leader and thereby maintained the value of interaction with him:

> We must . . . always remember that these relations are mutual: if interaction flows toward a man because he has high social rank, it is also true that he has high social rank in part because interaction flows toward him. The interaction pattern confirms his rank.[41]

Propositions 6 and 7 summarize this tendency within the Nortons for interaction to flow to and from the leader and other persons of high rank. Proposition 8 describes another evident but somewhat dissimilar phenomenon—namely, the formation of sub-groups, on the one hand among subordinates and on the other hand among those of high rank. '... the leader of the Nortons, with his chief lieutenants and friends, interacted with one another at high frequency. They saw a great deal of one another: they went around together. And the same was true of the followers.'[42] Homans argues that there are two patterns of social interaction related to social rank. In the first place, there is vertical interaction between subordinates and leaders whereby the latter come to acquire a wider range of interaction. Secondly, there is a pattern of horizontal interaction among those of roughly equal rank which produces dominant and subordinate groupings. Those with high rank will interact with *more* members of the group; yet, at the same time, any individual of whatever rank will interact more *frequently* with his equals. Indeed, Homans suggests, the actual pattern of interaction within a group will represent a balance between the two divergent processes summarized in hypotheses 6, 7 and 8.

Having used the Norton Street Gang study to confirm prior generalizations and to formulate additional hypotheses with special reference to social ranking, Homans moves on to an examination of the Tikopia family. He regards the data provided by Firth on the Tikopia as particularly useful because it is based on observation of numerous similar groups instead of one unique group.[43] In Homans' view this kind of data is more satisfactory as a basis for induction. To the extent that Tikopia families resemble each other, 'we must assume that this similarity is not a matter of chance, but that similar forces are producing similar results in all families'.[44] None the less, I shall not repeat here the analysis by means of which Homans provides additional support for his earlier propositions. I shall instead concentrate on two new hypotheses which connect the fundamental generalizations outlined above with the Homans and Schneider study of cross-cousin marriage.

9 The more frequently persons interact with one another, when no one of them originates interaction with much greater frequency than the others, the greater is their liking for one another and their feeling of ease in one another's presence.[45]

10 When two persons interact with one another, the more frequently one of the two originates interaction for the other, the stronger will be the latter's sentiment of respect (or hostility) toward him, and the more nearly will the frequency of interaction be kept to a minimum.[46]

The first of these two hypotheses is an amplification of proposition No. 1. It is based on a comparison, on the one hand, of the relationship between brothers and, on the other hand, of the relationship between father and son among the Tikopia. The former relationship is called by the Tikopia a *tautau laui*, or good relationship, while the latter is bad, or *tautau pariki*. The 'good' tie between brothers is typically close, easy and affectionate. This situation appears to endorse proposition 1: regular and intimate interaction has engendered strong sentiments of liking. But father and son interact frequently within the Tikopia household, if not quite as often as do brothers. How is it then, that interaction in this case appears to breed respect and an ambivalence frequently approaching hostility? Homans suggests that the respect and hostility of the son are a response to the father's authority. Regular interaction produces affection only under certain circumstances and on the basis of the evidence from Tikopia it seems that one of these conditions is the absence of authority:

> Not only do brothers interact frequently with one another; they also have scant authority over each other. No one of them gives orders much more often than any of the others, or, as we say in our technical language, no one of them originates interaction much more frequently than any of the others.[47]

Thus Homans is required by the evidence to modify the initial proposition one by introducing a conditional clause to the effect that interaction and sentiments of liking are positively related *only if* none of the persons involved originates interaction too often. Homans is also required to formulate a generalization which recognizes the positive relationship between authority (or initiation of interaction) and hostility or respect. This he does in the proposition No. 10, above. This proposition is entirely consistent with the Homans-Schneider hypothesis which postulates a negative relationship between the *locus* of authority and the development of positive sentiments.

In the present section we have, so far, reviewed Homans' inductive analysis of three case studies in order to appreciate the factual basis for his central empirical generalizations. Because little is added to these generalizations by the last two studies in *HG*, there is no need for us to examine further Homans' inductions. Nevertheless, before summarizing the content of this chapter and finally abandoning the inductive perspective, we should note what Homans considers to be the main characteristics and limitations of his generalizations.

Homans makes no claim that the propositions we have been discussing are original. He is more interested in validity than originality and suggests that if any of his hypotheses are valid they will almost certainly have been formulated before. In addition, he stresses that they are hypotheses, not theorems. They are intended as tentative generalizations based upon a limited range of data and, as such, will undoubtedly need to be modified in the light of further evidence. None the less, Homans' propositions are supposed to form a coherent series of related statements. Because they are related, each generalization qualifies the others. For example, there are certain circumstances in which interaction does not foster sentiments of liking. But this fact does not invalidate the first hypothesis, for those instances in which it does not apply are either covered by existing hypotheses, such as proposition No. 10 or can be covered by the formulation of new empirically substantiated generalizations. A serious danger faced by this kind of scheme is that new propositions may come to be introduced in an *ad hoc* manner to account for *any* divergence between factual data and existing theoretical statements. This danger can be minimized, however, by ensuring that hypotheses make use of a common language composed of first-order abstractions with clear empirical referents. As long as new generalizations have unambiguous empirical content, their inclusion within the scheme will be determined by their capacity to express definite empirical regularities rather than by the theorist's wish to remove theoretical inadequacies.

Although Homans regards his propositions and concepts as a considerable improvement on those of structural-functionalism, he is forced to admit that they are far from reaching the level of precision common in the physical sciences. In particular, he recognizes that his concepts are not themselves variables. They cannot be given a single series of numerical values, as can, for instance, temperature in physics.[48] Activity can vary in terms of output or efficiency; interaction can vary in terms of frequency and duration; while sentiments and norms each cover an even wider range of variables. Homans' terms, like those of everyday speech, vary along several dimensions. There is, therefore, no immediate likelihood of using such concepts to form simultaneous equations, though the theorist hopes in the long run to move in this direction. But surprisingly, instead of improving the precision of his scheme—for example, by developing techniques of quantification—Homans is more concerned to complete his deductive system. He appears to regard his inability to provide precise propositions as less important than his failure to *explain* these propositions. In *HG* there are many hints as to how this is to be done, and Homans refers recurrently to such psychological notions as reward and deprivation when giving exploratory explanations of his generalizations. In fact, reference to human psychology is even built into Homans' hypotheses. To make this point clear, it is worth comparing a proposition taken from the physical sciences with one from *HG*. Boyle's Law, for example, states that if the pressure of a gas is doubled, then the volume of the gas will be halved. Homans' first hypothesis states that the more frequently *persons* interact, the stronger *their* sentiments of liking will be. Boyle's Law is a flat statement. It states a precise relationship between two variables, but gives no indication of how this relationship is brought about. The problem of explaining the Law is left empirically open. Homans' generalization, in contrast, refers explicitly to the agents, in this case individual human beings, which are seen as establishing the relationship between interaction and sentiments. Thus in the very form of his hypotheses Homans indicates the kind of propositions from which his sociological generalizations should be derived. They will be propositions about persons *qua* persons.

V

Homans' long-term theoretical objectives are no different from those of the two functionalists treated in earlier chapters. Homans, like Parsons and Merton, wishes to construct a relatively comprehensive deductive system in relation to social phenomena. He does differ from them, however, in believing, as did Pareto, that the formulation of such a general deductive system must remain the immediate and central focus of theoretical work. He rejects the idea that we can best contribute to a general theory by developing comprehensive conceptual schemes or even by undertaking piecemeal explanatory analyses. For Homans the most profitable theoretical strategy is that of direct and systematic induction. Because his sole aim is to create a fully theoretical system without passing through such intermediate stages as categorial or middle-range analysis, Homans pays particular attention to describing what kind of theoretical scheme he is seeking. His envisaged theory must, when complete, constitute a logically valid deductive system or series of systems made up of propositions at three broad levels of generality, those at the highest level being psychological in character. This theory should have clear empirical referents and should be capable, under a variety of given conditions, of generating a wide range of explanations and predictions. Ultimately the worth of the scheme will depend on this capacity for producing precise and, as far as possible, quantitative, deductions about observable social events.

Before undertaking the inductive survey which constitutes a crucial phase in his theoretical strategy, Homans recognizes the need to come to terms with the excessive complexity of sociological data. Unlike Parsons, he makes no attempt to achieve complete conceptual coverage of the social world. Instead, he adopts the Paretian tactics of selection and simplification. In the first place, he decides to concentrate on face-to-face interaction and to regard more complex social groupings as unproblematic. Secondly, he reserves the right to make an arbitrary distinction between that social behaviour he will try to explain and that which he will take as given. Thirdly, he adopts a conceptual scheme which he regards as representing the fundamental, in the sense of most simple, observations made by sociologists in the course of their studies. Having thus limited his theoretical focus and effectively simplified his theoretical task, he undertakes a secondary analysis of five case studies in order to formulate the empirical generalizations required for the realization of his theoretical aims.

Systematic induction produces, not only a series of related generalizations, but also a depiction of certain processes occurring in the small group. Homans' account of these processes stresses that social interaction, when rewarding, leads to the elaboration and differentiation of group activities, to the standardization of these activities and to their embodiment in norms. He suggests that it is out of such interaction between individuals that complex structures have emerged historically. This emphasis on the way in which group structures develop out of simpler processes differs considerably from the perspective of the functionalists. For the latter, individual actors are born into ongoing social structures which mould their behaviour and constrain their activities. Consequently functionalism concentrates on the roles, norms and values of the social system itself and, when interpreting the actions of individuals, views them as structured responses to that system. From this viewpoint the only *universal* and, therefore, potentially explanatory features of social life must be certain characteristics of social systems themselves, such as their functional prerequisites. Largely as a result of strategical considerations, Homans concentrates on face-to-face interaction, and in so doing comes to stress that complex structures grow out of such interaction, which is itself dependent on certain psychological mechanisms. Consequently, he concludes, in complete contrast to the functional approach, that the true sociological universals are precisely those psychological mechanisms which guide all men in the course of direct social interaction. We must now examine the way in which Homans' deductive system is completed by the introduction of statements expressing these psychological uniformities.

7 A theory of social exchange: Homans

I

Most of the analysis in *HG* is inductive. It is concerned with expressing observed regularities in the form of generalized statements. In several instances, however, Homans does use his hypotheses deductively to explain specific social events and, in the course of these deductions, he begins to make explicit his underlying psychological assumptions. I shall examine Homans' explanatory use of his generalizations first in relation to his treatment of social control and then in relation to his analysis of social disintegration.

When sociologists investigate social control they are trying to account for regular recurrences in social behaviour. They are asking such questions as: Why do social structures persist? or Why do the members of a particular group comply with the norms of that group? Homans chooses to ask this last question with respect to the norm governing output in the Bank Wiring Room. His theoretical perspective requires him to *deduce* conformity to this norm by applying his hypotheses. This he attempts to do. But he approaches the problem by predicting the outcome of an hypothetical case of deviance. He argues that social regularities persist because any departure from regularity is met by resistance. If this is so, then an effective way of determining how such regularities are maintained is to examine what would happen were some deviation from the normal pattern to occur.

All the members of the Bank Wiring Room conformed, to some degree, to the output norm of 6,000 connections per day. Homans suggests that the degree of each individual's conformity was bound up with his position within the network of activities, interaction and sentiments of the group, and that any movement further away from his existing level of conformity would automatically change this network. He also suggests that the changes produced by any movement away from conformity can be inferred by applying his hypotheses. Thus, in the first place, a decrease in the degree of an individual's conformity would reduce the frequency of his interaction with colleagues. This follows from proposition 3, above, to the effect that the less alike are people's activities the less often will they interact. Secondly, by hypothesis 1, as interaction declines so the deviant will be liked less by his workmates. Furthermore, proposition 4 tells us that his rank within the group will tend to fall. These inferences are clear and unquestionable as long as we accept Homans' generalizations. Nevertheless, taken alone, they are insufficient to account for effective social control in the Bank Wiring Room. A decline in conformity may well reduce a person's frequency of interaction, lower his informal rank and make him less well liked. But we still have to explain why any individual should be prevented from acting by a threatened reduction in social activity, a loss in rank or by the disapproval of others. In order to fill this gap, Homans finds it necessary to introduce two additional assumptions. The first is that approval, rank and interaction were experienced as rewarding and their absence or reduction as a deprivation by the members of the Bank Wiring Room. The second is that people act to increase their rewards rather than their level of deprivation. These psychological assumptions underlie the following statement, in which Homans examines why Taylor, the incipient leader of the Bank Wiring Room, was effectively controlled by its norms:

> Taylor came closest to realizing the output standard of the group. He also had the highest social rank, received most interactions from other men ... and was the most influential member of the group. Any long-continued departure in his activity rate from the norm of the group would have brought about a decline in all of these other things. *So far as he enjoyed his social rank, his associations, and his influence, a change in his output rate would have hurt him.* In the relations of each of these elements to all the others in a system lies the fact of control.[1]

As long as we can presume or establish that the individuals being studied *value* social activity, then Homans' generalizations can be used to infer effective control. But it is clear that in situations where interaction is not rewarding these generalizations will lead to quite different deductions. For example, when social approval and interaction are experienced as punishments instead of rewards, nonconformity will be gratifying and will tend to increase rather than decline. It is clear, therefore, that Homans' hypotheses depicting the network of activities, interactions, sentiments and norms cannot alone account for the phenomena of social control. They must be supplemented by statements about the rewards and deprivations experienced by group members. Indeed, these psychological factors are so central to Homans' analysis that he builds them into his definition of social control:

> Control is the process by which, if a man departs from his present degree of obedience to a norm, his behaviour is brought back toward that degree ... control can be effective only when that degree of obedience is the one that produces the greatest amount of satisfaction of the man's sentiments possible under the existing state of the social system, so that any departure whatever from that degree brings a decrease in satisfaction, a net punishment.[2]

Homans refers to a situation in which control is effective throughout the group as a state of equilibrium. Full equilibrium exists when all group members have achieved a maximum level of satisfaction. He admits that it would be exceptionally difficulty to establish that a particular group was characterized by the greatest amount of satisfaction possible under the circumstances. Nevertheless, he asserts, it is clear that in a group where members *had* achieved maximum satisfaction any small change within the social system—that is, within the network of activities, interactions, etc.—would be followed by further changes tending to reduce the impact of the initial change. And this tendency for change to be minimized would be observable. Accordingly, Homans insists that equilibrium is something to be demonstrated empirically. Use of the term 'equilibrium' does not commit us, in his view, to presuming the existence in all social systems of mechanisms for attaining or preserving certain steady states. Equilibrium is rather a state of the system which, in particular circumstances, grows out of interactions within the group and is amenable to explanation by the combined use of sociological and psychological propositions. Similarly, disequilibrium states can be observed when small changes are fostered by the social system in a way which promotes further change. Furthermore, Homans maintains, his hypotheses deal as well with disequilibrium as with social control.

Homans selects to study disequilibrium in the form of social disintegration or social decline, partly because social disintegration involves exactly opposite processes to those of elaboration and differentiation with which his analysis is mainly concerned. In one sense the analysis of disintegration is inductive, for it does indeed express observed regularities in a more general form. But these 'new' inductions are mostly reversed versions of earlier hypotheses. Thus proposition 1, that increased interaction increases the intensity of social sentiments, is changed to: A *decrease* in the frequency of interaction will bring about a *decrease* in the strength of interpersonal sentiments.[3] On the whole Homans' interpretation consists of attempts to fit the facts of social decline to such reversed formulations of prior hypotheses. As a consequence, it is possible to treat his analysis of social decline in Hilltown as a deductive interpretation of social disintegration.[4]

During the nineteenth century Hilltown was a prosperous American agricultural community with complex patterns of internal interdependence, a strong normative structure and a thriving social life. As the present century progressed, however, certain changes occurred in Hilltowners' sentiments:

> ... changes in the technical and physical environment made Hilltowners poorer, in comparison with other people, than they had once been, while ... changes in the cultural environment made them anxious to get richer.[5]

At the same time, new opportunities to satisfy these sentiments emerged in neighbouring regions:

> As transportation improved, local industry declined, and milltowns grew up round about, the interests of Hilltowners led them to take part in organizations, such as markets and factories, outside the town rather than inside it.[6]

In other words, Hilltowners came to feel that certain activities, particularly economic activities, could be pursued more satisfactorily outside their own community; and as the level of relative deprivation involved in the pursuit of these activities within Hilltown increased, so its inhabitants increasingly undertook them where the reward was higher.

Once the occurrence of this change in the sentiments and a corresponding change in the activities of Hilltowners have been demonstrated, Homans' generalizations lead us to infer, other things being equal, that a cumulative decline in social life will ensue. The process proceeds in broad terms as follows: A change in sentiments reduces the number of activities carried out within the community. Reduced activity necessarily entails a decrease in interaction. The decline in both activities and interactions weakens positive social sentiments, which in turn further reduces activities and interactions. As social sentiments diminish norms become less clear, social ranking less definite and conformity less rewarding. In this way the incentives for social activity fade and a process of progressive social disintegration gradually takes shape.

This drastically simplified account of Homans' analysis of disintegrative change allows us to make one important point—namely, that psychological as well as sociological propositions are used. In the interpretation of social control Homans takes as given that interaction in the Bank Wiring Room was generally experienced as rewarding. By combining this assumption with his hypotheses, he is able to infer that control will be effective and that the group will be fairly stable. In the study of Hilltown, in contrast, Homans establishes that, at a particular point in time, interaction became relatively unrewarding. As a result, he is able to infer, using a reversed version of his generalizations, that social control will be progressively ineffective and that social disintegration will ensue. In both these analyses Homans takes as given participants' *values* —that is, what they experience as rewarding. When he postulates that a particular form of interaction is rewarding, his generalizations predict processes of elaboration and differentiation leading towards social equilibrium. When he postulates that interaction is relatively depriving, his propositions predict cumulative disintegration. The next theoretical task must clearly be a detailed consideration of those psychological givens which are so essential to his explanatory procedure.

II

In his search for general statements of psychological uniformities, Homans turns first to behavioural psychology whose adherents, owing to their use of precise experimental techniques, have been more directly concerned with the behaviour of animals, such as rats, than with that of human beings. Behavioural psychologists, in accordance with considerable evidence gathered by experimental methods, have come to view the activities of animals as responses to positive and negative reinforcement or, in more everyday terms, as reactions to the receipt of reward and punishment. Within this perspective, a number of general propositions have been put forward of which the following are important examples. The more fully an animal has been deprived of a reward the more often it emits activity previously reinforced by that reward. The more fully an animal has been satiated with a reward, the less often it emits the appropriate activity. The more often an activity is reinforced, the more often the animal emits that activity. The more often an activity is punished, the less often the animal emits it.[7]

Homans contends that such statements apply as well to human as to other animals and that, at the very least, human behaviour cannot be inconsistent with them. Nevertheless, he does not regard these generalizations as adequate in themselves to account for elementary social behaviour, for the simple reason that they are not *social* propositions; they take no cognizance of the fact that most human rewards and deprivations depend upon interaction with others who are themselves subject to the same psychological laws. He argues accordingly that supplementary propositions are required which express the processes governing the exchange of rewards and costs between human beings. Such exchange propositions have already been formulated in elementary economics. A good example is the law of supply, which states that the higher the price of a good, the more of it will a supplier sell. A related example is the law of demand: the higher the price of a commodity, the less of it will a consumer buy. These propositions, although limited to the realm of economic conduct, are laws of social exchange. They depict the actions of at least two persons, a buyer and a seller, each of whom, in order to maximize his own reward, provides his partner with some valued response. Homans regards such statements about human exchange as corollaries of the findings of behavioural psychology, but corollaries which need to be stated explicitly because they take into account the complications of mutual reinforcement. He suggests that by combining propositions of this kind from economics with those from psychology, and by expressing them in as general form as possible in order to make them applicable beyond the confines of purely economic behaviour, he can furnish the generalizations needed to complete his theoretical scheme. But these generalizations will do more than simply constitute the highest level within the logico-deductive system. They will also lead us to perceive social life in a particular way—namely, as a network of social transactions or bargainings:

> ... both behavioral psychology and elementary economics envisage human behavior as a function of its pay-off: in amount and kind it depends on the amount and kind of reward and punishment it fetches. When what it fetches is the behavior, similarly determined, of another man, the behavior becomes social. Thus the set of general propositions I shall use ... envisages social behavior as an exchange of activity ... between at least two persons.[8]

Before stating Homans' high-level exchange propositions we must first note certain conceptual modifications and additions which he finds it necessary to introduce in *SB*. The four basic concepts used in *HG* are retained, but they are now explicitly recognized as no more than *descriptive terms*, i.e. merely as names for categorizing the kinds of behaviour to be examined. None the less, Homans' definitions of his descriptive terms have been tightened and are couched strictly in behaviourist language. Thus interaction, sentiments and norms are all defined unquestionably as particular sub-types of human *activity* or *behaviour*. Sentiments are:

> *activities* that the members of a particular verbal or symbolic community say are signs of the attitudes and feelings a man takes toward another man or other men. . . . Sentiments are not internal states of an individual any more than words are. They are not inferred from overt behavior: they *are* overt behavior and so are directly observable.[9]

Similarly, the term 'interaction' is used 'when we are not interested for the moment in the particular sort of *behavior emitted*—whether it is an activity or a sentiment, or a particular kind of activity or sentiment—but simply in the fact that the behavior . . . is at least social'.[10] While a norm is 'a *statement* made by a number of members of a group, not necessarily all of them, that the members ought to behave in a certain way in certain circumstances'.[11]

These explicit behaviourist definitions seem to have been adopted because they are required by the emerging conception of social life as exchange. Whilst Homans was simply establishing inductive relationships between such factors as interaction and sentiments, there was no reason, apart from the need for reliable evidence, why such terms should not refer to inner states of individuals. But once we view social behaviour as exchange, an observable phenomenon must be found which is exchanged, for it is hardly possible to exchange internal states. Thus, given the important place which activity has held in Homans' scheme from the outset and its significance for the behavioural psychologists, it is reasonable for him to conclude that various kinds of activity are exchanged and to redefine his descriptive terms accordingly. Although these refined definitions are perhaps more systematic than the earlier formulations, they are not essentially different. The major conceptual innovation in *SB* is not the treatment of descriptive terms, but the introduction of certain variables—that is, terms which express some of the dimensions along which descriptive terms can vary. The two main variables chosen are quantity and value. Homans' intention is to state contingent propositions, of the form 'the quantity of X varies as the value of Y', about the relations between the various kinds of social activity.

Within any group various social activities occur more or less frequently during a given period of time. Their quantity varies. *Quantity* is a measure of the rate of emission of units of activity—whether in the form of sentiments or interaction or just plain activity—per unit of time. The rate of emission of activity is one of the variables which Homans builds into his explanatory propositions. The second variable, value, is more complex. *Value* refers to the degree of reinforcement or punishment that a person receives from a unit of activity emitted by another person. Homans regards it as relatively easy to attain crude measures of quantity, that is, of the frequency of units of activity. But the measurement of value is more difficult. One possible measure of the value of a reward is the quantity of activity that an individual will expend to gain the reward. But if we measure value in terms of quantity, if we decide that the value of a reward *is* the amount of activity emitted to attain it, then we will be unable to formulate *empirical* generalizations linking together these two variables.

> If we say: the more valuable a reward the more activity
> a man puts out that gets him that reward, and our only
> measure of value is in fact the quantity of activity put out,
> then our proposition turns into a tautology, for X and Y have
> the same measure: indeed they are simply the same variable.[12]

Thus Homans is forced to seek a measure of value which is independent of the quantity of activity expended in pursuit of what is valued. His solution is to examine the history of the groups or persons involved. If they sought a particular reward in similar situations in the past, then we have evidence that they will value this reward now. Similarly, if we know that they have recently been deprived of the reward, then we have good grounds for assuming that the value they put on the reward will be relatively high. In short, 'the past offers in principle the information we need to assess values independently of the amount of activity a man puts out to get these values at present'.[13]

Value is defined as the degree of positive *or negative* reinforcement received from a unit of activity. Subsequently, however, another concept is introduced which is closely related to the idea of negative reinforcement or negative value. This is the notion of cost. The term *cost* refers to negative value or unpleasantness incurred in the course of obtaining a reward and also to positive value attached to alternative courses of action which are forsaken and which thereby reduce the net reward attained. Costs may often be high in relation to rewards, but it is assumed that social relationships will not persist unless all parties involved are making a profit. *Psychic profit* is, of course, defined as reward less cost. Homans does not state explicitly whether profit or cost are variables or descriptive terms. However, they can hardly be regarded as names for the kinds of activities to be studied. They must, therefore, be variables and can probably be viewed most satisfactorily as sub-divisions of the term 'value'. This interpretation is borne out by Homans' decision not to present any *formal* propositions about cost on the grounds that such propositions are no more than corollaries of the more basic statements about value. In the following list of generalizations, two statements involving cost have been included, however, for the sake of clarity.[14]

(a) If in the past a man's activity has been rewarded in a particular situation, then the more similar the present situation is to the past one, the more likely he is to emit the same activity, or some similar activity, now.

(b) The more (less) often within a given period of time a man's activity rewards the activity of another, the more (less) often will the other emit the same activity.

(c) The more (less) valuable to a man a unit of the activity another gives him, the more (less) often he will emit activity rewarded by the activity of the other.

(d) The more (less) cost a man incurs in emitting an activity, the less (more) often he will emit it.

(e) The more (less) often a man has in the recent past received a rewarding activity from another, the less (more) valuable any further unit of that activity becomes to him.

(f) The more (less) often a man has in the recent past emitted a costly activity, the more (less) costly any further unit of that activity becomes to him.

These, then, are the generalizations which complete Homans' deductive theory. No attempt is made to justify them inductively. They are to be used to explain established generalizations of a lower order of abstraction, such as those put forward in *HG*. They are also designed to extend the scope and precision of Homans' analysis of particular case studies and experimental findings. These new propositions are to be substantiated deductively—that is, by their capacity for generating accurate predictions and explanations. We shall first examine how they are used to explain the two hypotheses (4 and 5) discussed earlier in relation to social ranking.[15]

Proposition 4 states that the higher the rank of a person within a group, the more nearly his activities conform to the norms of the group. In *SB* Homans shows how this hypothesis can be deduced from his more general explanatory statements. The deduction is roughly as follows. A norm is a statement describing behaviour which is prescribed within a particular group. From Homans' perspective, it is impossible to conceive that behaviour could be prescribed and yet not valued. Thus he assumes that behaviour which is normatively defined must be valued by those who endorse the relevant norms. Consequently, the greater a person's conformity to group norms, the greater is the reward he supplies to those other members of the group who hold the same norms. Now, although most group members will be able to conform to normative requirements to some acceptable degree, we can presume that the number of persons who can conform to any great, and therefore particularly rewarding, degree will be relatively small. This was true, for example, in relation to the output norm of 6,000 connections per day in the Bank Wiring Room. In most groups there will be certain norms conformity to which is highly valued, while at the same time there will be no more than a few persons capable of providing an unusual degree of conformity to these norms. Proposition C, above, enables us to infer that in such situations those persons in receipt of this highly valued conformity—that is, the majority of group members—will respond with some activity valued by the minority of exceptional conformists.

Some of those receiving highly valued conformity may be able to respond with exceptional conformity in relation to another norm or other norms. But in circumstances where exceptional conformity of all kinds is the province of the few, the majority of group members will be unable to reciprocate with any specially valued activity. Yet the few will not long continue their valuable activities unless appropriately rewarded (proposition B). The majority will, therefore, tend to reciprocate with rewards which are at the disposal of all men in all human groups. Homans contends that esteem is such a generally available reward. Consequently, he argues, it can be inferred from the basic propositions of social exchange that, under certain specific and common conditions, exceptional conformity by the few elicits high esteem from the many.

The association between high rank or high esteem and extreme conformity is strengthened by considerations of cost. Extreme conformity will generally entail high costs in terms of effort and in terms of alternative rewards relinquished. As a result, unless rewards corresponding to these high costs are forthcoming, in the form of social rank or in some other fashion, the profit of the 'élite' will be low and they will be prompted to abandon the conformity so highly valued by their colleagues. Thus both proposition F and proposition C provide strong support for the initial hypothesis about social ranking. Proposition F tells us that the costs of conformity for the 'élite' will tend to increase disproportionately when compared to the costs of other group members. Proposition C enables us to infer that the 'non-élite' will try to elicit the conformity of the 'élite' by providing them with sufficient esteem to outweigh their costs. These two propositions, plus those cited in the preceding paragraph, demonstrate that certain basic processes of social exchange underlie the tendency found in many groups for those persons who provide exceptional conformity (the 'élite') to receive high rank.

In *SB*, as well as explaining his prior generalizations, Homans provides considerable new documentation for them. For example, in relation to social ranking, he refers to the study by Moreno and others of the Hudson School for Girls, in which a relatively small number of girls were found to be at the same time highly esteemed and closely conforming to group norms.[16] Newcomb's study of Bennington College is also cited.[17] In this study it was established, Homans suggests, not simply that the girls with high esteem were the girls who measured up in high degree to the liberal norms of their college, but that the *greater* their degree of conformity the *higher* was their esteem. This new evidence can be expressed perfectly adequately in general form by Homans' initial hypothesis that persons who conform to a high degree tend to have high rank. Nevertheless, interpretation of this hypothesis in terms of social exchange does draw attention to certain inadequacies in its formulation. According to exchange analysis, it appears that it is not so much conformity which is important as the provision of a specially valuable activity. Thus even perfect conformity will not be rewarded with high rank as long as many members of the group conform to more or less the same degree. Furthermore, conformity to an important norm is more valuable than conformity to a norm less highly prized within the group and will, therefore, be rewarded with greater rank. At the same time, it is possible that those who conform closely to norms exceptionally significant for the group may, as part of their reward, be allowed to flout minor rules which govern the behaviour of the majority. It is also clear that, in some groups, behaviour which is highly valued may not have become normatively defined. Yet, as long as it remains rare and valuable, it is likely to be rewarded with social esteem. Considerations of this kind lead Homans to conclude that although his initial hypothesis summarizes an important overall relationship between rank and conformity, there will be many exceptions. He decides, therefore, to undertake a more detailed analysis of social ranking from the exchange perspective, in the course of which he intends, not only to explain more of his initial hypotheses, but also to refine and modify these limited inductions in the light of the more general notions of social exchange.

Homans first investigates the possibility that persons of high rank, although required to provide valued services, may be allowed 'some leeway in lesser things'.[18] He examines the results of a series of relevant experimental studies which indicate that persons of high and low rank are most likely to diverge from group norms, while those of middle rank are most likely to conform. These findings are then subjected to a detailed interpretation and it is suggested that the potential rewards, costs and profit attaching to conformity and nonconformity differ for each of the three ranks. High-ranking persons have relatively little to gain from further conformity. Their rewards are already high and any additional acts of conformity will have diminishing returns (proposition E). In comparison, acts of nonconformity, depending on how rewarding they are likely to be, will appear enticing (proposition E). Furthermore, the costs associated with nonconformity will be relatively low for those with high rank. They may indeed lose esteem, but they have a surplus on which to draw. Even if their rank is lowered, they will remain better off than most (proposition E). It appears, therefore, that the potential profits of nonconformity are likely to be relatively great for those of high rank and that, consequently, they will be likely to indulge in acts of nonconformity, at least in relation to the less central norms of the group.

The position of persons of middle rank is somewhat different. It is true that neither high nor middle ranks will gain much by conformity as long as most group members conform. But what the middle-rank person gains is more valuable to him (proposition E). At the same time, his potential losses from nonconformity are relatively high, for deviant acts could quickly reduce him to the lowest levels within the group (proposition D). Thus the balance between the profits of nonconformity and conformity favours the latter for the person of middle-rank. Persons of low-rank are less fully members of the group than either of the levels above them. Consequently, although they have little to gain by conformity (proposition C) the potential cost of nonconformity is equally low, and they will easily be tipped toward deviance by any activity which promises to be rewarding (proposition D). In short, the 'upper-status man has little to gain by conformity, the lower-status one little to lose by its opposite, and so for different reasons the behavior of both is biased in the same way'.[19]

Having reviewed and revised his initial hypothesis on the relationship between rank and conformity, Homans turns to a study by Blau for further material on social ranking.[20] Blau's study examines the social relationships among sixteen American civil servants concerned with the enforcement of certain Federal laws. The main task of these Federal agents was to investigate the activities of business organizations and to report their findings to a supervisor. On the basis of these reports, legal action against the firms was either undertaken by the agency or was deemed unnecessary. The degree of competence displayed in their reports was a major concern of the agents, because it largely determined their chances of promotion. Within the group, each agent's competence in formulating reports had become clearly defined and generally acknowledged. Officially, they were required to consult the supervisor rather than other agents when in need of guidance in writing up their reports. But in practice this rule was disregarded, and the agents had developed definite patterns of mutual help which were clearly linked to the informal system of ranking. In the first place, those agents who were defined as most competent were held in high esteem, except for two, who, although extremely knowledgeable, refused to supply helpful advice to the less-favoured. Secondly, the competent and highly-ranked officials were consulted by a large proportion of other agents, but did not themselves go regularly for advice to any one colleague. Thirdly, the majority of less-competent men tended to select a regular partner for mutual assistance from among their equals in competence as well as consulting regularly, but much less frequently, with one of the few highly competent agents.

Some of Homan's earlier hypotheses can be used to express certain of these regularities. For instance, the proposition that the higher a person's rank, the wider the range of his interaction is clearly exemplified in Blau's material. Nevertheless, much more can be gained, in Homans' view, from deducing Blau's findings from the generalizations about social exchange. Homans' analysis proceeds as follows:

Informal ranking in the Federal agency grew out of the network of consultations. Each consultation was itself an exchange of values. The highly competent agent gave advice which was valuable because it improved the calibre of recipients' reports. In return he was rewarded with esteem, which varied in amount depending on the frequency and the competence of his advice (propositions A, B, C). He was further rewarded by the opportunity to pick up useful information during consultations without incurring the cost of having to ask for help. Nonetheless, giving advice unavoidably entailed costs for the adviser because it kept him from his own work. This cost increased rapidly as more consultations were undertaken, while at the same time the value of additional esteem depreciated (propositions D, E, F). In short, the competent agent's profits from consultation were controlled by a cumulative increase in costs, coupled with a corresponding decline in rewards.

The number of consultations any individual was willing to give was limited, not only by his own falling profits, but also by the declining profits of the recipients. In the Federal agency the main cost facing the less-competent agents was the need to admit inferiority in order to elicit advice. Consequently, each additional demand on the highly-competent agents not only brought in advice of diminishing value, but entailed a relatively greater admission of incompetence (propositions D, E, F). Because exceptionally competent advice was so valuable, all the less-knowledgeable officials were willing to solicit it on occasion, at the cost of establishing a hierarchy in which they were placed in a comparatively low position. But as the profits of consultation declined so rapidly they were left continually with problems about which they needed advice, but which were not serious enough to make high-level consultation necessary. This need was satisfied by means of less valuable, but also less costly, transactions with their peers.

Homans' interpretation of this study illustrates his thesis that social behaviour is an exchange of more or less valuable rewards. It also shows that certain of the hypotheses formulated in *HG* can be deduced from the more general propositions about social exchange. For example, proposition No. 5 is shown to operate under certain conditions and to be deducible from statements relating reward, cost and profit; persons with high rank enjoy a wide range of interaction because they furnish their social contacts with valued services. But this deduction also demonstrates the need for a change of focus. It is no longer adequate to identify the rank of group members and their rates of interaction and to establish the relations between these elements. The crucial procedure in undertaking an exchange analysis is to identify those who actually supply and those who receive rewards of various kinds. For it is the exchange of rewards which is responsible for both ranking and interaction. This is exemplified by the two highly competent Federal agents, who, because they refused to give advice, were socially isolated and awarded little esteem. It is only by delineating the interchange of rewards that we can gain a detailed picture of the processes which underlie ranking and interaction, and in this way improve upon the crude relationships established inductively.

As well as refining and explaining existing hypotheses and interpreting new research material, Homans uses his exchange propositions to interpret some of the fundamental group processes discussed in his earlier work. Thus in his analysis of ranking within the Federal agency, as we have seen, he shows how the relative balance of horizontal and vertical interaction depends on the relative distribution of rewards and costs. Although, as he recognizes, the balance will differ in other social contexts, the principles involved have, at last, been made clear. In so far as these explanatory principles are adequate, Homans' exchange analysis is a definite advance on *HG*.

In *SB* the processes of social elaboration and standardization are also examined in some detail from an exchange perspective. In both cases Homans' approach is the same: to explain and modify his previous inductions in accordance with the principles of social exchange and in the light of new research. There is no need here to follow through the whole analysis, for the very uniformity of Homans' objectives and procedure makes it possible to exemplify accurately his general approach by examining solely his treatment of social ranking. Furthermore, although the present survey of Homans' deductions has been partial, this partiality will be remedied to some extent in the next chapter, where we deal with Blau, who builds upon Homans' work and who includes in his scheme much that has been omitted in this exposition of Homans' analysis of elementary exchange.

III

Homans' theoretical work is divided into two definite stages. The first is mainly devoted to induction and the second to deduction. In this appraisal of his theory I shall examine these stages in turn before putting forward certain general conclusions.

The central task of the inductive stage is the provision of a reliable basis for a relatively general theoretical system which will, in time, be capable of generating accurate deductions about social behaviour. If this goal is to be attained, certain requirements must be met. In the first place, analysis must cover a sufficiently wide range of social phenomena to make possible the formulation of a relatively *comprehensive* theory. Secondly, if the inductions are to furnish a reliable theoretical basis, the conceptual scheme must have unambiguous empirical referents. Thirdly, induction must produce precise empirical propositions, for without precise statements of the relationships obtaining between social phenomena the next stage, that of deduction, will be impossible. Finally, in order to constitute the basis for a general theoretical *system*, the hypotheses reached by induction must be systematically interrelated. We must examine to what extent Homans' work in *HG* satisfies these requirements.

Homans' inductive strategy closely resembles that of Pareto. But in certain respects he improves on the methods of his predecessor. For example, whereas Pareto's empirical material consists mostly of second-hand accounts of people's beliefs culled from a wide variety of historical sources, Homans' inductions are based almost exclusively on statements describing direct observations of social activity. The latter's generalizations are, therefore, more likely to provide a *reliable* formulation of empirical regularities. Secondly, Pareto tends to use a number of historically unrelated examples to substantiate each theoretical point and, consequently, fails to specify in the course of his inductions how social facts are systematically connected. Homans, however, chooses to investigate a series of empirical systems in detail and is thereby able to provide more convincing evidence of the systematic interdependence of social facts. This tactic also enables him to construct a single series of related hypotheses—that is, the beginnings of a theoretical *system* —which is closely connected with empirical material. Thirdly, whereas Pareto's inductions in many cases produce no more than non-explanatory categories, Homans does succeed in formulating general propositions which, at least in principle, can be used to deduce and explain social behaviour. In short, Homans' inductions appear to be more reliable, more systematic and more capable of forming part of a genuinely deductive theory than those of Pareto. Nevertheless, despite its merits, Homans' inductive survey is by no means free from serious defects.

The most obvious defect in Homans' scheme is its limited coverage. Like Pareto, Homans simplifies his analytical problems by ignoring whole areas of information acknowledged to be relevant. But whereas Pareto succeeds at least in producing a scheme which deals with complex social systems, Homans ends by concentrating almost exclusively on the relatively simple phenomena of elementary social behaviour. However, in view of Pareto's unquestionable theoretical failure, Homans' decision to focus on the simplest type of sociological data may well be counted as a point in his favour. Clearly our assessment of his selectivity will depend on our opinion of the results it produces. We must, therefore, postpone this question until we have judged the adequacy of his theory within the sphere it is designed to cover. In short, we must concern ourselves first with its reliability, empirical precision and explanatory power in relation to face-to-face interaction.

Homans prefaces his inductions with a conceptual reform which is intended to improve the reliability of sociological analysis by making its terms both simple and unambiguous. This attempt to replace the 'big abstractions' of structural-functionalism is not, however, entirely successful, for not only are Homans' terms more complex than he admits, but, more significantly, their empirical content is less clear.

Each of the four basic terms is said to be a first-order abstraction —that is, a name given to a single class of observations which cannot be further sub-divided. It is doubtful however, whether this claim is justified. Take, for example, the term 'sentiments'. Homans himself provides the following list of sentiments, to give some idea of the term's range: 'Affection, sympathy, indulgence, respect, pride, antagonism, scorn, nostalgia, hunger, thirst. . . .'[21]

The empirical content of this category appears to be remarkably diverse. In what sense, therefore, can we regard 'sentiments' as a single class of observations? Homans' answer is that all the terms listed above, as well as many others, refer to 'internal states of the human body'.[22] Yet if all internal states are to be regarded as sentiments, we can hardly regard the concept as incapable of further sub-categorization. Rather it appears to be a highly general term which subsumes a wide variety of distinguishable phenomena. It is by no means certain that such a concept is less complex than those used in the language of structural-functionalism.

However, it can be argued that it is not 'sentiment' which refers to a single class of observable data, but the terms denoting specific sentiments. This interpretation probably accords more closely with the theorist's intentions for each of Homans' hypotheses deals, not with sentiments in general, but with particular sentiments, such as friendliness or respect, sympathy or affection. But if we take this view, then Homans must be required to state clearly those sentiments recognized in everyday speech which are to be regarded as first-order abstraction. We cannot simply assume that terms varying from 'jealousy' to 'sexual desire' to 'the concern with making an economic profit' all have this logical status. Unless a clear statement is made in this connection, Homans' claim to be using first-order abstractions means merely that he has dropped the terms of structural-functionalism in favour of the terms of common sense. Unfortunately, Homans simply ignores the problem. Instead of attempting to furnish clear empirical referents for those classes of sentiments to be examined, he does no more than use the ordinary vocabulary of sentiments of an educated American, as if empirical clarity was thereby ensured. It is not surprising, therefore, that certain ambiguities arise in relation to the empirical referents of the term 'sentiments'.

In ordinary language the word 'sentiment' refers to unobservable, emotional states within individuals. Homans recognizes this in his initial definition of the term discussed above. But subsequently in *HG* he quotes with approval Firth's statement that sentiment 'describes a type of behavior which can be observed, not a state of mind which must be inferred'. 'This', says Homans, 'is a good working definition of sentiment. . . .'[23] In this second definition Homans is striving for the reliability, the scientific rigour which is the primary justification for his conceptual innovations. 'The behavior we include under the word "sentiment" must of course be observed, or we should not, as scientists, be entitled to make generalizations about it.'[24] If sentiment *is* a particular type of behaviour, then it can be unambiguously observed, reliably reported and fitted into scientific hypotheses with assurance. Nevertheless, having established that his use of the term 'sentiment' is scientifically reliable because its referents are purely behavioural, Homans is forced to make a revealing admission. Although sentiments may not *be* internal states of mind, inferences about such internal states are necessary if we are to identify correctly the various types of sentiment; although sentiments *are* activities we must, in order to interpret these activities, pay attention to the meanings attached to them within particular groups and societies. We must note 'inflections of the voice, the look of the eyes and carriage of the head, intimate little movements of the hands and arms'[25] and then label these activities as particular sentiments in the light of the inferences which participants themselves draw about the 'states of mind' involved. This procedure appears unlikely to be especially reliable. In order to formulate propositions about sentiments, we seem to require not only extremely detailed observations of actual behaviour, but also an intimate knowledge of the conventions governing these actions, plus accurate information on the way in which participants themselves define and interpret various kinds of expressive behaviour. Thus in relation to the term 'sentiment' Homans fails to realize his theoretical objectives. Instead of a simple first-order abstraction with unambiguous and directly observable referents, we are offered an unspecified range of everyday notions, the use of which necessitates a complex series of inferences involving unobservables. Of course, such difficulties can be reduced by ignoring the rich variety of human emotions and focusing on a small nucleus of crudely but easily identifiable sentiments, as well as by studying sentiments within the framework of conventions most familiar to the theorist and his audience. This, in practice, is what Homans does in *HG*, where he concentrates almost exclusively on sentiments of liking and esteem, and where four out of the five case studies depict aspects of American society. This tactic, however, is a way of avoiding the difficulties of constructing a reliable conceptual apparatus rather than a solution.

Sentiment is not the only term whose use entails difficulties. There is, in particular, one problem which pervades the whole conceptual scheme—namely, that of distinguishing the content of any one term from that of the others. The difficulty arises because sentiments, norms and interaction are all sub-divisions of the term 'activity'. Sentiment is activity in so far as this activity is regarded by those involved as expressing some emotional state. A norm consists of verbal activity defining what is experienced as rewarding within a group, while interaction is activity which stimulates some response in others. The most obvious point to be made is that, if interaction and so on are types of activity, then the term 'activity' cannot be a first-order abstraction, for first-order abstractions 'refer not to several classes of fact at the same time but to one and one only'.[26] As with sentiment, it may be argued that activity is not meant to be a first-order abstraction, but rather the multitude of specific activities, such as soldering, bowling, shopping, and so on, which are defined in everyday speech. But if this is so, Homans' conceptual clarity comes to depend once again on the ambiguities of ordinary language.

A more important problem, however, if we wish to formulate propositions expressing empirical relationships between the four types of activity, is whether there are clear criteria for distinguishing one type of activity from another. It seems possible to distinguish, at least in principle, between norms and sentiments. But the difference between activity and interaction is more difficult to establish. Undoubtedly there are occasions when particular human activities produce no response in others. The prayers of a hermit might be an example. Such isolated activity can be clearly distinguished from social interaction. But acts of this kind do not enter into Homans' analysis, which is concerned solely with *social* behaviour. Homans is interested only in those activities which actually involve interaction. Now, it is possible to make an analytical distinction between an activity, such as helping others at their work, and the interaction which accompanies it. But it is doubtful whether empirical evidence of the activity of helping can be supplied which is separate from the evidence of interaction.[27] Consequently, any hypothesis linking these terms will be a tautology. If it is impossible to distinguish empirically between interaction and activity, they will appear to vary together; but the relationship will be logical rather than empirical. Logically, the terms 'activity' and 'interaction' will be identical.

If this criticism is valid, Homans' generalizations about the interdependence of activity and interaction are empirically worthless.[28] Moreover, to the extent that the distinctions between other terms are blurred, all his propositions must be suspect. It is impossible here to conduct a close scrutiny of more than a few of Homans' inductions with this problem in mind. Nevertheless, we can briefly re-examine one of his analyses in order to discern just how distinct is the empirical content of the various terms.

In the analysis of Hilltown Homans tries to give empirical content to most of his hypotheses. We will examine three related statements and the evidence put forward to support them. Toward the beginning of his analysis Homans makes the following assertion: 'It is clear that in the course of Hilltown's history, *the number and strength of the sentiments that led members of the group to collaborate with other members had declined.*'[29] He then offers evidence for this statement:

> When the land had been cleared, and the barns and houses raised, the need for neighbors to work together became much less than it had been. As transportation improved local industry declined, and mill towns grew up round about, the interests of Hilltowners led them to take part in organizations, such as markets, and factories, outside the town.[30]

Within Homans' framework this evidence is adequate. He is concerned to establish the occurrence of a change in economic sentiments and, as sentiments *are* activities, his evidence consists of a description of changed economic activities. The next step, however, is less convincing. He argues that, as sentiments changed, so 'the number of activities that members of the group carried on together decreased'.[31] In this statement sentiments and activities are regarded as distinct elements within the social system of Hilltown. Yet the evidence offered to demonstrate the decrease in activities is virtually identical with that used to establish that economic sentiments had altered:

> The farm bees had gone: farming itself was in decline; the local industries . . . the factories, had been unable to survive; the general stores, once their customers began to trade in larger centers, lost money. . . .[32]

This is no more than a restatement of the facts cited above in relation to sentiments. The actual observations which provide the evidence for the change in sentiments as well as the decline in activities are, first, that farmers co-operated less and, second, that Hilltowners increasingly worked and shopped elsewhere. Finally, Homans argues that: 'As the number of activities that members of the group carried on together declined, so the frequency of interaction between members of the group decreased.'[33] It is not surprising to find that Homans offers no additional evidence to support this proposition, for, as was suggested above, interaction is seldom, if ever, effectively distinguishable from activity. Thus one set of observations is used three times to support different statements derived from Homans' series of hypotheses. This does not mean that all Homans' inductions are invalid. In many instances even in the Hilltown study his concepts are given relatively clear and independent empirical referents. Nevertheless, the example given above is far from being the only occasion on which the empirical relationships expressed in Homans' hypotheses are illusions created by conceptual overlap, and it must lead us to doubt whether his terminological reform has been as successful as he would have us believe.

We have seen so far that Homans' 'technical vocabulary' makes great use of common-sense terms and that, partly as a result, its empirical content tends to be imprecise, sometimes to the point of vacuity. Homans' failure to develop, in *HG*, a proper scientific vocabulary is also evident in his inability to formulate a series of variables. He himself admits that his basic concepts are not variables, but terms denoting 'elements of social behaviour',[34] and that his hypotheses are intended to indicate only very broad empirical relationships. Thus when variables are introduced into the generalizations they are used in a crude fashion. Take hypothesis 1: 'If the *frequency* of interaction between two or more persons *increases*, the *degree* of their liking for one another will *increase*.' This statement can be phrased in everyday language with no loss in precision or clarity as: The more often people meet, the more friendly they become. Moreover, the hypotheses themselves tend to be but restatements of common knowledge with the usual indeterminacy of such knowledge. Thus 'The more often people meet, the more they will like each other' is an acceptable generalization. But we, and Homans, know that it holds true only under certain conditions and that these conditions are difficult to specify. Not all of Homans' hypotheses are as commonplace as this one. But none of them is any more precise. Thus once again we are led to question the success of an inductive strategy which produces no more than a relatively small number of generalizations utilizing rather imprecise terms to summarize, often at the level of commonsense, certain broad empirical regularities derived from five case studies. Is this a proper foundation for further theoretical development? Although the implication of the analysis so far is clearly that the theoretical base is inadequate, we must appraise the second stage of the theoretical strategy before we can answer this question conclusively.

IV

If Homans had followed through the logic of his theoretical strategy, the second stage in the construction of his theory would have been to distil a series of more general explanatory propositions from an inductive survey of his own empirical generalizations. But, in view of the inadequacies of the latter, this procedure would have been difficult to follow. It is hardly surprising, therefore, that Homans prefers a simpler solution and adapts certain propositions, taken from psychology and economics, which bear some resemblance to the explanatory notions evolved in *HG*. Nevertheless, it *is* surprising to find that Homans chooses to refer to this method of obtaining explanatory propositions as 'induction':

> The process of borrowing or inventing the more general propositions I call *induction*, whether or not it is the induction of the philosophers; the process of deriving the empirical propositions from the more general ones I call *explanation*, and this *is* the explanation of the philosophers.[35]

In our terms, and those of the philosophers, Homans' higher-level propositions are not reached inductively. They are introduced, already formed, from other disciplines and, after some modification, are used to deduce prior empirical generalizations. It is, therefore, doubtful whether Homans achieves his original aim of using his initial generalizations as the dependable foundation for his theoretical system. The generalizations are merely *reconciled* with exchange propositions borrowed from psychology and economics. Furthermore, the exchange propositions remain constant, while any discrepancies between higher- and lower-level generalizations are eliminated by altering or even abandoning the latter. Thus the exchange propositions rather than the inductive base furnish the one stable theoretical component. At least this appears to be the situation. Unfortunately, we cannot be sure, because Homans nowhere states whether those hypotheses which are not subsequently deduced from the exchange propositions have been dropped or are merely in temporary abeyance. Given the theorist's own emphasis on the need for reliable and systematic procedures in the construction and use of theory, it is disconcerting to find that he presents no summary of extant propositions at all levels of generality nor a guide to their interrelations. Until this has been done, Homans' scheme cannot be regarded as a mature hypothetico-deductive system. Nevertheless, despite the fact that his strategy is not consistently inductive and the fact that the relationships between higher- and lower-level generalizations are by no means clear, Homans has produced a theoretical scheme which is recognizably a general deductive system capable in principle of generating explanatory inferences. And ultimately such a theory must be judged by the explanations and predictions it actually renders.

The deductive explanations offered by Homans depend on propositions taken from behavioural psychology. The use of such propositions in psychology is subject to certain severe limitations related to the techniques by which they are discovered. Unlike Homans' own inductive generalizations, they are expressions of regularities observed under rigorously experimental conditions. The environment of experimental animals is drastically simplified, so that responses to specific stimuli can be unambiguously observed and results checked by detailed replication. At the same time, variables are defined in clear and standardized fashion which makes possible accurate measurement.[36] When propositions derived under such conditions are applied in situations where such clarity and simplicity are absent, their value is considerably reduced. It may, of course, be assumed, as it is by Homans, that they underlie actual events. But until similar levels of precision and control are attained they cannot be used to provide unambiguous explanatory inferences. Although there is no reason why the propositions of animal psychology should not be extrapolated to the social behaviour of humans, they supply no more than an analogue until precise behavioural content for the propositions can be specified. Homans' second conceptual reform, in *SB*, is in fact an attempt to provide just this kind of specification. Its success, however, is more apparent than real, and we are offered the behaviourist rhetoric with neither its conceptual rigour nor the experimental control which accompanies its use in psychology.

Homans' first step in *SB* is to redefine his four basic concepts in unmistakably behaviourist terms. This has the advantage of removing any doubts we might have retained from *HG* about whether sentiments are internal emotional states and whether norms are ideas inside people's minds. They are not. They are activities. Yet although these redefinitions assist conceptual clarity, they supply no new techniques which might enable us to distinguish consistently between these different types of behaviour. There is no real advance here on the situation already discussed in relation to the inductive survey. None the less, Homans at last reaches a stage of conceptual sophistication where he can state and define his variables. Unfortunately, he has great difficulty in providing clear empirical indices of quantity or value and, consequently, in reconciling their use with his behaviourist outlook.

In the first place, Homans is forced to admit that value—that is, the degree of reinforcement a man gets per unit of an activity—is difficult to observe. As we have noted, he decides not to measure value in terms of the amount of activity a person will expend in order to obtain a particular reward, on the grounds that this would turn certain basic propositions into tautologies. But Homans' stratagem of establishing a person's current values on the evidence of his past actions does not in itself solve the problem. Measuring present value by the amount of activity expended in the past to obtain a particular reward does not obviate the tautology. Whether we look to past or present behaviour, we need to ensure that evidence for values is independent of the activities to be explained as products of these values. Secondly, cost seems to be even less amenable to a behavioural definition than value. The cost of an action has two components, the positively painful experiences incurred in carrying it out and the positively rewarding experiences foregone, neither of which is observable. As Homans admits, 'we infer costs and do not directly observe them'.[37] Nevertheless, he argues, 'the things from which we infer costs are no less observable than those from which we infer values'.[38] Costs, like values, are inferred from people's activities. But once again we must ensure that we have observable evidence of costs and that this evidence is independent of the behaviour to be explained. In many instances, Homans is unable to furnish such evidence. Let us examine an example in which both cost and value are involved.

Homans uses his exchange propositions to explain certain anomalous findings in a study of influence by Gerard.[39] The details of the study are complex and we deal here only with those facets immediately relevant to our interests. Gerard wished to examine the degree to which opinions could be changed within different types of small groups. The composition of these contrived groups varied along two dimensions. In the first place, groups were designed to be either rewarding or unrewarding independently of their members' opinions. Secondly, group members either shared certain opinions or were in varying degrees of disagreement. Having established a number of groups, with different degrees of internal attraction and agreement, the experimenter tried to change the opinions of all participants. In general, it was found that opinions changed least in highly-rewarding groups, especially where opinions were shared, and that they changed most in unrewarding groups. Not only did these results conform to the experimenter's expectations, but in Homans' view they can also be deduced from his exchange propositions, for the degree to which opinions resisted change varied directly according to the reward attached to maintenance of opinions. There was, however, one result which the experimenter regarded as anomalous:

> The 8 per cent figure for the low-attraction, strongly-disagree condition is perplexing. The figure is too low to be accounted for by chance. There seems to be no reasonable explanation for this inordinately low figure.[40]

The members of this type of group had been led to expect that membership would be disagreeable. In addition, the opinions of group members on the relevant topic were strongly opposed. Thus the experimenter had assumed that rewards would be low and that opinions would be easily influenced. From his perspective, the low rate of change was inexplicable. Homans suggests, however, that the response is unexpected only because we have not properly estimated the relative profits of the various groups by balancing out rewards and costs.

Homans begins his analysis by suggesting that there was a value affecting the behaviour of the experimental subjects which was not considered in Gerard's interpretation. This value, available to every participant, was the *maintenance of personal integrity* in the face of efforts to change his opinions. In Homans' view, those who maintained their opinions would experience thereby a positive reward, while those who changed their opinions would sacrifice this reward —in other words, they would incur costs. Having established that personal integrity must be included in the analysis as potentially both cost and value, Homans proceeds to compare the relative profits of various categories of groups. We will confine our attention to highly-rewarding groups with shared opinions, on the one hand,

and unrewarding groups with conflicting opinions, on the other hand, in both of which opinions had been resistant to change. Homans argues that members of the former type of group will have high profits. In the first place, their opinions will bring them approval from their colleagues, and this approval will be especially rewarding within high-attraction groups. The rewards attached to profession of their opinion will be high. At the same time, costs will be low because personal integrity is not being sacrificed. Thus individuals within such groups will maximize highly rewarding social approval and minimize costs by maintaining prior opinions. The situation facing members of unrewarding groups where opinions clash is quite different. The reward of maintaining their personal opinion is high in the face of so much opposition. To attain this reward they must, of course, forgo group approval. But then social approval is of little value in such a group and costs are, accordingly, low. Thus profit, the difference between rewards and costs, is high in both types of group, although for exactly opposite reasons. Homans suggests that because the profits associated with particular opinions are high in both sets of groups, their members will be unlikely to change these opinions unless they are offered a specially valuable response. He concludes, reasonably enough, that Gerard's anomalous finding is no longer an anomaly, but is deducible from the propositions of social exchange.

In the analysis described above reference is made to three kinds of evidence. First, there is evidence about the degree to which opinions changed during the course of the experiment. This material is supplied by the experimenter and is based upon direct observation of subjects' verbal responses. We have no reason to question its validity. Secondly, there is evidence about the value and cost of social approval within the various groups. This also is supplied by the investigator and appears satisfactory. Thirdly, there is evidence for the value and cost of personal integrity. The experimenter, however, can make no contribution here, because measurement of personal integrity was not part of the original experimental design: 'The investigator does not mention this reward, but we cannot make sense of the results without it, or something much like it.'[41]

The notion of personal integrity is introduced specifically to eliminate Gerard's anomaly. But unfortunately the experiment provides no independent evidence capable of indicating the magnitude or even the existence of this element. Homans provides, in fact, no evidence of personal integrity apart from the behaviour which it is supposed to explain. For instance, the only behavioural indication we have that members of low-attraction groups with diverse opinions found maintenance of personal integrity rewarding is the fact that they did not change their opinions. Now, Homans has argued that evidence must either be observable or inferrable from direct observations. Clearly, personal integrity is not observable. It must, therefore, be inferred from the sole observation of behaviour which is both available and relevant. However, if we infer that personal integrity was valuable from the subjects' tendency to maintain their opinions, our explanatory proposition becomes empirically vacuous. We are using the same evidence for participants' values as for the behaviour to be explained as a product of these same values.

It may be argued in Homans' defence that the criteria we are applying are too rigorous and that he is simply suggesting a plausible interpretation for further investigation. But if this is so, it should be made explicit. Homans tells us that he is providing deductive explanations. Consequently, we must take him at his word and apply the appropriate criteria. According to these criteria, Homans' deductions are totally inadequate. They either make use of analytic propositions which are not amenable even in principle to empirical test or they are merely unsupported *ad hoc* interpretations. Homans' failure in this instance to provide an acceptable explanation arises from the empirical indeterminacy of the concepts of cost and value. But this is not the only difficulty associated with the use of these terms. A further important problem is stated clearly by Deutsch and Krauss in the following words:

> Homans' theory implies that there is a common *currency* or a single dimension to which the value of different experiences ('getting a B+ on an exam', 'being kissed by one's sweetheart', 'hearing a Beethoven quartet', 'being served a cold beer') can be co-ordinated so that the value of a 'unit' of one such activity received can be compared with the value of another unit. If there is a common currency of 'value', it has not yet been identified. . . .[42]

We saw earlier that the notion of a currency which was both a means of exchange and a measure of value was an essential element in Parsons' exchange paradigm. Homans, in contrast, seems to ignore the problem. It would, of course, be possible to regard activity as fulfilling this role. If we were to adopt this approach, we would establish the relative value of a good exam. result and that of listening to Beethoven by comparing the amount of behaviour expended to gain each experience. But Homans cannot consistently use activity as the dimension along which to measure value, because he has himself argued that value and activity must be defined independently. Moreover, we have just seen that when Homans allows himself to use activity as an index of value his deductions do in fact become empirically vacuous. There is also a more practical difficulty. If we were to translate values into various quantities of activity for purposes of comparison, we would need a standardized measure of a *unit* of activity. For example, it may be that, although more activity is expended *in total* to achieve a good exam. result, listening to Beethoven may at a particular moment be more valuable *per unit* of activity. And it is the value per unit at a particular time that will determine behaviour at that moment. Unfortunately, Homans supplies no way of breaking down activities into standard units. Consequently, it is impossible either to compare the quantity of behaviour entailed in different activities or to measure and compare values in terms of one uniform dimension. Yet without the ability to make such measurements and comparisons, a term such as profit, the use of which assumes that cost can be subtracted from reward along a single dimension, becomes meaningless and the whole analytical scheme begins to collapse.

Before I conclude this appraisal of Homans' work, let me summarize the critical points made so far. In the first place, it has been argued that the basic conceptual apparatus is imprecise and that, as a result, the initial hypotheses are not always properly justified by empirical evidence. Secondly, it was suggested that the conceptual revisions introduced in *SB* do not substantially improve conceptual precision, so that the attempts at deductive explanation are often vacuous. Thirdly, Homans has been criticized for abandoning his professed inductive strategy and for failing to provide a formalized statement of extant propositions at all levels of generality.

This last criticism is particularly important because a formal theoretical exposition, as well as making clear which of the initial generalizations have been retained, would allow the theory to be used and thereby tested by independent investigators. This requirement is based on the assumption that a scientific theory should be sufficiently clear and reliable to furnish the same or closely similar inferences for all those competent to use it. Undoubtedly very few theories, and certainly no sociological theories, satisfy this requirement. The nearest we normally get to this situation in sociology is the attempt by a theorist to use his own theory to *predict*. A prediction is made when an inference is drawn from a theory *before* the theorist has access to evidence capable of confirming or invalidating the inference. It is without doubt a more satisfactory theoretical test than Homans' usual procedure of interpreting data *ex post facto*. This latter approach is defective in that, as long as a theory's terms lack empirical precision, it will often be possible to make sense of empirical findings after the event by extending the content of the terms in an arbitrary fashion to fit the facts. This is precisely what Homans does, for example, when he introduces the notion of personal integrity into the analysis discussed above. Such an approach does not properly test a theory's deductive capacity, simply because this capacity remains unspecified and can be varied to incorporate new findings as they are proffered for analysis. In contrast, predictions are more demanding because they are made before empirical results are available and are, therefore, independent of such results. As long as we can take the factual data as accurate, any divergence between data and prediction must be due to theoretical inadequacies. Because prediction is such a reliable theoretical test, we can use it to give some indication of the accuracy of the criticisms levelled above at Homans' work. If Homans uses his theory to generate a wide variety of satisfactory predictions, then our criticisms are almost certainly wrong. On the other hand, if the predictions are unsuccessful, the theory is probably defective and many of the criticisms are, perhaps, correct.

Homans informs us that his theory has been used to make a 'large number of predictions'[43] about social behaviour in the course of a study of an American factory. In *SB*, however, he examines only one of these, which is concerned with the relationship between status and informal ranking. The first step in making a prediction is to state the proposition or propositions to be used. Rather surprisingly, the nearest Homans comes to a formal statement of the proposition which is being tested is the following somewhat imprecise formulation:

> Since the ability to reward other members tends to be associated with outside status, and people who actually do reward others tend to get their esteem, then it should be a good bet that the order of members in outside status would also be their order in a number of measures of esteem or of things like interaction that are associated with esteem.[44]

This statement appears to include both the generalization to be tested and an attempt to deduce the generalization from the higher-level propositions of social exchange. Nevertheless, what Homans is predicting is fairly clear. It is that individuals or groups with high status within the wider community (high 'outside' status) will receive relatively great esteem within any more limited social context. And this proposition is itself explained by the assertion that ' "Outside" status is apt to be associated with experiences that make people especially able to reward others, and rewarding others gets them esteem'.[45]

Having put forward the proposition to be tested, Homans and his associates needed to provide empirical evidence for those descriptive propositions which must be taken as given before any prediction can be made. Strict precautions were taken to ensure that the predictions were not influenced by any awareness of actual behaviour in the department to be studied and the investigators took their givens from the company's personnel records before visiting the factory. On the basis of information taken from these records plus a 'general familiarity with American industry',[46] the four sub-sections within one large department were ranked in order of external status. The rank-order was as follows:

1 High-paid machinists.
2 High-paid assemblers.
3 Low-paid machinists.
4 Low-paid assemblers.

The investigators chose this rank-order for two reasons. In the first place, they thought that as 'pay is the most important measure of status, so the two high-paid sub-groups should rank higher than the two low-paid ones'. Secondly, they 'decided that machining would have higher status than assembly work because it requires more training . . .'. Finally, these givens were combined with the general proposition stating a positive relationship between esteem and external status, and it was predicted that 'the order of sub-departments in external status would also be their order in various measures of esteem'.[47] Subsequent research, however, produced the following rank-order in terms of intra-departmental esteem:

1 High-paid machinists.
2 { High-paid assemblers.
    Low-paid assemblers.
3 Low-paid machinists.

Homans makes the following general comments on these results:

> Analysis of the data thus collected showed that their predictions had turned out to be partly right. They were most nearly right at the top: in six out of eight measures of esteem and associated variables, the high-paid machinists ranked first, as they had predicted. They were most nearly wrong at the bottom. . . .[48]

In fact, only one of the four sub-departments was unambiguously placed in the correct position. Consequently, although we must agree that the predictions were partly right, the exercise hardly justifies any great confidence in the theory. Homans' response to these findings is to argue that an important variable—namely, status inconsistency—has been ignored and to attempt, in due course, to revise his analysis accordingly. This procedure is perfectly legitimate. But it would be more convincing if a series of further predictions had then been made which included this new factor. Moreover, despite the potential utility of prediction as a test of theoretical validity, Homans' approach to this task is far from rigorous. In the first place, the proposition being tested is never formally expressed. Secondly, the givens are established more on the basis of common-sense than reliable evidence. Clearly the company personnel records give no information on the external status of the four sub-sections. Thus the only justification offered for judging the 'outside' status of these sections solely in relation to their wages and training is the investigators' 'general familiarity with American industry'. Is this any different from or more reliable than common-sense? Thirdly, there are certain problems associated with the measures used to determine esteem. One of the measures is the ratio of contacts occurring within each section to contacts occurring outside the section. Homans argues that this ratio will be higher in groups enjoying high esteem because persons held in esteem will be mutually rewarding and will, therefore, interact more with each other than with persons outside the group. But it could be argued that this ratio is as good an index of external status as of esteem, for interaction between members of groups with high status would be rewarding, due to their status, and would therefore on Homans' assumption generate relatively high rates of internal interaction. Consequently, even if the predictions had come off, it could reasonably have been argued that they were empirically vacuous. However, in view of the predictive failure, we need only note that once again Homans experiences great difficulty in supplying distinct empirical indices for his terms. Homans' prediction is inconclusive because it is not properly implemented. Yet the very inadequacy of the test confirms our previous conclusion that the theory's conceptual indeterminacy prevents any clear application to the empirical world.

There is one further problem raised by this attempt at prediction —namely, Homans' use of 'the givens'. This is problematic in the first place because, under the heading of 'givens', Homans reintroduces the kind of big abstractions, in this case the concept of 'status', which were repudiated in his earlier work. Although no attempt is made to explain the givens, they still require reliable empirical evidence. It is surprising, therefore, in view of his earlier argument, that the provision of evidence of external status is treated in such a cavalier fashion. However, we have discussed Homans' conceptual deficiencies at such length that we can profitably turn from his failure or inability to supply proper documentation for the givens to a more general consideration of their theoretical role. In examining the givens from a wider perspective, we can supplement our conclusions about the scheme's inadequacies as a deductive system by coming to appreciate more fully the limited range of social phenomena which the theory covers.

A THEORY OF SOCIAL EXCHANGE: HOMANS

In applying his theoretical propositions, Homans takes as given a wide range of phenomena. In some of his analyses the givens are even non-social. This is so, for example, when he shows how the physical layout of a housing estate influences interaction and thereby plays an indirect role in determining friendship patterns within the estate.[49] More usually, however, the givens are social. In most of his deductions, Homans takes as given the normative structure of the group under study as well as any formal social relations, and uses these, along with his general propositions, to explain certain behavioural variations occurring within the social context provided by these givens:

> Much social science is rightly devoted to explaining why the rules are what they are: Why, for instance, the physician's role in our society is what it is. ... But this book will not undertake to explain the rules. Instead, taking the rules said to apply in a particular situation as given, it will try to explain the actual behavior. ... Doctors do not live up to their role equally well, and the role itself leaves plenty of room for variations. But it is the variations, that is, the actual behavior that [the student of elementary social behavior] would have to explain.[50]

Thus Homans' theory is concerned with explaining certain minor behavioural variations taking place within a given structural-cultural context. Whereas structural-functionalism concentrates on institutionalized behaviour, Homans' theory focuses on the sub-institutional: 'Since sociologists often call things like roles and their attendant sanctions *institutions*, and behavior so far as it conforms to roles *institutionalized* behavior, elementary social behavior might be called *sub-institutional*.'[51]

The distinction between institutional and sub-institutional behaviour pervades Homans' work. Thus in the predictive study examined above Homans distinguishes between the institutionalized status of the machinists and assemblers and the sub-institutional esteem generated within their work groups. Institutionalized status is, of course, for Homans unproblematic. The information on institutional behaviour is not to be explained, but to be taken as given and used to make predictions about the pattern of informal relations within the factory. Similarly, in the analysis of the Federal agency the formal authority of the supervisor is taken for granted, as is the agents' official role. General conformity by the agents to the main requirements of their institutionalized role is taken as given and explanation is offered only with respect to the patterns of informal helping and esteem, which are occasioned by the varying ability of individual agents to satisfy institutional expectations.

Even in the early investigation of cross-cousin marriage, the distinction between institutional and sub-institutional behaviour is implicit. In this study Homans and Schneider assume the existence of two institutions—namely, cross-cousin marriage and jural authority—and try to establish that the location of authority within the institutional network of kinship roles largely determines the direction of cross-cousin marriage. This, of course, is an analysis of institutionalized rules. However, the *explanation* of the relationship between authority and cross-cousin marriage refers indisputably to the sub-institutional level. For Homans and Schneider argue that the location of jural authority generates ties of affection which are not institutionally required, but which do, nevertheless, influence the pattern of institutionalized sentiments and thereby channel institutional behaviour.

In *Marriage, Authority and Final Causes* considerable attention is paid to the way in which sub-institutional behaviour forms institutions. But as Homans' theory matures this approach is dropped and institutional givens are increasingly used to explain sub-institutional activities. Thus Homans' theoretical strategy has entailed a withdrawal from sociology's long-standing interest in the institutional structure of societies, in favour of a consideration of relatively minor behavioural variations within small groups. This would perhaps have been justified if a reasonably satisfactory hypothetico-deductive system had been formulated in relation to elementary social behaviour, which could have provided a firm reference point for the investigation of more complex, institutionalized social structures. Unfortunately, as we have seen, Homans' theory of social behaviour has too many defects and ambiguities to act as a reliable basis for such a comprehensive sociological theory.

Although Homans is aware of his theory's limited scope, he makes no attempt to extend it beyond the realm of sub-institutional behaviour. Nevertheless, he does indicate what he regards as the major differences between institutional and sub-institutional behaviour. First, the processes of institutional exchange are indirect rather than direct: 'For instance, [a] man gets his pay at the end of the week, not from his own supervisor . . . but from a clerk who is himself rewarded by still another member of the firm.' Secondly, these networks of indirect exchange are maintained by generalized rewards, such as money and social approval. 'For instance, a man cuts wood, not because he needs it for his fire, but because a firm will pay him for cutting it.'[52] Thirdly, these standardized and complex patterns of institutional exchange are regulated by explicitly stated norms and orders. In addition, Homans suggests that elementary exchange and institutional exchange may, under certain conditions, come into conflict. When the costs of conformity to institutional requirements are high, sub-institutional behaviour may erode institutional exchange. If the restraints of institutional behaviour raise costs unduly, the profits from unorganized and, perhaps eventually, organized opposition will become relatively more attractive. And out of organized opposition may emerge radical institutional change.

Homans raises these themes, but does not pursue them. He never seriously attempts to expand his rather restricted theory into a comprehensive sociological scheme. This task is taken up by Blau, to whose work we now turn. Blau's attempt to extend the exchange perspective into the realm of complex and formalized structures is organized in part around the suggestions made by Homans. However, in developing these hints, Blau is forced to abandon Homans' short-run theoretical objectives and to retreat toward a theoretical strategy more akin to that of the functionalists. In his own words, Blau tries to steer between 'the Scylla of abstract conceptions too remote from observable empirical reality and the Charybdis of reductionism that ignores emergent social and structural properties'[53] by constructing a theoretical prelude or categorial system couched in terms of social exchange.

8 A conceptual elaboration of exchange theory: Blau

I

Of the theorists discussed in this study, Blau tells us least about his theoretical objectives or his theoretical strategy. Nevertheless, the few references he makes on this topic indicate that he is, like the others, working toward a comprehensive and empirically relevant deductive system. Although in making his contribution to such a theory Blau has been greatly influenced by Homans, he does not adopt the latter's theoretical strategy. He accepts that Homans has made a signal contribution to the analysis of elementary social behaviour and he makes great use of Homans' ideas at this level. But he does not regard Homans' theoretical strategy as suitable for the study of either simple or complex social relationships. This is evident in the fact that Blau himself retreats from Homans' short-term theoretical aims. He makes no attempt to construct a theory, even at the level of direct interaction, but is content to offer what he calls a theoretical prolegomenon.

Blau does not tell us in detail what he means by the term 'theoretical prolegomenon'. However, by observing his actual procedures we can glean a reasonably clear picture of what he has in mind. For instance, certain features found in Homans' scheme are omitted. In the first place, a theoretical prolegomenon seems to require no formal statement of explanatory hypotheses. Secondly, there is no systematic induction. Thirdly, no attempt is made to specify the empirical content of major concepts in any rigorous fashion. Finally, because one of Blau's main objectives is to generalize the insights gained by Homans and others in relation to direct exchange so that they can be used in the study of more complex social processes, analysis is not restricted to the sphere of direct interaction. Thus it is clear that Blau's theoretical strategy is quite different from that of Homans.

Blau is much less concerned with conceptual and propositional rigour and much more interested in including within his scheme a wider range of sociological data.

Blau's strategy resembles closely Parsons' attempt to prepare the way for a general theory of society by constructing a categorial system. For, like Parsons, he offers a general model of society, made up of a series of related concepts plus a number of propositions at various levels of generality and precision. In the theorist's own estimation, however, his prolegomenon avoids the conceptual formalism of Parsonian analysis while simultaneously overcoming the problem of limited empirical range associated with Homans' approach. Blau's strategy is designed to bridge the gap between Homans and Parsons. Thus the whole of his major work, *Exchange and Power in Social Life*,[1] is an attempt to extend the scope of exchange analysis beyond the boundaries of Homans' theory. At the same time he tries to demonstrate, by generating a number of 'empirically testable hypotheses',[2] that theoretical range has not been purchased at the cost of empirical vacuity. If we find that Blau does make satisfactory predictions over a wide range of sociological phenomena, we will have to recognize that his prolegomenon, although not a genuine theory in Homans' sense, is a considerable move in that direction.

Unlike his theoretical strategy, Blau's central *substantive* theoretical problem is inherited directly from Homans. In *HG* the problem was broached of how social activity elaborates upon itself to produce more complex and differentiated structures. But as Homans' deductive system developed this question was dropped and complex social structures were relegated to the status of unproblematic givens. Blau's prolegomenon returns to the earlier hints furnished by Homans about the way in which 'social life becomes organized into increasingly complex structures of associations among men'.[3] Blau's aim is to use the terms of social exchange, which in his view have been shown to be fruitful at the simplest level, to conceptualize relationships at higher levels of complexity. It is, in fact, this more general application of the exchange perspective which he regards as the distinguishing feature of his approach: 'It is this fundamental concern with utilizing the analysis of simpler processes for clarifying complex structures that distinguishes the approach here from that of other recent students of interpersonal processes . . .'[4]

Accordingly, the analysis proceeds in two stages. In the first stage, simple social relationships are analysed as processes of direct exchange. In the second, an attempt is made to show how complex structures 'grow out of' simpler associations as the networks of exchange become increasingly indirect. It is recognized that this crude division into simple and complex structures, or direct and indirect exchange, is little more than a convenient analytical device.

There is in reality within any large society a 'complex interdependence between substructures of numerous kinds, often intersecting, and on different levels'.[5] Blau tries to keep in mind throughout his analysis this complex interdependence between social levels. Nevertheless, he must begin somewhere, and his strategy requires him to start with the relatively simple processes governing direct social exchange.

II

Direct social exchange is a product of those psychological processes which lead people to undertake and to repeat activities experienced as rewarding, while avoiding activities associated with deprivation or punishment. In Blau's view these psychological propensities can be taken as given by sociology, which is concerned with explaining the structure and dynamics of social associations and not their psychological roots. None the less, because most human gratifications are provided by other people, the notions of reward and deprivation constitute a necessary starting-point for sociology. As long as we presume that people are typically motivated to associate with others because they expect to benefit thereby, it is essential that 'reward' and associated concepts should play a central role in sociological analysis.

Sociology, then, is concerned with the principles which govern the attainment of rewards through social activity. Blau argues that if we are to understand these principles we must supplement the idea of reward with that of cost. This is so because the production of the social rewards accruing to any one individual involves his partners in punishments and deprivations. He suggests that the exchange of rewards and costs in interaction is governed by the principle of reciprocity.[6] According to this principle, if individual A expects to find association with B gratifying he will attempt to please B by emitting valuable behaviour Y, in the expectation that B will reward him in turn in order to ensure the continuation of Y. Thus, when people engage in social activity with the expectation of reward, interaction tends to take the form of reciprocal exchanges whereby each person accepts certain costs so as to obligate others to respond with benefits which more than balance these costs. Blau, like Homans, has come to think of most, though not all, social association 'as an exchange of activity, tangible or intangible, and more or less rewarding and costly, between at least two persons'.[7]

Blau enlarges on the principle of reciprocity by combining it with two hypotheses taken over by Homans from economics. The first states that the more is received of a valuable activity the less rewarding its recipient finds it, and the second that the more an activity is emitted the more costly it becomes. Although Blau uses the ideas expressed in these hypotheses, he does not put them forward as formal propositions. Instead, he argues discursively along the following lines: When one individual supplies another with a valued experience the second person feels obligated to reward his benefactor in return. If both persons continue to value what they are receiving, they will supply further units of their own services in order to stimulate the other to supply further benefits. But as more and more benefits are received, the value of each additional unit will fall. At the same time, the cost of providing further incentives will rise. As a result, the profits from each subsequent exchange will decrease fairly rapidly until the cost of providing incentives equals the forthcoming reward. Adopting a version of the language of economics, Blau concludes that:

> Ultimately, the declining marginal utility of additional benefits is no longer worth the cost of obtaining them, and the point at which this happens for both partners . . . governs the level of transactions most advantageous for both at which the volume of exchange between them presumably becomes stabilized.[8]

These are the basic principles of social exchange, and in Blau's view they pervade social life. 'Social exchange', Blau notes, 'can be observed everywhere once we are sensitized . . . to it, not only in market relations but also in friendship and even in love. . . .'[9] Nevertheless, he is aware that if the idea of exchange is too loosely conceptualized it will be in danger of becoming vacuous:

> [T]he assumption of exchange theory that social interaction is governed by the concern of both (or all) partners with rewards dispensed by the other (or others) becomes tautological if any and all behavior in interpersonal relations is conceptualized as an exchange, even conduct toward others that is not oriented in terms of expected rewards from them.[10]

To avoid empirical vacuity, Blau attempts to provide a criterion which clearly defines the limits of social exchange. He states that social exchange refers only 'to actions that are contingent on rewarding reactions from others and that cease when these expected reactions are not forthcoming'.[11] This definition seems to include only behaviour that is emitted to bring forth rewards. Yet, as we shall see when we examine Blau's notion of power, he is greatly concerned with behaviour which is directed toward avoiding deprivation. We must assume, therefore, that the term 'reward' in this definition has both positive and negative connotations. If this interpretation is correct, the term 'social exchange' has potentially a very wide coverage. It is, therefore, not surprising that only two types of behaviour are specified which do not fall under its rubric—namely, behaviour produced by physical coercion and behaviour where the sole reward is that of self-approval.

This broad definition of social exchange appears to include economic transactions, which clearly involve expectation of reward. But the kind of behaviour that Blau treats in practice as social exchange differs significantly from strictly economic conduct and at one point he draws explicit distinctions between the two forms of exchange. Economic transactions are regarded as having three distinguishing characteristics. First, the goods and services exchanged have a value which is relatively independent of particular transactions; for any given commodity there tends to be one fairly uniform price throughout the market. Secondly, economic value can be expressed precisely in terms of a single generally accepted medium of exchange. Thirdly, it is usually possible to state explicitly and precisely all the obligations involved in any particular deal, as is done, for example, when a contract is drawn up. These three features are evident in the purchase of a new car, where the purchaser is required to pay a definite monetary price, in return for which he receives a product which is formally guaranteed to meet certain technical requirements. In contrast, Blau argues, these features are largely absent from social, as opposed to economic, exchange. In the first place, there is no market price and the rate of exchange varies from one transaction to another. Furthermore, the obligations entailed are largely unspecified. 'Thus, if a person gives a dinner party, he expects his guests to reciprocate at some future date. But he can hardly bargain with them about the kind of party to which they should invite him . . .'[12] Finally, the benefits exchanged have no exact price in terms of one medium of exchange. The value of a dinner party is not measurable, at least by the participants. Nor is there any obvious way in which its value can be compared with that of other social rewards. Blau concludes that the vagueness and incommensurability of social values 'is a substantive fact, not simply a methodological problem'.[13] The values people hold and the obligations they incur in relation to non-economic social exchange are inherently ill-defined and diffuse.

If social exchange involves obligations which are unspecified, it will be difficult to depict its characteristics in precise scientific language. Blau himself is forced to admit the difficulty of applying the economic principles of maximization of utilities to social exchange. For if we presume that people act to maximize their profits, it seems that we must be able to measure the values and rewards involved in order to decide when profits have been made and to compare their magnitude. But he points out that, even in economics, utilities (values) are seldom actually *measured*. They are, he suggests, inferred after the event. For example:

... if a scientist accepts an academic job at a lower salary than he could command in industry, the so-called psychic income he obtains from his university position is assumed to equal or exceed in utilities the difference in salary. Similar inferences can be made from the observable conduct in social exchange.[14]

At first sight this statement seems to limit exchange analysis to a series of plausible *ex post facto* analyses. The theorist, however, rejects this view. He argues that once we have made *ex post facto* inferences about the values specific rewards have for individuals, we can 'derive testable hypotheses concerning the group structures that will emerge. . . .'[15] This procedure undoubtedly raises once again the problem discussed in relation to Homans, of the need for independent evidence of values and of the phenomena to be explained or predicted by reference to these values. We shall return to this issue when we consider the success of Blau's attempts at prediction.

The points made so far in this section can be summarized as follows. Social exchange, in the broadest sense of this term, occurs when behaviour is oriented according to the rewards and deprivations expected from interaction with others. Although Blau is concerned with exchange at this general level, he concentrates on the non-economic varieties of social exchange, which are distinguished by an inherent lack of precision. Despite this imprecision, social exchange, in the narrower sense of non-economic exchange, is to be interpreted by certain definite principles taken in large measure from economics, the most important of which are the principle of reciprocity, the principle of the maximization of profit, and the principles of diminishing marginal cost and value. Blau suggests that these principles, when combined with inferred data about the values of individuals, can be used to generate testable predictions with respect to group structure. These predictions will constitute the final source of validation for the analysis of *social associations* in terms of exchange.

This outline of the basic mechanisms of social exchange has the same theoretical significance for Blau's prolegomenon as has Parsons' delineation of the two-actor paradigm for his categorial system. In both cases certain basic concepts plus an underlying theoretical perspective are introduced at the simplest possible level, as a foundation on which to build a more elaborate theoretical scheme. Yet Blau's approach differs from that of Parsons with respect to both strategy and content. Strategically, Blau comes closer than Parsons to an explicit formulation of explanatory propositions. Consequently, he is able to promise more firmly that the scheme will eventually generate hypotheses which will either confirm or invalidate its theoretical principles. At a more substantive level, Blau differs from Parsons in four important respects.

First, he places much less emphasis on shared values. Secondly, he conceives of direct interaction in a more dynamic manner. Thirdly, he introduces the idea of power in interpersonal relationships. Fourthly, he suggests that the basic unit of social life is the three-person rather than the two-person group. As these four notions affect the whole analytical scheme built up from Blau's interpretation of direct interaction, we must examine them briefly before we proceed further.

In Parsons' view, social interaction which is not subject to normative constraint will degenerate into open strife as each individual pursues his own self-interest regardless of others. Consequently, shared cultural prescriptions are seen as essential for the maintenance of regular social relationships. Blau's principle of reciprocity, in contrast, has quite different implications. For it indicates that stable social relations can develop independently of cultural prescriptions, as people regularly reward others in order to safeguard their own interest. Accordingly, from Blau's perspective shared values are not functionally necessary for the occurrence of stable social interaction: 'While structures of social relations are, of course, profoundly influenced by common values, these structures have a significance of their own, which is ignored if concern is exclusively with the underlying values and norms.'[16] The decision to investigate social exchange to some extent apart from normative factors is theoretically significant in itself. It gains in importance, however, by enabling Blau to furnish a more dynamic paradigm of simple interaction.

The typical situation facing partners in social exchange is that in which each participant *prefers* the other to make the greater contribution to the relationship, but is himself *willing* to make the major contribution rather than discontinue the exchange. Thus exchange partners have certain shared interests, but, at the same time, there are certain points at which their interests diverge. On the one hand, both participants wish the association to persist. On the other hand, both wish their partner to make the greater commitment. If both partners profit from the transaction, they have a common interest in maintaining it, while differing as to the ratio at which benefits should be exchanged. Blau argues that this situation faces both actors with a problem or dilemma: 'This situation poses the dilemma for each partner that he must put pressure on the other to make the greater commitment by withholding his own commitment up to the point where it would endanger the relationship but not beyond this point.'[17] The 'model' put forward here presents a view of simple interaction quite different from that of Parsons. Instead of two actors conforming to expectations which are complementary and normatively defined, we have two actors facing a similar dilemma arising out of a partial convergence and a partial divergence of interests. Blau maintains that such dilemmas pervade social life and are a fundamental source of social change.

Dilemmas are essentially dynamic because the tactics which are required to achieve balance within one transaction automatically produce imbalance in other transactions. Let us return to the dilemma posed above, where both participants are withholding their own commitment so as to induce their partner to offer a better price. Although both partners face a similar dilemma, it cannot be assumed that their situations are identical. In fact, in most transactions, one participant will enjoy a stronger market position. Not only will he provide the more valuable services, but he will, as a result, find the association relatively less profitable. Consequently, his partner will be forced to make a greater contribution. But such contributions are costly and high costs within one exchange can be met only by the withdrawal of resources from other transactions. For example, a man who is relatively incompetent at his job may have to purchase valuable advice from highly skilled colleagues by giving his advisers considerable compliance. Such compliance, however, will prevent him from following his own inclinations in relation to other transactions within the group, thereby unbalancing his exchanges with other colleagues. One dilemma has been resolved only through the creation of new dilemmas, which themselves may have dynamic implications for other social relationships. If we assume that the resources used in social exchange are scarce, and this must be so because otherwise exchange would be unnecessary, we can view social life as a continuous movement of resources from one association to another as new dilemmas emerge. Blau argues that no previous attempt to conceptualize social equilibrium and social change has fully grasped the fact that the attainment of balance in one association is achieved only by disturbing equilibrium in other associations. Accordingly, he puts forward as a general principle that 'balanced social states depend on imbalances in other social states'.[18] This principle is of central significance for the analysis of complex as well as simple exchange.

Blau's view of direct exchange stresses the tendency for participants to try to control the behaviour of others in their own interests. In many associations, because both partners have valuable resources to contribute, only very partial control can be achieved. In other words, exchange is reciprocal. However, in many situations, 'one person needs something another has to offer, for example, help from the other in his work, but has nothing the other needs to reciprocate for the help'.[19] The person in need has several strategies open to him in principle. He can force the other person to help him. He can get help from somebody else. Or he can learn to do without help. But if he is unable to adopt any of these alternatives he has no option but to subordinate himself and to comply with his benefactor's wishes. 'Power' is the term Blau uses to refer to this ability of persons with unilateral control over resources to require compliance by their exchange partners. It is clear that the notions of power and partial equilibrium are related. For associations based on power will be unstable to the extent that, should any of the other alternatives become available to the subordinate partner, a radical change in the pattern of exchange would be likely to occur. Thus Blau suggests that power is an important and recurrent social phenomenon which needs explicit conceptualization at all levels of social life.

The preliminary analysis of simple exchange, power and social dilemmas has one further implication—namely, that the basic social unit is the triad rather than the dyad. It is clear, even from the brief statement above, that power and compliance depend on the social alternatives open to the members of an association. As a result, power can only be covered in the paradigm of direct exchange if we include some reference to at least one actor outside the minimal dyad who can provide such alternatives. If we begin with a two-actor paradigm we are likely to omit the fundamental phenomenon of power at this crucial stage and, perhaps, thereby exclude it altogether from the theoretical scheme.[20] Similarly, balanced exchange between two persons is only attained through the use of resources gained in other social contexts. Thus conceptualization of interpersonal relations which fails to recognize these wider social connections will miss the dynamic implications for other transactions of the achievement of equilibrium within the dyad. Blau concludes his preliminary account of direct exchange therefore by emphasizing that if we are to recognize the existence of power and the dynamic implications of social dilemmas we must make a basic distinction between a pair and any group of more than two: 'It is essential, in the light of these considerations, to conceptualize processes of social association between individuals realistically as finding expression in networks of social relations in groups and not to abstract artificially isolated pairs from this group context.'[21] We must turn now to examine the way in which Blau depicts the processes governing the networks of social relations in groups.

III

Blau's use of empirical evidence to support his exchange analysis is much less systematic than that of Homans. His objective is to investigate the implications of viewing social behaviour as exchange rather than to produce fully verified propositions. Consequently, instead of a series of documented inductions, he offers a description, linked frequently but irregularly to factual data, of certain general group processes. In the exposition to follow, few references will be made to Blau's empirical material. We shall be concerned more with the processes than with the evidence used to illustrate them.

People associate because they expect to find it rewarding. They are attracted to situations where the potential profit seems highest. In line with the principle of reciprocity, a person who is attracted to others will attempt to impress them with the value of his own qualities, for the rewards which they supply to him will depend on their anticipation that association with him will be gratifying. In order to make a good impression, it is necessary to decide which qualities are most highly valued in a particular group and to behave in a way which implies that one has such qualities. This process has been studied by Goffman under the heading of the presentation of self.[22]

Presentation of a favourable self-image with the intent of maximizing rewards is found in virtually all social associations. However, like many basic social processes, it is most clearly evident in unstabilized relationships—for example, when strangers enter an existing group or when new groups are formed. In new groups members tend to compete in order to place themselves in a favourable light. In doing so they draw attention to those capacities which they believe are most useful to the group and in which they regard themselves as most gifted. Because members are rewarded for specializing in that sphere in which they appear to be of most benefit to the group, a functionally differentiated structure of interpersonal relationships emerges. Thus the development of functional differentiation in face-to-face associations can be seen as a predictable outcome of elementary processes of social exchange.

As participants gradually discover which social arrangements are most profitable, functional differentiation becomes established and regular patterns of exchange become crystallized. Certain of these recurrent transactions are limited to instrumental services. For example, in a research team one member may supply mathematical knowledge, while another furnishes an ability to design experiments. Such contributions towards fulfilment of group objectives will act as rewards to all members and will, consequently, foster integrative bonds of interdependence within the group. Nevertheless, in most groups certain members make instrumental contributions which are so valuable that they can only be balanced by such generalized responses as esteem and compliance. Thus differentiation in terms of power and social ranking, as well as functional differentiation, are the almost inevitable products of direct social exchange.

Individuals differ in the extent to which they can provide others with valuable services. In any group, the principle of reciprocity requires that an attempt be made to recompense more highly those who make the more valuable contribution to group life. Yet those whose services have little instrumental value will be unable to offer any specific benefit which will pay their social debt. Consequently, they will have no alternative but to offer some generally available response which is universally experienced as rewarding. In Blau's analysis there appear to be four such generalized reinforcers: money, approval, esteem or respect, and compliance. Money is clearly inappropriate as a means of repaying diffuse social obligations. Simple approval, however, although an acceptable social reward, is not usually in sufficiently short supply to constitute an adequate reward and incentive for important services to the group. Thus the scarcer and therefore more appropriate responses of esteem and compliance tend to be forthcoming. The differential distribution of esteem among group members constitutes a system of social ranking. In time the internal hierarchy will become recognized and accepted by most participants. And as social ranking becomes increasingly definite and generally endorsed within the group, so individual deviation becomes less possible: 'Public recognition of the relative respect deserved by various members of the group makes the prestige structure a social reality independent of the attitudes of specific individuals.'[23]

In temporary groups or groups with fluctuating membership hierarchical differentiation may not reach this stage. But in groups of longer duration esteem is unlikely to prove an adequate incentive for those making particularly valuable contributions to the group. This is so because, as the low status of persons paying respect for valued services becomes clearly defined, so the value of their respect declines. As a result, low-status members are obliged to repay their benefactors in some new and more rewarding fashion. At this stage, Blau suggests, the only alternative open to those in receipt of valued benefits is to defer to the wishes of the person or persons who supply them.

The requirement of reciprocity is met by compliance with the preferences of superiors. Thus out of these processes whereby important contributions from some meet with compliance on the part of others a differentiated power structure begins to emerge. Blau defines power as the ability to control the behaviour of others through the use of negative sanctions. It is: '. . . the ability of persons or groups to impose their will on others despite resistance through deterrence either in the forms of withholding regularly supplied rewards or in the form of punishment, inasmuch as the former as well as the latter constitute, in effect, a negative sanction.'[24] Power grows out of an exchange relationship when one partner is more dependent on the transaction than the other. For example, employers and employees are engaged in *asymmetrical* exchange which often makes the employee more vulnerable to the withdrawal of rewards. Thus, being fired from his job will be experienced by the employee as a punishing deprivation.

But, while he acts as an isolated individual, his withdrawal of labour will have little effect on the firm's management. In this exchange relationship, therefore, the employee is more dependent than is the employer and accordingly more effectively controlled by the threat of negative sanctions. Power and exchange, then, are intimately related. But the degree to which exchange gives rise to power is limited by four factors. In the first place, power is reduced to the extent that the recipients can supply some valued service in return. Secondly, compliance will be less if recipients have access to alternative suppliers of the same or closely similar services. Thirdly, power is eliminated to the extent that the recipients can use physical force to obtain the service. Finally, the recipients may learn to do without the service and in this way, by stopping exchange, avoid dependence and the need to comply. Subject to these conditions, power becomes concentrated in the hands of those group members who furnish the greatest benefits for other participants.

Before clearly defined ranks have emerged in a group, competition for power, prestige and approval takes place among all members. But as the status structure crystallizes, low-status members drop out of the competition for major rewards. Exchange relationships between persons of high and low status persist, but competition for power and leadership becomes restricted to a relatively small group who supply important instrumental services and who are generally esteemed throughout the group. In short, as the group's hierarchical structure becomes stable, so exchange transactions tend to operate vertically while competitive relationships operate horizontally. Those at the top can, of course, use the compliance of those obligated to them to strengthen their own claim for domination. Blau argues that the leaders use up their power as they call upon subordinates to comply with their demands. The more compliance is required the more costly it becomes. Clearly, it will only be forthcoming as long as costs do not exceed rewards. However, the powerful are in an advantaged position because they can use the compliance of subordinates in ways which further benefit the group. An emergent leader 'can use his power to organize their activities more effectively to achieve various objectives. The benefits that accrue to them due to his effective leadership further obligate others to him and strengthen his power over them.'[25]

So far Blau has argued that out of certain basic processes of social exchange four important features of small groups emerge. These are functional differentiation, integration through interdependence, social ranking and the differentiation of power and leadership. His next step is to examine, along the following lines, how integration is fostered by the development of norms, which, in turn, make possible the development of authority structures.

As a group's structure becomes relatively stable its members come to expect that past rewards will be regularly supplied. As long as people conform to these expectations, explicit norms are not required. However, we can assume that in any group members will sooner or later try to increase their profit by departing from customary activities. When such departures affect only minor transactions or relatively few members, they will be met with small alterations in the current rates of exchange. But when 'a group member's action that furthers his interest . . . directly harms the interest of the rest or of the group as a whole . . .'[26] explicit norms are likely to develop as part of the attempt at control. These norms define those actions which are experienced as rewarding by most group members or by the more powerful members. They assist social control by making more evident the costs, in terms of disapproval and withdrawn benefits, of nonconformity. But Blau, unlike Parsons, is not greatly concerned with norms and values as sources of social integration. He is more interested in their link with power and authority. In this connection, he turns to a more detailed examination of norms of fairness and norms of legitimacy.[27]

All collectivities, from the small group to the whole society, develop norms that stipulate fair rates of exchange in social transactions. Whole groups of men come to expect that the reward for a particular service should be proportionate to the costs undergone in its production. Given the diffuse character of social exchange, these norms of fairness can never be precise. Nor are they constant from one social context to another. Nevertheless, in Blau's view, people do compare their investments as well as their rewards in accordance with standards specifying what is a fair return. But norms of fairness are only one factor influencing social transactions, and in many instances people are unable to realize a 'proper return' on their investments. One important reason for this is that many social associations require a commitment which is not easily reversible. Blau refers to occupational choice as the most obvious example:

> The investments made in occupational training are irrevocable and create strong occupational commitments. . . . If the demand for the services of a given occupation should decline, and with it the rewards received for them . . . the persons in the declining occupation . . . pay the cost of the process of adjustment. Their commitment to the occupation, which precludes mobility to other occupations for most of them, means they receive unfair returns for their investments. . . .[28]

Because satisfaction with rewards depends just as much on their meeting standards of fairness as on their amount, people who are deprived of a fair return by forces of indirect exchange beyond their control are likely to react with resentment and hostility toward their superiors. In contrast, those whose expectations are met or even exceeded will respond with approval and greater willingness to comply with their leaders' directives. In the former case, opposition and conflict will tend to develop. While in the latter a formal authority structure is liable to emerge.

Compliance with the directives of the more powerful members of a group is experienced by subordinates as a cost, which is assessed in relation to norms of fair exchange. Demands which appear unjust according to these standards engender disapproval. But where leaders' demands are regarded as moderate relative to their contribution to group life, and where subordinates' returns are above what is expected on the basis of their investments, leadership is generally approved. And out of this approval develop norms which make leadership legitimate:

> If the benefits followers derive from a leader's guidance
> exceed their expectations of a fair return for the costs they
> have incurred, both by performing services and by complying
> with directives, their collective approval of his leadership
> legitimates it.[29]

As a result of regular benefactions, subordinates come to expect their superiors to make decisions on behalf of the collectivity and to expect other subordinates to carry out these decisions. Thus norms emerge within the group prescribing compliance with the policies of the leaders. These norms, Blau suggests, make the exercise of power legitimate from the perspective of those within the collectivity. He uses the term 'authority' to refer to the exercise of power which is regarded as legitimate by those subject to it.

As power becomes mediated through legitimating norms, the processes of exchange involved become increasingly complex and indirect. Before power has been recognized as legitimate there is a relatively direct exchange between persons of high and low status. Those with high status provide valuable services while those with low status respond with esteem and compliance. Once power is supported by social norms, however, a new type of transaction develops among subordinates. For subordinates now receive approval from their peers, as well as from their leaders, for complying with the directives of those in authority. The act of compliance is no longer solely a means of rewarding one's superiors for valued services; it is also a request for approval from the collectivity at large. These transactions with peers introduce additional pressures for compliance. For they constrain individuals inclined to resist particular directives to submit rather than forgo the approval of their colleagues.

Competition for social rewards, functional differentiation and interdependence, the formation of prestige hierarchies, differentiation of power, and social norms develop out of elementary exchange in all enduring groups. But authority emerges almost exclusively within collectivities where subordinates have some overriding common objective towards which leaders can make a discernible contribution. A leader cannot achieve a position of authority on the basis of separate transactions with the individual members of the group. For in such a situation recipients share no common debt to their benefactor and the possibility of shared norms of legitimacy does not arise. Furthermore, any person who improves his own bargaining position *vis-à-vis* the leader does so at the expense of fellow-members. Thus shared feelings of loyalty to superiors and shared norms of legitimacy develop only where there are common interests and where, consequently, leaders can contribute to the common welfare of the group. Accordingly, authority structures tend to form in the attempt 'to organize collective effort on a large scale in pursuit of ends commonly accepted'.[30] But, Blau stresses, commonly accepted ends are not necessarily common ends. Because this point is crucial to his analysis it is worth elaborating with a lengthy quotation:

> Commonly accepted ends are not necessarily common ends. Some organizations, such as unions, are designed to further the common objectives of the membership. The objectives of other organizations, such as business concerns, are those of the owners or of management. The majority of members whose services are bought in order to achieve these goals are expected to accept them as valid guides for operations, although they are not their own objectives. In either case, the members make contributions in exchange for rewards, but whereas the union member's rewards result from and are contingent on the achievement of the union's objectives, those of the firm's employee come from the salary he is paid for his services, which does not *directly* depend on the firm's profits, that is, on the achievement of the organization's objectives.[31]

When large numbers of men come together to realize commonly accepted goals it is no longer possible for them to interact freely in pursuit of personal rewards. Instead, social resources must be channelled and combined so that they further the collectivity's long-term objective. Obedience to the orders of those responsible for running the organization replaces the striving for direct social gratification. Since collective ends cannot be attained unless the internal structure of the collectivity is stable and predictable, those in authority tend to formulate relatively detailed prescriptions designed to govern the specialized activities of subordinates in a co-ordinated fashion. The kind of collectivity which emerges is called a 'formal organization'. It is exemplified in trades unions, business organizations, many religious associations, military groups and so on. Within such organizations, owing to the formal control of behaviour, indirect exchange predominates. For instance, official A fulfils his formal obligations to official B, not because official B rewards him for doing so, but in order to satisfy official C, who is recognized as having the right to control his behaviour within the organization. Nevertheless, formal rules originating from those in authority can never be sufficiently detailed to regulate all the activities of the participants. Consequently, direct exchange persists within the interstices of the formal organization, as we saw when we examined in ch. VII Blau's study of the law-enforcement agency.

So far this discussion of authority has focused on the situation in which subordinates approve the actions of their superiors. But, particularly in the larger and more complex organizations, leaders frequently experience great difficulty in maintaining general social approval. This difficulty arises because the commonly accepted ends, which are the main concern of those in authority, are not necessarily the *prime objectives* of all or even any of the subordinate groups. Thus those who exercise formal control within the organization are often faced with the problem of balancing the divergent and competing demands of a variety of internal sub-groups. In meeting the demands of any one group, the authorities are likely to offend against norms of fairness endorsed in other groups or even, in principle, throughout the organization. And when norms of fairness are contravened those concerned are likely to react with hostility, opposition and sometimes with a denial of legitimacy. Blau sees these processes operating especially clearly in business organizations where, once earnings reach a certain minimal level, workers become concerned as much with wage differentials—that is, with the question of fair distribution—as with the actual purchasing power of their income: 'As management yields to the pressures of one group to avert active opposition in the form of a strike or possible defections to other companies . . . it satisfies the demands of one group but creates dissatisfaction in others.'[32]

In Blau's view the managing group of virtually any complex organization will be faced with an inescapable exchange dilemma, or, rather, a continuing series of dilemmas. He argues that, given limited resources, it is only possible for management to balance one exchange relationship by unbalancing others. As one group gains a relative advantage, other groups are roused into opposition; and as resources are used up to balance one transaction, more resources are needed to deal with the new demands provoked thereby. Thus Blau argues that change within formal organizations tends to take a dialectical form as the intermittent refocusing of conflict and consensus is accompanied by realignment of internal exchange relationships.

In this section we have been concerned with what Blau calls 'microstructures'—that is, social structures composed of interacting individuals. In his analysis of microstructures Blau tries to show how certain features of group structure—namely, integration, differentiation, organization and opposition—are the outgrowths of the elementary processes governing direct exchange. The approach developed, although similar to that of Homans, is by no means identical. In particular, it places much greater emphasis on formal organizations and the related phenomena of power, authority and opposition. Formal organizations play a particularly important role in Blau's scheme because they constitute a major link between microstructures and macrostructures. The latter are structures composed of interrelated groups or collectivities. Although formal organizations are not the only type of collectivity operating at this level they are regarded by Blau as specially important. One reason for this is that the transactions between organizations are seen as generating new levels of power and authority as well as a dialectical pattern of societal change. By focusing on formal organizations, Blau is able to show how many of their internal processes are repeated, in modified form, at those higher levels of social complexity to which we now turn.

IV

There are many parallels, some of which will become evident as this section progresses, between the social processes taking place in microstructures and those occurring in macrostructures. But there are also certain fundamental differences. First, exchange in macrostructures is indirect rather than direct, and is possible only in collectivities where mediating values are held in common. Thus the study of macrostructures cannot proceed without an examination of shared values. Secondly, the network of exchange in macrostructures tends to become institutionalized, thereby constituting a historical reality which is passed on from one generation to the next, determining to some extent the elementary processes of exchange. Thirdly, the components of macrostructures are themselves social structures with their own internal dynamics. Consequently, owing to the institutional constraints on elementary exchange and to the impact of elementary exchange upon collective processes, any full understanding of macrostructures requires us to consider more than one level of social organization. In order to account for the operations of macrostructures, we must consider both the internal processes and the external relations of their component collectivities. We shall now explore these points of difference between microstructures and macrostructures in more detail.

Blau's analysis of cultural values is greatly indebted to Parsons and is undertaken from a noticeably functional perspective. His main thesis takes the following form: In large communities there can be no direct interaction among the great majority of members. Consequently, direct attraction, which integrates interpersonal associations in small groups, is inoperative. Yet, despite the absence of personal attraction, there is a coherence and stability in large social aggregates. There must be, therefore, some functional equivalent to integration through direct exchange. This equivalent, Blau suggests, is provided by shared values which can be conceived of as 'media of social transactions' that expand the compass of social interaction in the same way that money extends the network of economic relationships.

Blau does not provide a definition of 'cultural value'. However, he seems to use the term in the usual sense as meaning a commonly accepted standard for judging the propriety of social conduct. If this meaning is borne in mind, there does appear to be a definite similarity between money and cultural values. Money provides a commonly-agreed-upon standard for assessing the worth of economic commodities. As long as it is in general use, it enables people to enter into complex and extended chains of indirect economic exchange. For example, a man can work in a factory which produces one single commodity, yet remain confident that he can use the money earned there to acquire a wide variety of products and services. Similarly, Blau argues, as long as commonly accepted values and norms guide social behaviour, people can be confident that their participation in complex networks of social exchange will receive its expected rewards.

In his analysis of norms Blau continues to use the functional approach adopted in relation to values. Norms are more specific prescriptions than values and provide a more detailed indication of the behaviour required in particular circumstances. The basic argument put forward is that there is a need for social norms prohibiting those forms of conduct conflicting with 'fundamental cultural values'[33] and that norms do tend to emerge to satisfy this need. It is not suggested that norms develop whenever they are required to safeguard important values, but that, when they do exist, they operate to prevent people violating basic values in the pursuit of self-interest.

The conduct prompted by individual self-interest often diverges from that required by the values and interests of the collectivity. In such situations, norms tend to emerge which channel self-interest in the direction required by the collectivity. Blau gives the example of voting in a democracy. Democracy is itself in certain societies either a basic value or it stands for a variety of more particular values, such as freedom of speech, freedom of association, etc. If democracy is to operate and if these values are to be attained, it is necessary that a good number of citizens express their political choice by voting in elections. However, individual self-interest will not lead a man to vote, for his single vote can have no appreciable influence on the outcome of the election. Voting involves costs in terms of effort and alternatives forgone, but brings no rewards. Thus the rational individual will choose not to vote. Consequently, if all men pursue individual self-interest, no voting will take place and democratic values will become defunct. But if voting is normatively defined the rewards of indirect social exchange will outweigh the costs for at least some citizens. Where voting is prescribed by social norms men will enter into an indirect exchange in which they give their vote to a political candidate in order to receive the approval of their fellows. Of course, in the long run, political activity may bring other rewards, such as economic benefit, which reinforce people's political commitment and strengthen their tendency to vote. None the less, social norms and the associated processes of indirect exchange play an important part in moulding behaviour in support of democratic and other major values.

Blau's treatment of norms and values has strong functional overtones. In the first place, he argues that a functional alternative to direct attraction appears to be required in large collectivities and that cultural values perform this function. Secondly, it is argued that individual self-interest must be controlled in a way which furthers the attainment of collective ends and cultural values and that social norms and associated mechanisms of indirect exchange satisfy this need. However, Blau makes no attempt to explain the existence of particular norms and values by showing that they fulfil social functions. Like Parsons, he is concerned with the more limited objective of clarifying the effects of cultural values in social life. For Blau, values and norms serve to integrate the complex patterns of exchange both within and between macrostructures. He recognizes that cultural values and their supporting norms are of several types and that each type is associated with a different form of integration and a different kind of collectivity.

Following Parsons, Blau distinguishes between particularistic and universalistic values: '... attributes that are valued by people regardless of whether they possess them reflect universalistic values, whereas preferences for attributes like one's own reflect particularistic values.'[34] Particularistic values foster integration among those who share a given characteristic. Nationality, for example, promotes feelings of identity and loyalty among large aggregates of people. Thus, in place of the direct personal attraction found in small groups, shared particularistic values unite the members of a collectivity into a cohesive unit even though the majority of members have no direct contact. In this way they extend the scope of social integration within collectivities, while, at the same time, erecting boundaries between them. Universalistic values, in contrast, are applied by actors irrespective of their own status. They constitute impersonal criteria for assessing social standing and social rewards. Educational attainment, for example, provides a universalistic standard which is defined as important by entire communities. Because it is a general impersonal criterion, different people are able to satisfy it to different degrees. Blau argues that universalistic values in general tend to differentiate between people and to make them eligible for differentiated rewards. Universalistic values are, therefore, most evident in the processes governing the distribution of economic goods and social status: 'Universalistic values and the processes of differentiation to which they give rise find expression in the society's distribution systems, including notably the class structure as the basic manifestation of the differential distribution of major social rewards . . .'[35]

Blau identifies two further types of values—namely, legitimating values and opposition ideals. The former make possible the development of extensive authority structures. By making the exercise of power legitimate, they help ensure compliance and in this way they serve to extend the scope of social organization. Legitimating values are, of course, operant in all administrative and political structures. Finally, there are opposition values, which fulfil a similar function to legitimating values, but in relation to collectivities directed toward reorganization and social change.

So far in this section we have been discussing the first distinguishing characteristic of macrostructures, the mediation of indirect exchange through cultural values. We must now turn to the second distinguishing feature, that of institutionalization. For Blau institutions are those social arrangements which persist over long periods of time and institutionalization refers to the processes which bring about this persistence of social forms. He suggests that there are three main factors involved. The first of these is that social procedures in macrostructures tend to become formalized. As people become dependent for their important rewards on networks of indirect exchange, there is a pressure to express the norms governing exchange in explicit terms in order to ensure receipt of expected benefits. In pre-literate societies the rules governing important social relationships are formulated orally and passed on by word of mouth. But in literate societies they tend to be written down as well as embodied in formal arrangements, such as religious rituals, military traditions, legal procedures, and so on. Once the principles controlling social conduct have been formally established in this fashion they provide a social framework which is transmitted from generation to generation and which exerts an external constraint on the behaviour of individuals.

Social institutions are also perpetuated because the values and norms by which they are made legitimate are internalized during the process of socialization. Many fundamental values and beliefs are learned during childhood so that formal social arrangements appear to the individual, not only as external constraints on his self-interest, but also as morally justified constraints. Socialization, of course, continues throughout life in so far as individuals enter new collectivities, such as business organizations, trades unions, friendship cliques, and so on. Because full membership of such collectivities is often conditional on acceptance of group norms and values, many normative commitments which are not made in youth are acquired later in life. Thus the participants in institutional arrangements learn to see them as right. And once people have come to believe in their institutions in this way they will pass on their beliefs to others and they will resist change.

The account of institutionalization offered so far is little different from that of Parsons. Blau does differ, however, in arguing that a third factor which helps maintain social institutions is the active support of the powerful. He suggests that powerful groups in a societal collectivity or in its sub-collectivities will be closely identified with existing institutional arrangements and with associated cultural values, if only because they are the major beneficiaries of the existing order. Consequently, it can be assumed that they will use the negative sanctions over which they have control to command obedience from many subordinates who would otherwise deviate from institutional requirements.

Institutions, then, are formalized social arrangements which, because they constrain individual actors from outside, because they are widely held to be morally justified, and because they are supported by those in power, persist for long periods of time. The differences between institutionalized behaviour and elementary social behaviour can be clearly seen in relation to authority. Authority develops out of face-to-face interaction as the power of an individual over a group, or of a group over a larger collectivity, is legitimated by the dependents. Thus authority in microstructures is generated by the power structure. In contrast, institutionalized authority is itself a source of power. It endows individuals and groups occupying particular social positions with power and gives them the right to use their power to perpetuate existing institutional forms, to maintain existing social relationships and to defend their own place within the power structure. Similarly, the normative standards underlying institutional authority do not grow out of social exchange. They are, instead, learned in the course of socialization. Many of the basic attitudes which lead people to regard as legitimate directives issuing from the occupants of certain positions are acquired during childhood. This is true, for example, in relation to paternal authority, religious authority and political authority. Thus people develop quite early in life feelings of moral obligation to conform to commands from legitimate sources. These culturally defined obligations are not formed during interaction within the relevant collectivities, but are internalized particularly within family and school, and are brought to the institutional context by the individual.

It is clear from the discussion above that normative beliefs are central aspects of all institutions. Blau suggests accordingly that institutions can best be classified in terms of the values they embody. His typology corresponds closely, but not exactly, with those four functional imperatives around which Parsons regards institutions as differentiating. The first type is that of integrative institutions, such as kinship and religion, which perpetuate particularistic values by teaching people to identify with familial, religious and national collectivities. This type corresponds approximately to Parsons' functional imperative of pattern maintenance. The second type of institution is the distributive. Distributive institutions, such as those in the economy, the educational structure and the stratification system, focus around universalistic values and perpetuate the mechanisms by which essential facilities and rewards are distributed. They correspond closely to the functional imperative of adaptation. The third type of institution is the organizational, which centres around values of legitimacy and includes political, military, legal and other institutions concerned with co-ordinating collective effort in pursuit of commonly accepted objectives. This type corresponds to Parsons' imperatives of goal-attainment and integration.

Finally, unlike Parsons, Blau contends that each cultural system contains a 'counter-institutional component', made up of those widely-held values which have not been expressed in institutional form. These values provide a focus for organized opposition to existing institutions and to the associated distribution of rewards and power. Furthermore,

> The very cultural values that legitimate existing institutions contain the seeds of their potential destruction, because the idealized expectations these values raise in the minds of men in order to justify the existing social order cannot be fully met by it and thus may serve as justification, if need be, for opposition to it.[36]

Opposition movements may sometimes be legitimated by means of values introduced from outside the collectivity. But many such movements, and particularly those intended to challenge political authority within a whole society, make use of paramount values which have not been fully institutionalized. Both institutionalized values and unrealized values current within a collectivity are cradles for incipient institutions. Shared values themselves provide a factor contributing perennially to social change. Precisely how opposition movements and new institutions emerge will become clearer as we consider the final feature distinguishing macrostructures from microstructures.

The third feature which distinguishes microstructures from macrostructures is that, whereas the former are composed of interacting individuals, the latter are composed of interrelated social structures. A general theory of society, Blau suggests, in treating the relationships between the various sub-structures which make up a societal collectivity would have to take into account the internal organization and dynamics of these sub-structures. It would have to combine the analysis of microstructures with that of macrostructures. In Blau's view there are four kinds of sub-structures. First, the members of a society can be allocated to categories on the basis of any one or more socially relevant criteria. For example, people may be classified as male or female, black or white, high-income or low-income, and so on. Each of these categories is socially significant, at least in our society, because it is associated with distinct patterns of social conduct. The more of these categories we use the more their membership will overlap and the more complex will be the connections between them. Secondly, societies can be divided into communities—that is, into organized collectivities located within specific geographical areas. Owing to their territorial base, communities are relatively separate and distinct. However, categories of the first type often cut across geographical boundaries. Thirdly, there are organized collectivities which are not restricted to particular spatial areas. Such collectivities vary from small, fairly informal groups to large-scale, institutionally-organized bureaucracies. Most people belong to several such collectivities at the same time. Furthermore, there is a constant movement in and out of them as some collectivities become more attractive while the rewards others offer decline in value. Thus the relations between organized collectivities tend to be ill-defined and to fluctuate over time. Fourthly, there are abstract social systems. Blau, like Parsons, distinguishes social systems from collectivities. The latter are composed of men associated together in an ordered fashion. Social systems, in contrast, consist not of the social relations in specific groups of individuals, 'but of analytical principles of organization, such as the economy of a society or its political institutions'.[37] But Blau differs from Parsons in devoting much more of his attention to collectivities than to social systems. 'The most important substructures for this analysis', he suggests, 'are organized collectivities. . . .'[38] In particular, his analysis centres upon the role of *formal organizations* in macrostructures. There appear to be two reasons for this focus. The first is that they are more amenable to interpretation in terms of exchange. The second is that Blau regards them as being mainly responsible for the dynamics of macrostructures. For the rest of this section we shall be mainly concerned with Blau's analysis of the interrelations among formal organizations and the connections between their internal and external social processes.

Formal organizations are formed to achieve given objectives. Once they exist, social transactions take place between them. These transactions are of two kinds. On the one hand, there is competition and, on the other hand, exchange. Organizations compete for social support and resources of various types. For instance, firms compete for customers and economic facilities, while religious groups compete for converts and religious commitment. Thus competition tends to occur among organizations with similar objectives and it produces hierarchical differentiation between those which are more and those which are less successful.

Competitive success has several important effects for the internal structure of an organization. In the first place, it furnishes members with rewards, which in turn justifies their compliance and increases their loyalty. As a consequence, the control of those in authority is strengthened and they are able to use the increased compliance of subordinates to improve even further the competitive position of the organization. As the successful organization expands its resources, it appears increasingly attractive to members of less-successful groups and becomes, at the same time, increasingly able to absorb them. There is, therefore, a continuous movement of people, throughout society, out of contracting and into expanding organizations. The resultant changes in organizational size have, of course, further effects upon the organizations' internal structures. Blau even goes so far as to assert that this flow of personnel, a by-product of the processes of competition and exchange, is the most important source of interdependence among substructures within a collectivity: 'The mobility of individuals between social segments and organizations in a society may be considered the core of the relations between substructures in a macrostructure, through which the internal structures as well as their boundaries in the larger system are continually modified.'[39]

In addition to competition among organizations there is exchange. Where competition produces hierarchical differentiation between successful and unsuccessful collectivities operating in the same field, exchange springs from and promotes specialization in different fields. In short, organizations, like individuals, concentrate on doing that which brings them greatest profit and, once having specialized, they become dependent on other organizations for essential services. Many, if not most, of these exchange relationships are indirect. A university research team, for example, may be involved in resolving certain scientific problems. The information it gathers during its research will be passed on to the professional journals and there published. Some of this information is likely to be acquired by industry, if it has technological implications, while certain members of the team will almost certainly transfer to industrial research, if only temporarily. Thus industry 'feeds off' the pure research undertaken in the university and uses it to change and improve its own products which, after passing through the hands of marketing and retail organizations, will eventually reach the consumer. At the same time as these exchanges are taking place, the consumer, in his role as taxpayer, will be paying for the initial research via various government departments and grant-giving bodies. This simplified example gives some idea of the complexity of indirect exchange between differentiated organizations. In many cases some form of central control is necessary to complete the network of transactions. This is so in the instance above where government agencies link the consumer with the research team. In fact, government agencies are often set up with the aim of mediating the indirect exchange of services and resources in accordance with common values and with the task of ensuring that important community needs are met.

Organizational exchange sometimes leads to coalitions and mergers. For example, separate trades unions may strike 'in sympathy' or may, if it promises a better bargaining position, form one single representative body. Similarly, competition often leads to the elimination of competitors. This can be seen, for example, in the history of the Catholic Church, which, from being one sect among many in imperial Rome, achieved a position of religious dominance in medieval Europe. Thus out of exchange and competition exceptionally large and powerful organizations emerge in various spheres. And in the same manner that powerful individuals in microstructures compete among themselves for dominant positions, so the relatively small number of powerful organizations, although operating in different areas of social life, compete for generalized resources, such as money, legitimacy and personnel. Furthermore, in macrostructures, as in microstructures, an overriding authority structure emerges to regulate these processes of exchange and competition.

Blau offers no detailed examination of the development of societal authority out of the competition and exchange among organizations. He simply states that:

> The existence of a differentiated structure of relations among organized collectivities creates the conditions for its formalization and the explicit establishment of an overall political organization in order to maintain order and protect the power of the organizations and ruling groups . . . against being overthrown by violence, which is the major threat to it.[40]

In macrostructures, then, political organizations tend to be created with authority over other organizations. This authority is accepted as legitimate, of course, only to the extent that it is seen as an expression of cultural values. Such political organizations have various objectives. First, as we have seen above in relation to scientific research, they attempt to regulate the complex networks of indirect exchange to ensure a fair and productive distribution of facilities and rewards. Secondly, they operate to control competition among powerful organizations by institutionalizing the distribution of scarce resources. For example, a government might try to use its authority to implement a policy controlling prices and profits, on the one hand, and wages and wage-increases, on the other hand. Or it might try to suppress certain kinds of religious groups while favouring others. Thirdly, certain organizations, such as political parties, will be developed to represent the interests of competing groups in the institutionalized competition of the political arena. Finally, political authority will be exercised to support existing institutions and the position of the powerful against encroachment and particularly against attempts to change the macrostructure through violence. But, Blau argues, the very exercise of political authority itself generates opposition and gives rise to strenuous attempts 'originating' within microstructures to change the network of social relationships at the macrostructural level.

Opposition movements tend to arise within groups undergoing various forms of deprivation. The exercise of political authority leads to the formation of such movements because political control necessarily involves exerting constraints, which are often experienced by recipients as deprivations and which easily give rise to frustration and hostility. Even when those in authority wish to satisfy all fair demands for resources they find that, in acceding to one set of demands, not only do they alter thereby the demands of other groups, but in many cases they expend the resources which could have been used to meet the latter claims. This is essentially the same dilemma faced by those exercising authority in microstructures. But the members of a society have little opportunity of escaping from the collectivity, and it is, therefore, frequently possible for those in authority to deprive one section of the community in order that the demands of the majority or of the more powerful may be met. On other occasions political authority generates opposition through simple exploitation. For in some circumstances those in authority find it more profitable to ignore norms of fairness altogether and to take what their power allows from dependent groups. Exploitation, oppression and the failure to meet culturally induced expectations, all create sentiments of hostility and aggression and, in this way, provide the basis for movements organized to oppose existing political authorities.

Opposition movements typically develop in socially distinct and isolated groups. This is true, for example, of the American Negroes, whose case fits Blau's analysis in most respects. The members of such groups share, at the outset, a common identity and an experience of deprivation based on a comparison of their investments and rewards with those of other groups. Out of this experience develop feelings of frustration and aggression, plus a need to express these feelings. Communication to other members of the group of these negative sentiments against outsiders is experienced as rewarding and, in due course, norms are formulated which define these attitudes, not just as acceptable, but as a requisite for membership of the group. At this stage political activists begin to formulate collective aims and to separate from those less strongly motivated. In order to justify their political objectives, the activists tend either to compose or to adopt a 'revolutionary ideology'. In most cases this ideology will show clear traces of values current but not fully implemented within the wider collectivity. As the group's goals become relatively explicit, so its organization crystallizes and a surplus of gratifications is generated internally which enables members to press for the realization of their ideals and to withstand the negative sanctions applied by those in authority.

As long as opposition groups continue their struggle, the social structure will remain unstable. Yet the very success of any such group will generate imbalance in other groups whose interests and norms of fairness have been violated thereby. Thus the attainment of balanced exchange between the political authorities and any one group fosters new problems and needs in other groups. A period of latency tends to follow during which these new pressures lead to internal reorganization of the collectivities now subject to relative deprivation. Then, once the forces of opposition have been mustered, the authorities are faced with demands for concessions from the new quarter. This process is, by its very nature, self-perpetuating. Consequently, the radical social change produced by organized opposition recurs at irregular intervals, as pressures generated within the macrostructure meet a response within microstructures, which reappears in due course in the form of new demands for change at the 'original' macrostructural level:[41]

> The existence of conflicting forces that pull in different
> directions itself would be reflected in social change in the
> direction of the resultant force, but in combination with the
> need for a latency period before opposition forces can
> realize their potential, it leads to structural change
> characterized not so much by continuous adjustments as by
> intermittent reorganizations. Structural change, therefore,
> assumes a dialectical pattern.[42]

V

Blau's scheme depicts society as composed of a multiplicity of social relationships between individual agents and between collectivities. These relationships can be studied at various levels of complexity. But a basic distinction is made between the relatively simple associations occurring within microstructures and the more complicated relationships within macrostructures. At both levels interaction is conceived as an exchange of rewards and costs; and at both levels this exchange perspective is used to interpret such social phenomena as competition, functional differentiation, the emergence of status hierarchies, and the development of power and authority. Yet, despite these similarities between microstructures and macrostructures, there are certain features which emerge as exchange becomes more complex and which can be investigated in detail in the study of macrostructures alone. Blau concentrates on the indirect nature of exchange in macrostructures, the shared values which mediate indirect exchange, and the development of institutional forms regulating such exchange.

Within any society the microstructural and macrostructural levels are linked in a complex fashion. Thus as the values current in macrostructures are internalized by individual members they come to guide direct as well as indirect exchange. Similarly, the institutions and networks of indirect exchange characteristic of macrostructures mould, though they do not determine, the nature of face-to-face interaction taking place within them. This process is exemplified in the way in which the exercise of political authority generates responses within microstructures leading to organized opposition and to a dialectical pattern of social change. The growth of political opposition is one specially important instance of how direct exchange is influenced by and reacts back upon associated macrostructures. But similar oppositional processes operate within all organizations, thereby changing social relationships throughout society. At the same time, there is a constant social flux as individuals are attracted from one organization to another by the possibility of greater psychic profit. Thus direct exchange is seen by Blau as operating continuously in the interstices of institutionalized exchange, feeding back upon and altering the institutional structure and periodically producing what appear to be sudden shifts in structural alignment.

This theoretical scheme is not intended as a general theory of society, but as the prelude to such a theory. It offers a series of related concepts for describing complex networks of social associations plus a number of broad propositions about the processes which both maintain and change social structures. In doing this it poses some of the substantive problems to be answered by a general theory without offering definite answers to such problems. It indicates, for example, that a general theory should include empirical generalizations in relation to both microstructures and macrostructures. It indicates also that these generalizations should deal with social differentiation, integration, organization, opposition, and so on. But no claim is made that a finished deductive system has been presented. As a consequence, Blau's theoretical prolegomenon is difficult to evaluate—even more difficult, in fact, than Parsons' categorial system, for Blau makes no systematic statement about his short-term objectives. None the less, he does state clearly that he is attempting to extend the scope of exchange theory while maintaining close contact with 'observable empirical reality'. He also asserts that his scheme is sufficiently mature to generate testable hypotheses. I shall, therefore, discuss briefly the scheme's theoretical maturity, the clarity of its empirical referents and its empirical coverage.

Early in *Exchange and Power* Blau examines the processes of competition occurring in emergent groups. He argues that initially all potential group members try to present a flattering image of themselves in order to establish their position within the group and to draw forth valuable responses from colleagues. In time, however, Blau suggests, social strategies change. Those who have achieved high status by supplying specially beneficial services tend to find that they have become a status-threat to their inferiors. And as the ranking system crystallizes, the costs of membership for low-status persons may even become high enough to threaten the continuance of the group. Consequently, it is claimed, those with secure positions of high rank will no longer emphasize their attractions indiscriminately. Instead, they will minimize their contributions to group life with respect to certain less important activities, thereby reducing their subordinates' costs in terms of professed inferiority, while never allowing any doubt about the value of the services upon which their status is primarily based. As a result of the use of this latter strategy by those offering highly-valued services, subordinates will respond not only with esteem or respect, but also with that approval and liking without which the group's continuation is in jeopardy.

Having put forward this analysis, Blau presents some experimental studies under the heading, *Testing Some Inferences*. In the first study he argues as follows:

> Common sense would lead one to expect that the group member two of whose attributes others find attractive is more likely to be befriended by the rest than the member who has only one of these two positive qualities. . . . The inference derived from the theory presented, in contrast, is that group members who have positive characteristics on a salient attribute,

which make them attractive, but *negative* ones on a less salient attribute, which also make them approachable, have the best chance to win informal acceptance. . . .[43]

Before we look at the relevant experimental findings, there is one important point to note about this inference. The experimental hypothesis states that the reward for having positive characteristics on salient attributes plus negative characteristics on less salient attributes will be *informal acceptance*. The preceding theoretical analysis, however, states that high-status persons who mitigate the burden of their subordinates' inferiority by not insisting on maintaining their superiority over them in every way win the *approval* and *loyalty* of low-status members.[44] It appears, therefore, that if the hypothesis being tested is a genuine inference from theory, we must regard 'informal acceptance' and 'approval and loyalty' as synonymous. In other words, Blau is referring to a reward which is very crudely conceived and which can be indicated equally well by a variety of everyday terms.

Interview data from twelve work groups in a welfare agency were used to test Blau's inference:

The sixty caseworkers in these twelve groups were classified, for each comparison made . . . on the basis of two characteristics as the independent variables and their informal acceptance as the dependent variable, the measure of the dependent variable being whether others in his own group were on a first-name basis with a given individual. Sociometric measures, such as popularity and being respected among colleagues, were used to indicate the more salient attribute, and background characteristics such as seniority and class origin as the indications of the less salient attribute. The prediction implied by the theory is that first-name informality is most prevalent among individuals who have a positive quality on the more salient and a negative one on the less salient factor and that first-name informality is least prevalent among those positive on the less and negative on the more salient attribute. Of 18 cross-tabulations examined, 15 confirmed this prediction.[45]

In our earlier discussion of the predictive tactics open to Blau we saw that there were two possibilities. One was the precise measurement of costs, values and profits as a means of making predictions about group processes. The other approach was to use *ex post facto* interpretations of costs, values and profits in the same way. In accordance with his prior conclusions, Blau adopts this second approach in the study just cited.[46] There is, however, some doubt whether this particular *ex post facto* analysis is adequate. For, to say that popularity, respect, class origins and seniority were more or less salient attributes within the groups under study appears to mean that these characteristics were experienced as more or less rewarding and costly by group members. Yet no evidence is given establishing a link between the salient attributes identified by the researchers and the subjects' values, costs and profits. For example, no evidence is provided to indicate that class origins were generally known or that they were associated with distinct patterns of behaviour. Yet without this kind of data, demonstrating that class background was a socially significant factor within the groups, its inclusion in the research design is unjustifiable. It appears that the prediction is based not on a systematic use of data to make inferences about actual values, costs and profits, but upon intuitive judgments as to which attributes were more or less 'important' in this social context. Nevertheless, the prediction *is* validated. If the criticism just levelled at Blau has any substance, how can we account for this apparent success? The answer is that the validation is spurious; it is no more than an outcome of conceptual confusion.

Blau's hypothesis is that persons who provide one highly-valued service but who rank low on other less important attributes will receive friendship as well as respect from their colleagues. Verification of this hypothesis requires the identification of certain positive and negative attributes of individuals and the demonstration that a particular combination of positive and negative attributes is associated with the social response of friendship or acceptance in any of its various forms. In order to identify the less salient attributes Blau notes *definite characteristics* of each individual, such as seniority and class background, which he presumes are relatively unimportant as sources of rewards. But in identifying the more salient attributes Blau turns from actual characteristics of individuals to group responses, using the latter as indicators of the existence of valuable attributes. Whereas seniority and social class are determined independently of the reactions of the group, respect and popularity are measured solely by the responses of others to certain (unidentified) attributes. Blau then shows that responses like popularity and respect, which are supposed to denote the existence of salient attributes, are associated with the additional response of first-name informality, which is taken to be an indication of social acceptance. But this association is meaningful only if the indices of salient attributes are independent of the index of social acceptance. If these two sets of indices are not independent the hypothesis tested takes the vacuous form 'If X then X' instead of 'If X then Y'. And in fact it does appear that the indices used by Blau are theoretically indistinguishable. For informality as well as popularity and respect is a reward given to those who furnish valuable services. Consequently, all three elements could equally well have been used as indices of salient attributes. Indeed, popularity and informality seem to be indices of the same variable—namely, social approval (or social acceptance or liking or friendship). The verification would, therefore, not have been less successful had popularity and informality been interpreted in exact reverse of Blau's actual procedure—that is, it would have been just as convincing to use first-name informality as an index of highly salient attributes and to use popularity as an index of group acceptance. Thus the statistical relationship is meaningless. It is simply a product of the failure to specify clear and independent empirical content for such terms as 'salient attribute' and 'group approval'.

Blau attempts more theoretical tests than does Homans. But, like the example just examined, they are seldom entirely convincing. Even the best of the studies designed as tests for the scheme are, as the theorist himself on occasion admits, 'somewhat equivocal' and no more than 'very suggestive for the theory presented'.[47] But equally important is the fact that the formulation of testable hypotheses is confined to the sphere of microstructures. Not once does Blau try to validate in this manner his analysis of macrostructures. It is worth investigating why this should be so.

Blau's prolegomenon is divided into two sections, each having a distinct theoretical structure. In the first section a number of principles supposed to govern direct exchange are put forward and used, not always explicitly, to deduce the occurrence of certain social processes in microstructures. Thus the analysis of microstructures produces a scheme broadly resembling the kind of deductive system envisaged by Homans and Pareto and, although the notion that the scheme constitutes a *mature* theoretical system is expressly repudiated, its deductive organization does allow the formulation of hypotheses which are, in principle, testable—though in practice they are vitiated by conceptual indeterminacy. In contrast, Blau's analysis of macrostructures is much less deductive. He does not argue that the processes of competition, combination, differentiation, and so on in macrostructures can be deduced from the principles governing interpersonal behaviour.[48] Nor does he offer an equivalent series of explanatory principles at the macrostructural level. Because he does not try to construct a deductive system at this level, Blau is unable to support his analysis by inferring testable hypotheses from general analytical principles.

At the macrostructural level Blau tends to replace deductive explanation with two substitute procedures. The first of these is the construction of a series of related categories—for example, the typology of substructures and the linked typologies of values and institutions. On the whole, little attempt is made to use these categories to form contingent and explanatory propositions. Indeed, Homans' critique of such big abstractions indicates that they are unsuitable for application in this way. Furthermore, given that many of the terms used in these typologies and elsewhere in the study of macrostructures are taken directly from Parsons, there is no reason to expect that Blau's categories will be any better in this connection than the concepts of structural-functionalism in general. The second alternative to explanation adopted by Blau is that of showing how many of the processes occurring in macrostructures parallel those in microstructures. For example, he maintains that 'Transactions among organized collectivities . . . may give rise to social ties that unite them, *just as* social exchange among individuals tends to produce integrative bonds.'[49] To point out analogues between the two levels is quite different from the provision of explanations, and Blau undoubtedly uses this procedure as a substitute for explanation, though it is not clear to what extent this substitution is an intentional theoretical manœuvre.

Although Blau's macrostructural analysis is not generally deductive, one broad explanatory sketch is essayed. This is the interpretation of social opposition. But even here attention focuses on those *microstructural* processes whereby organized collectivities arise in response to deprivation. Furthermore, the genuinely macrostructural problem of the structural sources of opposition movements is discussed only in very general terms. It is suggested that opposition develops when the competition for politically controlled resources produces relative deprivation. But the structural correlates of successful competition, on the one hand, and deprivation, on the other hand, are never examined in detail. We are offered a highly abstract account of the genesis of opposition movements, with no point-by-point application to specific cases. Blau's explanatory sketch consists of a highly general elaboration of implicit assumptions about exchange between organized collectivities plus occasional empirical illustrations, rather than an attempt at deductive explanation of systematically observed empirical data.

Blau's long-term theoretical objective is undoubtedly that of explaining the characteristics of complex structures by deducing them from the principles governing elementary exchange. But in *Exchange and Power*, which is merely a prolegomenon, he is still preparing the way for this final phase. At the microstructural level this scheme is organized loosely as a deductive system, but its conceptualizations are imprecise and its propositions seldom formally expressed. The analysis of macrostructures is even less theoretically mature and consists of various sets of related categories, descriptions of features in macrostructures analogous to those in microstructures, and explanatory sketches, often empirically unsupported and at a high level of generality. The very looseness of Blau's scheme, however, is the source of its main advantage. For it enables Blau to bring together within one theoretical framework many of the central notions appearing in the disparate theories discussed above. For example, he shares Parsons' concern with the emergent phenomena appearing in social associations and, accordingly, he uses many Parsonian terms for describing social structures and cultural systems—terms like 'institutionalization' and 'functional differentiation'. At the same time, Blau continues Homans' stress on the importance of psychological factors in social relationships and retains the latter's distinction between direct interaction and the institutionalized context within which it takes place. In addition, he finds it possible to combine these divergent perspectives with a Paretian view of dialectical change being generated by the exercise of political authority. As well as combining the substantive conceptions of prior theory, Blau's scheme tends to be more complete than its predecessors within each limited area. Thus Blau's treatment of direct exchange goes farther than that of Homans or Parsons in dealing with asymmetrical exchange or power. Similarly his macrostructural analysis extends beyond that of Parsons in furnishing a provocative account of the processes leading to sudden, disruptive change. At certain points, particularly in the interpretation of the link between authority and opposition, Blau's analysis even seems to promise a reconciliation with the sociological tradition of conflict theory stemming from Marx.[50] But these gains in empirical coverage and the reconciliation of theoretical perspectives which previously appeared quite disparate are accompanied by, and to a considerable extent made possible by, the conceptual imprecision of Blau's scheme, the looseness of its theoretical structure and the absence of systematic documentation.

There is no need to examine the defects of Blau's framework in any greater detail, because the operation of the strategical dialectic is to be pursued no further here. We need only note that Blau's strategy, like those of his predecessors, brings no nearer the conceptual clarity and precision without which conclusive theoretical advance is inconceivable. The strategical dialectic evident in the work of these five theorists, although it has produced a considerable number of conceptual innovations and although it has fostered the development of several distinct sociological perspectives, has not produced anything remotely approaching a comprehensive and rigorous theory of society. In the next chapter, after a summary of the discussion so far, I shall discuss the possibility of devising a more satisfactory theoretical strategy than those examined above.

9 Sociological theory and theoretical strategy

I

The present study examines how the theoretical strategies of five sociologists influence the content of their theories and also how each theorist develops a new strategy in response to the failure of his predecessors. It begins with Pareto, who, having judged prior sociological analysis to be empirically and theoretically inadequate, decides to model his strategy and much of the content of his theory on those disciplines which have already demonstrated their scientific maturity. Pareto's scheme is a useful point of departure for several reasons. First, its strategy is relatively simple. Secondly, the strategy furnishes an important reference-point for both Parsons and Homans. And, thirdly, it produces an extreme example of that conceptual indeterminacy which sociological theory has as yet been unable to avoid.

In Pareto's view, the theories of the advanced sciences are composed of deductively arranged propositions which are both logically consistent and empirically justified. In order to ensure that theoretical propositions are reliable expressions of empirical regularities, it is preferable to accumulate them carefully and systematically on the basis of accurate observations of actual events. Thus the general strategy of any science must be to construct inductively a precise deductive system. But systematic induction is not in itself a sufficient guarantee of theoretical adequacy. Ultimately theories are judged, not by the propriety of the method of their construction, but by results—that is, by the success of the explanatory and predictive deductions which they make possible.

This inductive-deductive strategy is copied by Pareto from the formative periods of disciplines such as classical mechanics and astronomy. These sciences apply their strategy to empirical systems which are made up of interrelated units, such as atoms or planets.

Analysis of these systems proceeds by the identification and measurement of certain variable features of their internal units—for example, the mass and velocity of planets—and by the formulation of simultaneous equations expressing the relationships between these variables. Pareto follows these disciplines, not only in pursuing their supposed strategy, but also in adopting the accompanying model of empirical systems. As a result, he assumes that social as well as physical systems are composed of interacting units, each of which varies along several dimensions. The units of social systems he takes to be individual human organisms; and in the course of his inductive survey he identifies their most important variables as residues, interests, derivations and social heterogeneity. These variables are either characteristics of individuals or can be inferred from characteristics of individuals. Pareto uses statements about the relationships between these 'psychological' variables to *deduce* the underlying dynamics of human societies, in the same way that in classical physics the characteristics of physical systems are deduced from information about the mass and velocity, etc., of their component units. In this way Pareto's theoretical strategy is a major determinant of the content of his theory. Because his whole approach to theory construction derives from his interpretation of physical science, he is forced to follow the assumption of these sciences that induction must focus on the nature of system units in order to produce generalizations which can then be used to infer the structure and dynamics of the systems under investigation.

In trying to implement this theoretical strategy, Pareto finds that he is faced with two major problems. The first is his inability to measure significant variables, which makes impossible the use of simultaneous equations. Pareto introduces cycles of interdependence as a partial substitute, but this is a qualitative and cumbersome technique, suitable only for small clusters of variables and likely to produce oversimplified analyses of complex empirical systems. The second, and related, difficulty is the complexity of social systems and the great variety of such systems to be found in the course of human history. Given the crudity of the analytical techniques available as well as the lack of prior empirical and theoretical studies, there must be considerable doubt about the possibility of constructing a scheme which can account for the great diversity of historically recorded conduct. Nevertheless, Pareto believes that in due course such a theory will be successfully formulated and that the most effective way of contributing to it is to present a first approximation. He admits, however, that this can be done only by the application of a radical policy of selection and simplification.

In accordance with this policy, Pareto proceeds to ignore certain factors which undeniably influence the organization of any social system—for example, its relations with other societies. He also simplifies the internal examination of social systems to such an extent that he operates with only four basic categories. Pareto justifies these tactics by arguing that all sciences rely on idealized statements which simplify events occurring in the real world. It is necessary, he suggests, to begin the construction of any scientific scheme by expressing certain underlying uniformities at a very general level. Only when this has been done is it possible to build up a sophisticated body of theory by distinguishing more detailed and complex relationships. He argues, therefore, that although his analysis is highly selective and drastically simplifies actual events, this is not a defect, for it is to be expected of any scheme which claims to be no more than a first theoretical approximation. Unfortunately, the results of Pareto's actual application of this policy fall far below his own criteria of theoretical adequacy. This theoretical failure occurs, on the whole, because Pareto is forced to apply so vigorously the policy of selection and simplification.

In the first place, the extensive cultural variety among societies is dismissed as 'mere derivation' and as largely irrelevant to social conduct. In this way the obvious and marked cultural differences between societies become theoretically insignificant, and Pareto is able to regard as unproblematic precisely those cultural differences which appear to make social systems so much more difficult to explain than their physical counterparts. Pareto's notion of 'derivation' considerably simplifies his analytical problems, for it allows him effectively to ignore the great bulk of sociological data and to concentrate on identifying and classifying what he regards as the underlying psychological uniformities. Accordingly, the diversity and complexity of human aggregates comes to be seen as a façade produced by man's tendency to rationalize his few relatively simple psychological proclivities—the residues. And the main task of the sociologist comes to be that of showing how the apparent complexities of social systems can be reduced to the interplay between large numbers of 'residual' acts. But the policy of selection and simplification does not stop even here. For although Pareto devotes a whole volume to the classification of residues, his deductions utilize only the exceptionally broad categories of 'combinations' and 'persistence of aggregates'.

In a similar manner to that in which the roots of social conduct are systematically reduced to two basic impulses, the second most important element in Pareto's scheme, that of social heterogeneity, is restricted in practice to a political, and occasionally an economic, context. Consequently, although he rejects mono-causal theories in principle and emphasizes the complex *inter*dependence within social systems, in practice he focuses on the impact of political factors upon the remainder of society. Pareto's policy of constructing a radically idealized model of the social system thus leads him to try to derive the structure and dynamics of societies from the operation of two human propensities largely within the political sphere. Eventually, when the theorist reverses his tactics and tries to use his simplistic scheme to account for a wide range of social activity, he is able to retain some semblance of empirical relevance only by abandoning the dictates of rigorous scientific procedure. Thus we find him denying the need for evidence, failing to specify the empirical referents of major terms, assuming instead of demonstrating that political changes reverberate throughout society, and in general departing from the very principles of clarity, reliability, consistency and empirical precision which he himself puts forward as the corner-stones of science. Consequently, subsequent theorists have virtually abandoned the content of Pareto's scheme, except for such highly abstract notions as social system, social equilibrium and governing élite. Pareto's greatest mistake can be seen to be that of attempting too much too soon; and his theory's main contribution to sociology is to provide a warning of the dangers of an over-ambitious theoretical strategy.

Parsons' long-term theoretical goal is the same as that of Pareto. But, in attempting to devise an appropriate strategy, he has the major advantage of being able to learn from the mistakes and failures of the preceding generation of sociologists. Consequently, he rejects Pareto's policy of aiming immediately for a logico-deductive system and decides instead to prepare the way for a genuine theory of society by developing a comprehensive, consistent and well-articulated system of concepts. Parsons argues that this categorial strategy will combine full conceptual recognition of the empirical complexities within social systems with the formulation of a conceptual framework which is empirically clear and reliable; and that only after these two requirements have been met will the construction of a satisfactory deductive theory become feasible.

The effects of Parsons' decision to avoid excessive conceptual simplification pervade his work, leading him to produce a network of interlocking categories which, by Paretian standards, is exceptionally complicated. For example, where Pareto makes no clear distinction between psychological and structural elements within social systems, Parsons distinguishes three levels of analysis (the psychological, the social and the cultural) which are interdependent, yet which require separate and detailed conceptualization. However, although his concepts have proliferated as he has tried to conceptualize explicitly every logically possible variation at all levels, Parsons' framework has been organized from the beginning within the limits of certain simplifying techniques. For Parsons uses structural-functional analysis as a means of simplifying in an organized manner the task of constructing a general conceptual apparatus for sociology.

Parsons argues that sociology cannot at present take as its data the vast range of minute variations in activity occurring within complex societies. He suggests, therefore, that we should reduce the task by concentrating on those widespread and recurrent activities which can be regarded as constituting the structure of a society. If the resultant structural concepts are to apply to societies in general, they will necessarily be highly abstract. Nevertheless, we can ensure their empirical relevance by deriving them from the social action framework which, in Parsons' view, emerges from several previous theories which are empirically well-founded.

In the long run, of course, Parsons wishes to use his structural concepts to express, in the form of contingent propositions and perhaps eventually as equations, the regularities observed within empirical systems. For the time being, however, he accepts that this is impossible and that we must remain content with conceptualizing the more important empirical variables and provisionally indicating the links between them. He realizes that this approach has its own dangers. In particular, it provides no guarantee that all empirically significant factors are included, nor does it deal with the interdependence and dynamics within social systems. But these difficulties can be resolved, Parsons suggests, by combining the use of structural concepts with a functional perspective. Functional analysis plays a role in Parsons' scheme equivalent to that of cycles of interdependence for Pareto. It is essentially a non-mathematical technique for demonstrating the importance of empirical variables and the relationships between them. Functional analysis prevents *over*-simplification by ensuring that the more empirically significant variables are covered. For it requires as a minimum that all structural units essential to the system are selected for attention. At the same time, by showing how a wide variety of structural units contribute to the same social system, it offers a preliminary account of structural interdependence and internal system dynamics.

In putting into operation this categorial plus structural-functional strategy, Parsons inevitably produces a scheme quite different in content from that of Pareto. The latter sees society as resembling a mechanical system formed by units whose features are, on the whole, determined independently of the system. Consequently, his theory focuses on biological or psychological impulses which can be taken as constant and which are only marginally influenced by the system. At the same time, such factors as cultural beliefs, which are system variables rather than individual variables, are regarded as mere by-products of impulsive action and therefore as theoretically peripheral. It is accepted, of course, that each individual's activities are affected by the organization of the total system. For example, persons characterized by group aggregates residues act differently when members of the governing élite than they do when striving for power.

Yet it is not so much the system which provokes these differences in activity as the actions of other individuals impelled by contrary residues. Thus for Pareto it is the propensities of individual units which, by their interplay, determine the structure and dynamics of the total system.

Parsons' approach to theory, in contrast, leads him to regard social aggregates as much more like organic systems in which the system's form must be taken as the constant and in which it can be presumed that the activities of individual components will be moulded to fit the requirements of the system. Thus in the same way that molecules develop within certain limits to meet the structural requirements of the biological organism to which they belong, so, according to Parsons, people learn to perform within limits those activities required for the continuance of their society. From the Parsonian perspective, societies are not mechanical aggregates, but systems which learn to respond to changing internal and external problems, largely through the medium of accumulated culture. Culture provides solutions not only to individuals' problems of choice, but also to society's problems of self-perpetuation. Accordingly, system variables, and in particular shared cultural beliefs, occupy a central position in Parsons' scheme. His strategy, focusing as it does on the notions of social structure and system requirement, is more easily applied when its associated content treats sociocultural systems as primary and when human personality and its biological bases are regarded as separate levels of analysis.

Structural-functional analysis is adopted by Parsons because it promises to combine an acceptable degree of conceptual simplification with a comprehensive and clear coverage of sociological data. In working out this strategy, he constructs an elaborate series of related categories organized in terms of an organic model of society. The resulting scheme improves on that of Pareto in being conceptually more elaborate. In this sense Parsons' prolegomenon gives greater recognition to the complexity and diversity of human societies. But its theoretical adequacy is difficult to judge because it offers few contingent propositions which can be compared with empirical observations. None the less, it is not difficult to establish that the scheme is in some respects inconsistent, that it tends to exclude certain kinds of dynamic factors, and that its concepts are too complex and abstract to have clear empirical content.

Some of these theoretical defects appear to be, to some extent, remediable by use of the terms of social exchange. But Parsons' strategical commitment to structural-functionalism hinders systematic development of such notions. Furthermore, use of the double-exchange paradigm in no way resolves the fundamental deficiency of conceptual formalism which is an almost inevitable by-product of the policy of extensive elaboration upon a small number of concepts derived from an unreliable inductive base. The conclusion is inescapable that Parsons' network of structural-functional categories fails to achieve its objective of providing a firm foundation on which to build a general deductive theory for sociology.

Judged by the ultimate criteria of scientific adequacy—namely, conceptual precision and the generation of empirically verified deductions—Parsons' scheme fares no better than that of Pareto. If we are to make a case for Parsonian theory's being a theoretical advance, we must look to such factors as its relative conceptual richness and its partial reconciliation of much prior work in sociology and in related fields, such as psychology and anthropology. Along with many other sociologists, Merton clearly regards Parsonian theory as a comparatively fruitful source of theoretical ideas, and he makes use of a number of conceptions similar to those in Parsons' system. Nevertheless, he rejects the idea that the terminology of structural-functionalism necessarily entails the adoption of a categorial strategy. In Merton's view, any form of general theory can be undertaken at the present stage of intellectual development in sociology, only at the cost of conceptual ambiguity and an enervating lack of empirical content. General theory can supply provocative speculations and a modicum of useful concepts, but, at the moment, virtually no established statements. He argues, therefore, that the successful general theory of the future will have to be built up gradually by accumulation of less spectacular but more empirically-grounded middle-range theories.

The long-term objective of sociology is, in Merton's view, the formulation of an extensive series of related and precise statements about social events. Taking this goal as given, he argues that we should begin by constructing theories with limited coverage whose empirical reliability can be established at the outset. In due course gradual synthesis of these special theories will produce a relatively comprehensive theory with firm empirical foundations. This middle-range strategy is, Merton argues, by no means the only conceivable way of building a general theory, but it is the most efficient because it ensures that each special theory makes an empirically supported contribution which, although likely to be modified as new theoretical ideas and new facts emerge, is never entirely wasted.

If this middle-range strategy is to operate effectively, the piecemeal formulation of unrelated theories must be kept to a minimum. Merton sees this problem, but is unable to adopt the obvious solution of linking special theories together by means of general theoretical assumptions, for his strategy is designed explicitly to eliminate such assumptions. He decides instead to devise a *method* of investigation which involves few substantive implications. This method is stated in the paradigm for functional analysis which Merton derives from a critique of the theoretical principles of certain social anthropologists who had earlier tried to implement in their field a theoretical strategy similar to his own.

In the course of this critique, virtually all the theoretical presuppositions of the anthropologists are abandoned, and along with them any possibility of an overall model of the social system. After having adopted a middle-range strategy, Merton is unable consistently to make any definite statements about the general character of human society. Functional analysis, when combined with a middle-range strategy, becomes merely the search for the objective consequences of recurrent social activities without prejudgment as to whether these consequences will be positive or negative, intended or unintended, relevant to the wider society or not.

The application of the functional paradigm by Merton to a variety of restricted empirical areas has stimulated a great deal of research. Nevertheless, Merton's approach, as an overall theoretical strategy, is not entirely successful. For his theoretical analyses, although limited in scope, are not rigorous theories on a small scale, but rather speculative interpretations designed to provide guide-lines for further more detailed research. Until this research is undertaken and its findings expressed in the form of empirically precise deductive systems, the middle-range strategy is no more demonstrably effective than that of Pareto or Parsons.

One difficulty with the notion of middle-range theory is that it is a residual category; and residual categories are typically susceptible to further sub-division. Merton's definition of middle-range theory is no exception. For a middle-range theory is any conceptualization or interpretation which is less than a comprehensive theoretical system yet more than a mere undeveloped hypothesis. Consequently, such theories can be pitched at many different levels of empirical complexity and theoretical generality. Furthermore, they can vary from a non-explanatory typology to a genuine attempt at systematic deduction. There is, therefore, no guarantee that use of a middle-range strategy will bring either clarity of empirical referents or simplicity of theoretical conceptions. Certain relatively narrow studies may achieve these aims, while other, equally middle-range, analyses fail to cope effectively with their more complex material. It is quite misleading of Merton to argue that his strategy necessarily combines theoretical interpretation with empirical reliability. For even within the limits of the middle-range approach, a choice must often be made between empirical precision and theoretical significance. And Merton in practice, just like Pareto and Parsons, chooses on the whole to relinquish precision in order to deal with problems which he regards as theoretically important. Thus in most instances Merton's strategy is used to formulate broad theoretical sketches which require considerable modification and empirical specification before they can be used as the reliable basis for a general theory of society.

Merton's strategy, unlike that of Parsons, does not preclude attempts at explanation. And the functional paradigm is in fact regularly used to formulate loosely explanatory analyses. These explanations are seldom entirely satisfactory, owing to conceptual ambiguity. Yet even if we regard Merton's analyses as no more than proto-theories, we would expect them to have a logically consistent and distinctly functional form. In practice, the logical form of Merton's explanations is somewhat confused, partly because no attempt is made to link the functional paradigm explicitly to the task of drawing deductive inferences and partly because Merton abandons those assumptions about negative feedback and maintenance of end-states which alone make functional explanations logically appropriate. In practice he offers two distinct types of explanation without himself distinguishing between them. In some studies he tries to demonstrate simply that certain items have observable consequences. But no attempt is made to show that these consequences feed back upon the original items. Consequently, Merton appears to be providing a straightforward causal analysis of the form: If we observe X, then we will observe its consequence, Y. There is no reason to regard this kind of explanation as functional. In other studies Merton comes closer to the functional form. But these analyses require to be supplemented by explicit recognition of exchange processes. Unfortunately, Merton himself makes little use of the notion of social exchange. Thus Merton fails to use the functional paradigm to generate logically acceptable functional explanations of sociological data.

Merton's brand of functional analysis does not eliminate those conceptual defects which vitiate Parsonian theory. Despite the attempt to lower the level of abstraction, gaps persist between theoretical statements and empirical data. Furthermore, Merton's theoretical preludes indicate that functional explanations are difficult to formulate successfully in sociology. In the schemes of both Merton and Parsons, however, there is a slight but definite indication that these conceptual and explanatory deficiencies can be reduced, although certainly not eradicated, by the introduction of some version of exchange analysis. But systematic development of the notion of social exchange is not easily reconciled with a strong commitment to the functional perspective. Accordingly, this task is left to Homans, who begins, however, not by rejecting the content of functional theories, but by repudiating the accompanying strategy of theoretical preparation.

Homans maintains that both Parsons and Merton misunderstand the true nature of scientific theory. He suggests that they err in regarding a theory as no more than a series of interrelated concepts and that, as a result, they are unable to furnish acceptable explanations. In his own view, Homans differs from the two functional theorists in appreciating more fully that a theory is composed of a number of deductively arranged propositions and that the first and last task of theory is to provide empirically precise deductions. There is undoubtedly a genuine divergence here between Homans and the functionalists. It is not, however, as the former supposes, a difference over the logical structure of theories, but a difference of opinion about theoretical strategy. Both functionalists, in fact, agree with Homans that a proper theory is made up of propositions formulated in terms of a conceptual framework, and they share with him the long-term objective of creating a comprehensive system of explanatory propositions for sociology. But in the functionalists' view such a theoretical system will not emerge without a great deal of preparation, much of which will contribute only indirectly to the completion of the long-term project. Homans seems not to understand that Parsons and Merton are primarily engaged in such theoretical preliminaries. This misunderstanding appears to arise because, for Homans, the only way to produce a satisfactory theory is to engage actively in the construction of a deductive system.

Homans' conception of theory and theoretical strategy is essentially the same as Pareto's—that is, to construct inductively a system of generalizations which can be tested and refined by means of deduction. The abstractions of structural-functionalism are rejected as inappropriate for this strategy. Their empirical referents are too complex for the reliable formulation of universal generalizations. Homans is, consequently, forced to devise a series of simpler terms. It is conceivable that, even after his drastic conceptual innovations, Homans could continue with some form of functionalism. But he is convinced that functional analysis requires phenomena to be explained by their consequences, either for the total system or for other system units, and that this is logically inadmissible. Accordingly, Homans abandons the functional perspective and, using a method of analysis closely resembling Pareto's cycles of interdependence, concentrates on producing a classic series of empirical generalizations modelled on those used in the physical sciences.

Having constructed inductively a series of generalizations, Homans turns to the task of completing the theoretical scheme by the formulation of a smaller number of higher-level principles, from which the generalizations can be deduced and in accordance with which they can be refined. In the light of the analysis which accompanies the inductive survey, he decides that it is appropriate to take over and modify certain exchange propositions from economics and psychology. He argues that his empirical generalizations and a wide range of additional sociological data can be inferred from these principles of social exchange and that they provide concise expression of the regularities underlying a great deal of social life. The principles are tested, in Homans' view successfully, by the deduction of various research findings and by occasional attempts at prediction. In this way Homans produces a theory made up of propositions at several levels of generality, which is built up more or less inductively and which is capable of generating empirically relevant deductions.

Homans' theory succeeds in avoiding some of the deficiencies of functional analysis. Thus the logically questionable procedure of explaining phenomena by their consequences is dropped, whilst most of the big abstractions of structural functionalism are abandoned. Furthermore, Homans goes further than Parsons in *using* his concepts to construct a deductive system which can in principle predict and explain, and further than Merton in formulating a *relatively coherent series* of related propositions. Nevertheless, despite these theoretical gains, Homans' scheme is far from satisfactory.

The fundamental defect of Homans' theory is its conceptual inadequacy. His analyses, of course, often achieve face-validity. But this is largely because he uses many of the everyday terms with which we ordinarily converse. Close inspection of Homans' concepts shows them to be hardly less indeterminate than those of Parsons or Pareto. For example, the content of his terms is so ill-defined that the same data are sometimes used as empirical referents for both factors in a proposition, thereby making such propositions vacuous. Because the conceptual framework is so imprecise, the attempt at deductive validation amounts to no more than a loose and intuitive reinterpretation of research findings. A more convincing validation is impossible without considerably greater conceptual rigour. Furthermore, Homans is able to construct a deductive system at all only by applying Paretian tactics of simplification and selection to such an extent that he offers not a theory of society, but a theory of behavioural variations occurring within given social contexts. Where Pareto deals with cultural variation by treating it as a theoretically insignificant by-product of basic impulses, Homans accepts that it influences the elementary processes of exchange, but allows it to enter his deductive scheme only as an unproblematic given. Homans' strategy, although facilitating a limited advance over the functionalists in terms of theoretical structure, produces a pronounced narrowing of theoretical content.

Although Homans' strategy produces neither a general sociological theory nor even a rigorous theory of limited range, it does foster a perspective on society which differs markedly from that of the functionalists. The initial decision to formulate a series of universal generalizations inductively leads Homans to search for a conceptual apparatus composed of simple terms representing single classes of direct observations. The resulting scheme necessarily focuses on directly observable interaction in small groups. Interaction itself is perceived as being governed by participants' values and resources, and by the transactions whereby values are exchanged. From this point of departure a series of propositions is formed which depicts the structure of small groups as developing out of and as being constantly renewed and modified by face-to-face interaction. Large social aggregates are regarded as differing only in so far as exchange processes are more complex and indirect.

Thus societies are to be conceived not so much as systems with relatively stable structures which direct the activities of participants in appropriate ways, but as organized patterns of interaction which, although constraining individual action are themselves continuously subject to pressures generated in face-to-face situations. This model of society resembles that of Pareto in viewing the organization of complex social systems as a derivative of certain variable characteristics of individuals engaged in interaction. But in Homans' scheme this model is not fully developed and, in fact, becomes less evident as Homans comes increasingly to take as given the social context of direct exchange. It is left to Blau to complete the picture of society strongly implicit in Homans' work.

Blau depicts social life as operating at two broad levels of complexity—that of direct and that of indirect exchange. The analysis offered of direct exchange in microstructures closely resembles the account given by Homans, although more attention is paid to the way in which relatively stable networks of social associations grow out of and are continuously affected by interpersonal transactions. Blau stresses that out of interpersonal exchange emerge phenomena, such as power and status hierarchies, which are characteristics of collectivities rather than of individual participants. In his view, the main task of sociology is to show how these emergent phenomena are produced by the processes of exchange between individual men.

The analysis of macrostructures is less clearly deductive than that of microstructures. Although it is maintained that networks of indirect exchange develop out of simpler transactions, no attempt is made to infer the characteristics of macrostructures from propositions about interpersonal behaviour. Instead, Blau points out certain analogues between the two levels while at the same time delineating the features which distinguish macrostructures. This conceptualization of the wider social context within which direct exchange takes place allows Blau to examine the dynamic interdependence between the two levels, in a way hinted at but not developed by Homans. But this successful conceptual extension of the exchange framework is achieved only because Blau is not committed to the pursuit of a consistent theoretical strategy.

Blau is the only theorist examined in this study who fails to formulate a definite strategical policy. He does state that he is constructing a theoretical prolegomenon, but this term is so vague as to leave him effectively free of strategical constraints. The very elasticity of the strategy does make possible the combination, in a provocative fashion, of a wide range of theoretical content which hitherto appeared irreconcilable. But it produces no improvement in scientific rigour. Blau's work, like that of his predecessors, consists of a series of concepts, typologies and broad propositions which are only loosely linked to observable events.

Exchange theory, then, is no more satisfactory as a theory than functionalism. Blau would probably claim in its defence that exchange theory can conceptualize more systematically and convincingly such problem areas as power and radical social change, which have always proved recalcitrant to functional analysis. But if we accept this argument, we are not choosing that scheme which we see as providing a rigorous deductive system. We are instead favouring that framework which is conceptually more comprehensive and well-articulated. Parsons, of course, argues all along that these are the kinds of theoretical criteria which must be applied at present in sociology. If we are driven back to Parsons' position after having considered Homans' attempt to replace functionalism with a fully explanatory approach, it adds support to the original functionalist thesis that at the moment it is premature to strive for the Paretian type of logico-deductive system. The very failure of the exchange framework to achieve its initial objectives adds weight to the functionalist assertion that sociological theory should be concerned, not with actually putting together a comprehensive deductive system, but with the conceptual and methodological preliminaries to this task.

In support of this contention, much historical evidence can be cited to show that a stage of theoretical and conceptual preparation tends to occur early in the development of scientific disciplines. Thus Toulmin summarizes in the following words the findings of a survey of intellectual growth in the physical sciences:

> If the growth of science has had a number of phases demanding quite different methods of work, that should not surprise us. For the business of science involves more than the mere assembly of facts: it demands also intellectual architecture and construction. Before the actual building comes the collection of materials; before that, the detailed work at the drawing-board; before that, the conception of a design; and, before that even, there comes the bare recognition of possibilities. No wonder science has included, and must include, much *a priori* study of possible forms of theory,

developed without immediate regard to the particular facts of Nature.

Unless these possible forms of theory are eventually applied to explain the actual course of events, our *a priori* studies will of course bear no positive scientific fruit. Yet they are a part, and a legitimate part, of scientific enquiry now as in previous centuries.[1]

Toulmin refers, for example, to the conceptual elaborations of the medieval scholastics as theoretical contributions without which Galileo's achievement in physics would have been inconceivable. If we accept that a period in which attention is focused on an empirically tenuous exploration of possibilities is essential for later more rigorous scientific growth, then we must also accept that the scholasticism of Parsons[2] and, to varying degrees, the other theorists discussed above, may well prove to be fruitful theoretical preparation. Yet, as Toulmin himself stresses, sooner or later a strategy must be devised which establishes a reliable link between theory and observation. In the course of the next section I will outline a strategy designed to facilitate the use of existing theoretical resources, as well as new ideas, in detailed empirical research.

II

Now that the strategical dialectic has been followed through a full cycle, it is possible to consider whether there is any evidence of scientific advance. In this connection it is clear beyond doubt that, if theoretical progress has occurred, it has fallen far short of producing an acceptable general theory. None of the schemes under discussion satisfy the more rigorous criteria of theoretical adequacy. It is pointless, therefore, to make our criteria of scientific advance too demanding. Consequently, in order to estimate the degree of scientific growth, I shall merely pose the following relatively crude questions: Is there any indication of improved empirical specification since the time of Pareto? Has there been an increase in the conceptual resources current in sociological theory? To what extent are there signs of theoretical agreement? There are other indices of scientific advance which could have been examined. Nevertheless, these simple questions are adequate for my present purposes. For if we could give a clear affirmative to these questions we should have demonstrated the existence of a definite movement toward theoretical maturity in sociology. I shall argue, however, that evidence of improved theoretical preparation is sparse and indicates, at best, only marginal gains.

Since Pareto's day there has been a considerable accumulation of empirical data, and some of the more recent schemes discussed above utilize this body of increasingly detailed empirical information. For example, recent empirical studies are used in Homans' inductive survey and in the attempts of both exchange theorists to test certain of their propositions against experimental findings. This reference to an increasingly wide range of empirical material, it might be urged, is an unambiguous indication of theoretical improvement. Yet the theoretical use of these data has been far from satisfactory. The more general schemes of Parsons and Blau make very selective use of available data and many of their speculations are proposed with no more than passing factual illustration, whilst the work of Homans and Merton achieves a higher level of empirical content mainly by means of a restriction of theoretical scope. Even Merton, despite his severe limitation of abstract speculation, sacrifices empirical precision in order to retain an interest in theoretically significant issues. To appreciate the true character of recent developments in sociological theory it is necessary to distinguish between, on the one hand, the quantity of data referred to in the construction and testing of theory and, on the other hand, the empirical specification of theoretical terms. Only the latter indicates theoretical maturity and, unfortunately, although sociologists have access to an increasing range of empirical findings this material has not been used to provide firm empirical content for even the most modest of recent theoretical analyses.

The imprecise nature of sociological theory has been demonstrated so frequently above that it requires no further documentation. Yet it may still be argued that there has been a marked increase in 'conceptual richness' and that this signifies a definite move toward scientific maturity, despite the ambiguities of this increasingly complex conceptual apparatus. The discussion in earlier chapters provides much support for this argument. Thus whereas Pareto's scheme is conceptually simplistic and relies greatly on notions taken over with only slight modification from the physical sciences, the four subsequent theorists build up a wide-ranging series of terms designed specifically to depict the complexities of social life. In so far as growth of conceptual resources is a requisite for scientific advance in sociology, there appears to have been a *potential* theoretical improvement. However, it is only too easy to introduce new terms whilst the propositions which they furnish are not clear enough to be tested. Conclusive demonstration that the conceptual innovations since Pareto constitute a scientific advance must await their use in the formulation of empirically and logically rigorous deductions. It is impossible to reach any rational decision about the scientific value of such a conceptual increment until clear deductions begin to emerge.

A further argument exists, however, to strengthen the claim that sociological theory is becoming increasingly mature. For in the last few years it has frequently been asserted, not simply that the conceptual resources of the discipline have been gradually extended, but also that there are growing signs of a broad theoretical agreement. Recent work in the history of science, particularly that of Kuhn,[3] indicates that theoretical consensus is often a useful index of scientific maturity. Consequently, if a theoretical *rapprochement* were evident in sociology, it would furnish support for the claim that recent theoretical developments are likely to prove productive, despite their current lack of rigour. This claim closely resembles Parsons' thesis, put forward in the 1930s, that there was then a convergence toward a theory of social action which promised imminent and important theoretical improvements. We have seen that this argument is based on false premises and that it has been belied, not only by Parsons' use of functional and exchange concepts to supplement the original social action framework, but also by the scheme's failure, after thirty years of development, to show any clear sign of theoretical fruition. I suggest that recent assertions of theoretical convergence in sociology are no more indicative of theoretical maturation than were those of Parsons.

The discussion in previous chapters has shown that there is at the moment no emergent theoretical synthesis, in the sense of the formulation within separate perspectives of validated generalizations which have been demonstrated to be supplementary. If there has been a convergence, it has taken some other form. The following quotation, taken from an attempt to reconcile structural-functionalism and conflict theory, shows what the proponents of the convergence thesis have in mind:

> Functionalism and the Hegelian-Marxian dialect each stress one of two essential aspects of social reality, and are thus complementary to one another. My procedure will be to examine in turn the basic postulates of functionalism and the Hegelian-Marxian dialectic, show the limitations of *each theory* as a complete *model of society* . . . and finally by retaining and modifying elements of the *two approaches*, search for a *unified theory*.[4]

The most obvious characteristic of this statement and the ensuing argument is that it is undertaken at a level of abstraction even higher than that of Parsons in *The Structure of Social Action*. For instance, functionalism is treated as a relatively unified theoretical perspective consisting of six or seven basic postulates, and differences among the various adherents of functional analysis are ignored.[5] Furthermore, no attempt is made to distinguish between a theory, a model of society and a theoretical approach. Arguments as broad as this are not intended to demonstrate genuine theoretical convergence, but merely to establish that certain basic theoretical presumptions, in this case from functionalism and 'Marxian theory', are not necessarily contradictory. Even if we were to accept the arguments presented, they would provide no evidence of theoretical maturity. For the analyst is striving for no more than a preliminary clarification of underlying principles as a preparatory step towards the eventual construction of a general theory of society. The fact that such discussions are still required in sociology and are regarded as useful contributions to theoretical development, is a clear indication of a lack of scientific maturity rather than a sign of imminent maturation.

Blau's scheme could be cited as a more convincing example of substantive theoretical convergence, for it does bring together within a single framework notions from structural-functionalism and exchange analysis, and uses them in a way which closely resembles certain versions of 'conflict theory', particularly that of Dahrendorf. But although Blau does achieve at least a preliminary synthesis of several previously separate theoretical perspectives, it would be misleading to regard this as a sign of increasing theoretical maturity; for Blau attains this theoretical reconciliation only by abandoning any attempt at consistency of theoretical structure and by using a conceptual apparatus which is neither clearly defined nor well articulated. It appears, therefore, that present-day claims for a theoretical synthesis in sociology are no more justified than was that of Parsons thirty years ago and no more acceptable as a reliable index of scientific maturity. We must agree with Bottomore, who, in the course of a much wider review of the literature than that undertaken here, decides that 'There is not, at the present time, any general body of sociological theory which has been validated or widely accepted'.[6]

It is difficult to demonstrate conclusively the occurrence of a theoretical advance either in relation to empirical specification, conceptual richness or theoretical synthesis. No matter which of these theoretical facets is explored, we find claims of improvement vitiated by the same major deficiency—namely, the failure to provide clear and consistent empirical content for theoretical terms. There are certainly signs of increased documentation, of conceptual growth and of conceptual reconciliation. But it is impossible to estimate the scientific value of these developments until theoretical statements can be compared unambiguously with observable events. So far not even exchange analysis, which initially appeared so promising, has begun to produce results of this kind.

Empirical specification of terms is, as Pareto emphasizes, a requisite for any significant form of theoretical development. Consequently, it appears that empirical specification is the fundamental problem upon which theoretical strategy in sociology has foundered. In the rest of this section I shall make some suggestions for improving the empirical specification of general sociological theory and, generally, for making theoretical strategy more productive.

Merton's strategy of retreating from broad theoretical speculation in order to promote, instead, limited analyses with relatively clear empirical referents is a direct response to the problem of empirical specification and to the failure of prior theory to find a solution. But, as we have seen, this decision to lower the level of abstraction produces no conclusive gain in conceptual precision.[7] None the less, I suggest that Merton is substantially correct, first, in recognizing that general theorists can neither undertake sufficiently comprehensive inductive surveys nor remain in close touch with an increasingly complex body of factual data; and, secondly, in deciding that the only way of giving detailed theoretical expression to these data is by constructing a series of special theories. If conceptual indeterminacy is brought about by the complexity of empirical material, it should be possible to increase conceptual precision by reducing the range of theoretical interpretation. It must be accepted, however, that this reaction to the central problem of sociological theory, although a reasoned response, can no more be justified conclusively in advance than any other theoretical strategy. In addition, it must be recognized that the middle-range strategy has not yet been vindicated by successful implementation and that it appears to be necessary to lower the level of abstraction further than does Merton.

Although the middle-range strategy promises to reduce the extent of the divorce between theory and research, in comparison with the strategies of Pareto, Parsons and Blau, Merton's failure to achieve an unequivocal conceptual improvement indicates that rigorous special theories are unlikely to emerge in the near future. There is still a great deal of exploration and preparation to be undertaken at this level. Yet if we presume that a fairly comprehensive sociological theory is possible in principle, then special theories must also be possible and, in view of the relative simplicity of their data, comparatively easy to construct. The attempt to merge various isolated hypotheses with the findings of empirical research at low levels of generality may be an *inefficient* way of constructing a wide-ranging theory. There may be alternative procedures which would produce the same result more quickly and with less effort. But it seems unlikely that it can be permanently ineffective, unless sociological data are simply not amenable to scientific interpretation. Thus I shall presume from now on that a general theory of society is likely to emerge, if at all, out of the gradual synthesis of numerous special theories.

Although Merton's formulation of the middle-range strategy is correct, as far as it goes, it is nevertheless incomplete. Concentration on relatively concrete analyses does not eliminate the need for theoretical activity at higher levels of abstraction. Merton himself does not advocate that general theory be entirely abandoned. In fact, he states clearly that there should be 'an enduring and pervasive concern with *consolidating* the special theories into a more general set of concepts and mutually consistent propositions'.[8] However, he makes no positive recommendations about how this consolidation ought to be effected, nor does he stress that such consolidation itself entails theoretical analysis beyond the middle-range level. To some extent, Merton intends to foster theoretical synthesis by the use of his functional paradigm. But we have seen that the paradigm is logically suspect and that its substantive assumptions about the general nature of human society are insufficient to promote the convergence of empirically separate analyses. Some other method must, therefore, be devised whereby numerous restricted theoretical preludes can be consolidated. Furthermore, Merton's strategy makes no mention of the need to bring to bear upon the problems of middle-range theory those broad speculations which, as Toulmin shows, often contribute invaluably to intellectual growth. This is surprising in view of the fact that many of Merton's own analyses depend on the conceptions of more speculative theorists. It appears, therefore, that the middle-range strategy must provide for the formulation and refinement of relatively general conceptions and for their productive use in diverse areas of research. Consequently, I suggest that there are at least two and possibly three theoretical activities which must be deliberately undertaken, yet which cannot be carried out effectively at the middle-range level. These are the search for theoretical synthesis, the provision of theoretical guidance, and the promotion of extensive theoretical innovation.

Large numbers of separate analyses will never merge into one unified theory unless there exists a class of specialists which regards theoretical synthesis as its special province. If most theoretical work in sociology is to be done at the various middle-range levels, it must be the task of the general theorist to seek reconciliation among these restricted analyses at a more inclusive level and, in the light of prior theory, to try to modify and refine such analyses. Merton's middle-range strategy, if supplemented in this way, implies the establishment of active interdependence between general and special theory. While each middle-range interpretation would aim at rigorous treatment of a limited range of empirical data, the general theorist would be concerned with moving gradually toward a unified and comprehensive theory in the course of a series of critical dialogues with more specialized contributors.

At the same time, general theory should provide theoretical guidance in the light of considerations and information beyond the purview of those immersed in the detail of special theory. It should, for example, construct a reservoir of critically evaluated theoretical resources for use in specific substantive fields. To some extent this relationship between general and middle-range theory exists already. We have seen, for instance, that much of Merton's analysis in *Social Structure and Anomie* derives from the work of more speculative theorists, such as Durkheim and Parsons. I suggest, however, that the provision of concepts and analytical advice should become an explicit part of general theoretical strategy. Furthermore, because there is a danger of middle-range theory developing in a piecemeal and unsystematic manner, these contributions should encourage theoretical co-ordination. If a general theory is to grow out of middle-range analysis, the general theorist must help, not only by extracting hypotheses for more general formulation, but also by trying to co-ordinate developments within various special areas of study.

In suggesting these additions to Merton's middle-range approach I am, in effect, recommending a new theoretical strategy. This strategy could not, at the moment, be associated with any one theoretical perspective, for one of its major justifications would be its capacity to allow the more specialized theorist considerable freedom of thought, whilst at the same time furnishing necessary theoretical support at a more general level. Such a policy of theoretical eclecticism would assist the development of conceptual precision by reducing the tendency to fit recalcitrant data into a narrow set of existing categories. The theoretical content of any particular analysis would be determined more by the empirical problems discovered there and by the theoretical creativity of those involved than by pre-established notions. This creativity would be encouraged by the general theorist, who would be concerned to foster new ideas, for example, by pointing out resemblances between empirical and theoretical developments in separate fields. In this way the present strategy would promote theoretical fertility by increasing cross-fertilization among sociological specialties.[9]

The middle-range approach, although necessary to encourage close contact between theory and empirical research, is incomplete as a means of building a general theory of society. Merton, of course, has always been aware of this. Not only does he advocate a continual search for theoretical consolidation, but he also designs the functional paradigm as a means whereby distinct analyses can share the same theoretical form. I am suggesting, however, that verbal support of the search for theoretical synthesis is not enough and that the functional paradigm makes no effective contribution to this end. If middle-range analysis is to be consolidated, it must be supplemented by theoretically uncommitted work at higher levels of generality in accordance with a definite policy. This policy should be to offer theoretical assistance in numerous special areas of study, to draw attention to the relevance of findings in each specialty for other sociological specialties with the aim of fostering theoretical innovation, and to formulate any general schemes which begin to emerge. For the sake of convenience, I shall call this policy of trying explicitly to reconcile general and middle-range theory the 'preparatory strategy'. In order to clarify its distinctive features and its potential advantages, I shall compare it in turn with the inductive-deductive strategy, the categorial strategy, and Blau's loosely structured approach.

We have examined two variants of the inductive-deductive strategy. As applied by Pareto, it consists of a relatively extended survey of historical material, followed by the formulation of a series of psychological generalizations which are used to explain and predict a wide variety of social events. This approach encounters several intractable difficulties. The coverage of the inductive survey, for instance, is inevitably inadequate as the basis for a general theory and, in the search for coverage, the quality of data tends to suffer. The crudity of the empirical material and of the accompanying analytical techniques necessitate the use of an exceptionally simple conceptual apparatus, which can be reconciled with the apparent diversity of social events only by making concepts and hypotheses highly inclusive and, consequently, vague. Conceptual ambiguity in turn leads to conceptual inconsistency, logical error and analytical confusion; and as theoretical statements become increasingly vacuous so it becomes necessary to disguise their empirical irrelevance by abandoning the basic scientific rule requiring systematic provision of evidence. The end-product is a scheme which, instead of opening up new problems for detailed investigation, achieves a spurious theoretical closure.[10] These are defects to which the preparatory strategy appears to be less exposed.

In the first place, the preparatory strategy would provide a firmer empirical base by replacing Pareto's single large-scale inductive survey with a series of surveys undertaken within limited substantive areas. In this way, not only would each area be investigated in much greater detail, but there would be more opportunity for designing inductive surveys in accordance with the quality and quantity of data available in each specialty. Secondly, there would be no compulsion to compress this empirical material into the narrow limits of any one comparatively simple theoretical model. Much analysis would in fact take place at what can loosely be called the middle-range level, where theoretical perspectives would be free to vary in accordance with the decisions of the specialists concerned. The tasks of the general theorist would be to search for genuine convergences and interrelations between the various special analyses, to try to express and develop these analytical connections in relatively general form, and to seek out and formulate theoretical-empirical problems at various levels of generality in ways which would promote further research. Thirdly, although the preparatory strategy would hardly avoid inconsistencies and ambiguities, one of its central aims would be to guide sociological analysis at middle-range levels towards greater clarity and empirical specification of theoretical notions. At the very least, by avoiding Pareto's policy of radical selection and simplification, it would be less predisposed toward theoretical indeterminacy. Fourthly, the preparatory strategy would differ from the inductive-deductive strategy most notably in its recognition that theoretical closure should not be a primary objective during a period of theoretical preparation. Pareto achieves closure by developing a method of analysis whereby any social event can be interpreted as a direct or indirect by-product of the circulation of political élites. The preparatory strategy, instead of eliminating empirical problems in this way, would concentrate on fostering new ideas—for example, by pointing out similarities and inconsistencies between separate but related middle-range analyses. In short, whereas Pareto's inductive-deductive strategy sacrifices theoretical rigour, theoretical fertility and full recognition of empirical complexity in order to construct a formally mature theoretical structure, the preparatory strategy reverses these priorities, placing little immediate value on theoretical structure and emphasizing the need for theoretical flexibility and fertility.

Homans' use of the inductive-deductive strategy differs from that of Pareto in that the immediate construction of a comprehensive theory is regarded as out of the question. But for Homans there is only one alternative approach, and that is the formulation of a deductive system which, although of limited dimensions, is broad enough to furnish a firm base for the erection of a fully general theory. Consequently, Homans restricts his inductive survey and his attempts at deduction to the realm of elementary social behaviour. The task of constructing a comprehensive theory is put off until after the successful completion of a theory devoted to the simpler data of direct interaction. Unfortunately, the original long-term theoretical objective is eventually forgotten or abandoned. As he completes his analysis of direct interaction, Homans comes to regard the great mass of sociological data as unproblematic. In this way Homans, like Pareto, achieves theoretical closure and an appearance of relative theoretical maturity, but at the cost of ignoring most classes of sociological data. Furthermore, despite its narrow empirical range and its formal maturity, Homans' scheme does not avoid reliance on a policy of radical selectivity and simplification. The result once again is conceptual vagueness and inconsistency and the usual difficulties of empirical specification.

Homans' modified version of the inductive-deductive strategy, because it requires drastic conceptual selectivity and simplification, because its associated theoretical content is indeterminate, and because it dismisses from consideration so much empirical material, appears hardly more promising than that of Pareto as a positive preparation for general theory. Like Pareto's approach, it seems likely to be inferior to the preparatory strategy in relation to empirical range, empirical detail, inductive support, and in its capacity for guiding and linking together many levels of sociological investigation. It may be argued, however, that Homans' scheme has at least been theoretically fertile. It has stimulated the formulation of Blau's more general version of exchange analysis and has, in this way, shown itself to be a potentially fruitful contribution to general theory. Yet, although there can be no doubt that Homans' efforts have helped promote Blau's interesting speculations, Homans' theoretical *strategy* actually hinders this extension of exchange theory. For Homans' insistence on constructing nothing less than a deductive system forces him to regard complex social structures as unproblematic and, thereby, prevents him from developing the implications of his own analysis with respect to social macrostructures. The effect of Homans' strategy is clearly demonstrated by the fact that Blau is able to furnish a relatively general prolegomenon only after abandoning Homans' strategy. Blau succeeds in extending the content of exchange analysis because he recognizes that the preparation for a general theory of society cannot proceed according to the dictates of the inductive-deductive strategy.

Parsons is strongly aware that a general theory of society can be constructed only after extensive theoretical preparation at a high level of generality and that the inductive-deductive strategy is inappropriate for this purpose. He recognizes the tendency toward oversimplification and conceptual ambiguity built into the latter strategy, and tries to devise an alternative approach which combines greater theoretical complexity with conceptual clarity and completeness. Parsons' solution, the categorial strategy, assumes that a satisfactory inductive base has been provided by prior research, and proceeds to work out systematically and consistently the conceptual ramifications of a small number of supposedly established theoretical presumptions. This strategy, however, is based on two inconsistent estimates of the level of scientific maturity reached by prior theory. On the one hand, the strategy of categorial preparation is required because existing theory is empirically suspect and vague. On the other hand, the strategy is likely to succeed to the extent that the basic notions taken over from previous theories are sufficiently precise and empirically well-founded to make detailed specification possible. Parsons does not resolve this dilemma. Consequently, as we have seen, his conceptual elaborations degenerate into theoretical formalism.

Parsonian categorial analysis is inadequate as a theoretical preparation because it creates and perpetuates a gap between available empirical data and the abstract notions of general theory. Merton correctly diagnoses this fault and tries to counter it by stressing the need for middle-range interpretations closely linked to actual observation of social events. But Merton fails to realize that, because middle-range 'theories' can be formulated at many levels of generality, theoretical maturity and interconnectedness continued theoretical analysis at the most general level is essential if these separate interpretations are to grow together into an eventual synthesis. The preparatory strategy alone combines the strong emphasis on empirical specification in middle-range analyses advocated by Merton with the theoretical guidance for all specialties and continuous concern with theoretical synthesis so important to Parsons and so necessary for the development of sociology.

The preparatory strategy is a more flexible method of theoretical preparation than the categorial approach, thereby making possible a closer contact with empirical research. In the first place, it does not rely on one inductive survey of prior theory, but attempts to build up and revise regularly its theoretical notions on the basis of a continual scrutiny of middle-level analyses. Moreover, it does not presume that all sociological specialties are at similar levels of development and in need of the same type of theoretical treatment. Accordingly, the preparatory strategy allows the general theorist freedom, for example, to codify the findings in one field into a tentative deductive system whilst, in other areas, offering no more than broad suggestions about which variables should be investigated. In this way the preparatory strategy can be adapted to the quality and quantity of existing data. Furthermore, this flexibility extends to theoretical content. For the preparatory strategy presents no barriers to the use of divergent concepts and models in the study of different aspects of social life. Parsons, in combining within one scheme several divergent terminologies, appears to adopt the same tactic. But he is forced by the requirements of his strategy, not only to limit this conceptual variation, but also to define each conceptual innovation so that it can ultimately be derived from the original action framework.[11] The preparatory strategy differs in allowing flexibility of content with no need for *a priori* justification. Each variation is to be judged more by its empirical rigour and theoretical fertility than its concordance with pre-established assumptions.

Several of the strategies we have discussed serve, at a relatively general level, to guide, synthesize and stimulate sociological thought. But all have important defects brought about by strategical rigidity. Thus the commitment of the inductive-deductive strategy to the immediate construction of a mature theoretical structure leads to inductive unreliability, extreme selectivity and over-simplification. Similar deficiencies are produced by the inability of the categorial strategy either to jettison basic preconceptions taken over from prior theory or to establish reciprocal interdependence with more empirically grounded studies. The flexibility of the preparatory strategy promises some relief from these deficiencies. In the first place, the preparatory strategy makes possible the provision of a more satisfactory inductive base. This is because it does not rely on a single inductive survey, but attempts to revise its content as new research leads to theoretical modifications at middle-range levels. In this way general theory remains in regular, although indirect, contact with basic empirical material and the dangers of conceptual formalism are partially averted. It is not, of course, intended that general theory should become a mere amalgam of special theories, for general theory would endeavour to bring to bear its own theoretical heritage as well as trying to refine and generalize from lower-level innovations. Secondly, the preparatory strategy, because it is committed neither to a particular kind of theoretical structure nor to a uniform model of society, is able to recognize all the empirical complexities revealed by a detailed investigation. Moreover, while it does not force unsuitable material into a deductive strait-jacket, it does not dismiss the possibility of crude explanation and predictions in the more theoretically advanced areas. Thirdly, the preparatory strategy is peculiarly fitted to ensure theoretical growth. For it is designed to promote theoretical innovation through the cross-fertilization of ideas between separate specialties while at the same time searching for genuine theoretical convergences and seeking to develop generally applicable theoretical schemes. In short, the preparatory strategy would contribute toward a wide-ranging sociological theory by guiding, stimulating and synthesizing the great variety of special analyses in accordance with a policy of theoretical and strategical eclecticism; and if such a theory is impossible, the strategy would at least make valuable contributions to some of the various sociological specialties. The products of this strategy are unlikely to be theoretically symmetrical, but they are likely to reflect more accurately than previous general theory the real state of development of the discipline of sociology.

Of the strategies which we have examined in operation, that used by Blau most closely resembles the preparatory strategy. Thus Blau's prolegomenon is intended as no more than a preparation for general theory; and although it makes no claim to satisfy the extreme criteria of scientific rigour, it is designed to reduce the gap between theoretical abstraction and empirical material found in Parsonian theory, while achieving greater empirical coverage than that of Homans. To gain these ends, Blau chooses to be strategically undogmatic—that is, he combines a quasi-deductive approach in relation to direct exchange with an analysis of macrostructures which is comparatively primitive. This strategical eclecticism is balanced by a willingness to unite various theoretical perspectives. For example, although primarily an exchange theorist, Blau does not hesitate to introduce structural-functional notions where they seem appropriate. In several ways, then, the flexibility of Blau's implicit strategy parallels that of the preparatory strategy.

To a limited extent this policy of flexibility pays off. For it enables Blau to produce a scheme which, although irregular in structure, provides a fairly comprehensive theoretical model. It is doubtful, however, whether he succeeds in furnishing a framework any better than his predecessors' in terms of empirical precision. Particularly in relation to macrostructures, Blau substitutes passing reference to illustrative material in place of a systematic attempt at empirical specification; and it is, of course, precisely in connection with complex social structures that the problems of empirical specification are most severe and in need of a definite policy. At this level of empirical complexity Blau's strategy differs little from that, advocated by Parsons, of elaborating on basic theoretical assumptions without immediate regard for empirical evidence. The preparatory strategy, however, offers an alternative suggestion—namely, that specification of abstract theoretical speculation be fostered by a continual interplay between general and middle-range theory. If Blau had adopted this approach, he would have coupled his analysis of macrostructures with a systematic examination of less general studies of complex social structures and in particular those which already applied some version of exchange theory. If this had been done, not only would Blau's prolegomenon have gained empirical support and greater empirical clarity, but it would also have provided clearer guidance for future empirical research. Thus a crucial constituent of the preparatory strategy which is absent from Blau's implicit strategy is the idea of a dialogue between general and middle-range theory, a dialogue which both guides and stimulates middle-range analysis whilst clarifying the empirical referents of the more general theoretical conceptions.

Blau neither states his strategy in detail nor attempts to justify it. We are, therefore, unable to judge to what extent he condemns the strategies of his predecessors and, accordingly, to what extent he is perpetuating the strategical dialectic. Nevertheless, it is clear that on the whole Blau is following the sociological tradition of theoretical insularity. In other words, he is engaged primarily in a dialogue with other theorists, especially with Parsons and Homans. It is true that Blau's prolegomenon bears definite traces of his earlier middle-range work on formal organizations. But he undertakes no systematic survey of relevant middle-range analyses; and the information acquired at this level is used to construct a scheme intended as a response to the merits and deficiencies of other general theoretical schemes and other general theoretical strategies. It is this aspect of Blau's approach, and indeed of all the strategies we have discussed except that of Merton, that is rejected most strongly by the preparatory strategy. For the latter requires that the interplay between the practitioners of general theory, which has dominated theoretical development in the past, be largely replaced by a deliberate dialogue between general theory and the remainder of the discipline.

Within sociology 'general theory' has become a separate subdiscipline with a relatively autonomous pattern of development.[12] Such intra-disciplinary specialization is not always ineffective. For example, in solid-state physics today there is a clear distinction between 'theoreticians' and 'experimentalists' which, although it sometimes makes communication difficult between the two sets of specialists, has not prevented considerable scientific achievement. But this partial separation between theory and empirical research works effectively in solid-state physics only because theory has already attained high levels of mathematical precision and because techniques for operationalizing theoretical statements have become firmly established. In sociology both precise theoretical statements and generally accepted techniques for translating such statements into unambiguous empirical measurements are lacking. Consequently, the present separation in sociology between the empirical and theoretical realms must be regarded as premature and, because it perpetuates the gap between observation and interpretative speculation, as constituting a major barrier to scientific advance.

The preparatory strategy offers one way of reducing this gap. For it requires general theorists to be closely involved with the work undertaken in a number of empirical areas and to organize their theory in response to the developments occurring there. If this strategy were implemented, sociological theory would inevitably become a less separate specialty and the strategical dialectic would tend to give way to dialogue between general theory, on the one hand, and various less comprehensive specialties, on the other hand, focusing, not on strategical issues, but on problems of theoretical content.

The outline given here of the preparatory strategy is by no means complete. In particular, certain obvious difficulties have been ignored, the most important of these being that of specifying the principles according to which the general theorist would select middle-range analyses for attention. Furthermore, although use of the preparatory strategy has been advocated as a *suitable* response to the deficiencies of existing theory, the inadequacies of previous strategies and the general state of sociology, I have not tried to formulate a conclusive justification. Like any other theoretical strategy, it can only be vindicated by successful application. The preparatory strategy, then, is put forward here in schematic form as a tentative solution to some of the problems underlying that strategical dialectic which has been an effective, though often a misleading, theoretical catalyst in sociology.

Notes

Chapter 1 Introduction

1 See Demerath, N. J., and Peterson, R. A., eds., *System, Change and Conflict*, New York: The Free Press, 1967. This book either reprints or refers to most of the important papers in the debate over functionalism.

Chapter 2 A general theory of society: Pareto

1 Pareto, V., *The Mind and Society*, New York: Dover Publications, Inc., 1963, 5. References throughout are to this two-volume edition of Pareto's *Treatise on General Sociology*.
2 Ibid., 72.
3 Ibid., 56.
4 Ibid., footnote, 1,436.
5 Ibid., 1,435.
6 Ibid,, 1,438.
7 Ibid., 7.
8 Ibid., 87.
9 Ibid., 511.
10 Ibid., 519.
11 Ibid., 598.
12 Ibid., 661.
13 Ibid., 807.
14 Ibid., 1,406.
15 Ibid., 1,406
16 Ibid., 1,407–8.
17 Ibid., 1,419.
18 Ibid., 1,423.
19 Ibid., 1,549, 1,551.
20 Ibid., 1,644.
21 Ibid., 1,735.
22 See Borkenau, F., *Pareto*, London, 1936. This is an excellent appraisal of Pareto's work which provides support for several of the points made below.
23 Pareto, V., op. cit., 7.

24 See Moser, C. A., *Survey Methods in Social Investigation*, London: Heinemann, 1958. It could be argued that, in the formulation of a first theoretical approximation, Pareto need only concern himself with the 'theories' of the social élite which he regards as the most important segment of society. However, this argument *presumes* the validity of Pareto's view of élites, a view which Pareto's strategy requires him to establish on the basis of an unbiased survey of empirical material.
25 For a discussion of residual categories see Parsons, T., *The Structure of Social Action*, New York: McGraw Hill, 1937, ch. 1.
26 Pareto, V., op. cit., 661.
27 Ibid., 1,644.
28 See Pierce, A., 'Empiricism and the Social Sciences', *American Sociological Review*, April 1956.
29 See Braithwaite, R. B., *Scientific Explanation*, London: Cambridge University Press, 1953. The nature of explanation in sociology will be discussed further in subsequent chapters.
30 Pareto, V., op. cit., 1,742.
31 Ibid., 1,744.
32 Ibid., 1,744–5.
33 This is evident throughout ch. XIII of *Mind and Society*. See also Stark, W., *The Fundamental Forms of Social Thought*, London: Routledge, 1962. He maintains—correctly, I think—that ' "residue" is, critically considered, no more than a label affixed to an action after it has been done' (p.134).
34 Pareto, V., op. cit., 1,282–3. Italics added.
35 Parsons, T., *Essays in Sociological Theory*, New York: The Free Press, paperback edition, 1964, 225. Italics added.
36 Ibid., 226.

Chapter 3 Structural-functionalism as a theoretical alternative: Parsons

1 Parsons, T., and Shils, E. A., eds., *Toward a General Theory of Action*, Harvard University Press, 1951, Part II, Introduction. Reference will be made throughout this book to the Harper Torchbook edition, 1962, cited below as *TGA*.
2 Parsons, T., *Essays in Sociological Theory*, New York: The Free Press, 1949, 216. Reference will be made here to the 1964 Free Press paperback edition, cited below as *Essays*.
3 *Essays*, 216.
4 *TGA*, 51.
5 Parsons, T., *The Structure of Social Action*, op. cit. Reference will be made to the 1968 Free Press paperback edition, cited below as *SA*.
6 *TGA*, 50.
7 *Essays*, 215.
8 Ibid., 217.
9 Parsons, like Merton, was influenced by the use of structural-functional analysis in physiology. See Cannon, W. B., *The Wisdom of the Body*, New York: W. W. Norton & Co., 1932, and *Essays*, 218–19.
10 *Essays*, 217–18. Italics added to the phrase 'the only way'.
11 See Durkheim, E., *The Elementary Forms of the Religious Life*, London: Allen & Unwin Ltd., 1915, and Radcliffe-Brown, A. R.,

Structure and Function in Primitive Society, London: Cohen & West Ltd., 1952.
12 *TGA*, 75.
13 Ibid., 7.
14 Durkheim, whose work greatly influenced Parsons, had come to similar conclusions many years earlier. See Durkheim, E., *The Rules of Sociological Method*, The Free Press of Glencoe, 1938, and *SA*, ch. 8–11.
15 See Part 3 of *TGA*, where E. C. Tolman writes about the use of the action framework in psychology; also Parsons, T., 'An Approach to Psychological Theory in Terms of the Theory of Action', in Koch, S., ed., *Psychology, a Study of a Science*, iii, 612–709.
16 See Mead, M., *Sex and Temperament in Three Primitive Societies*, New York: W. Morrow Inc., 1935.
17 Weber, M., *The Theory of Social and Economic Organization*, New York: The Free Press, second edition, 1947, and *SA*, chs. 16, 17.
18 *SA*, 202.
19 *TGA*, Part I, ch. 1.
20 Parsons' use of such terms as 'orderly' and 'systematic' is not intended to imply that social behaviour is never disruptive or chaotic. Thus in *TGA*, p.5, footnote, we find the following statement: 'The word *system* is used in the sense that determinate relations of interdependence exist within the complex of empirical phenomena. The antithesis of the concept of system is random variability. However, no implication of rigidity is intended.' Nevertheless, it has been argued convincingly that, whether intended or not, the implication of rigidity is present in Parsons' work. See Buckley, W., *Sociology and Modern Systems Theory*, Englewood Cliffs, New Jersey: Prentice-Hall, 1967, 23–31. This question will be discussed in section VI of the next chapter.
21 *TGA*, 21.
22 *SA*, 238.
23 *TGA*, 15.
24 Ibid., 24.
25 Parsons, T., *The Social System*, New York: The Free Press, 1951. Reference is made here to the 1964 Free Press paperback edition, p.39, cited below as *SS*.
26 Parsons, T., Shils, E., Naegele, K., and Pitts, J. R., eds., *Theories of Society*, New York: The Free Press, 1963, 39–40. Cited below as *TS*.
27 *TS*, 44.
28 Ibid., 45.
29 See Bales, R. F., *Interaction Process Analysis*, Cambridge, Mass.: Addison-Wesley, 1951.
30 *TGA*, 76.
31 Ibid., 77.
32 Ibid.
33 Ibid.
34 Ibid.
35 Ibid. For later modification of this scheme see Black, M., ed., *The Social Theories of Talcott Parsons*, Englewood Cliffs: Prentice-Hall, 1961, 323–6.
36 Parsons' resistance to exchange theory is expressed most strongly in *SA*, which is an extended critique of utilitarianism, itself a form of exchange theory.

NOTES

37 *TS*, 62.
38 Ibid.
39 Parsons, T., and Smelser, N. J., *Economy and Society*, London: Routledge, 1956, 53.
40 Merton, R. K., Broom, L., and Cottrell, L. S., eds., *Sociology Today*, Harper Torchbooks 1965, 17.
41 Ibid., 20.
42 Ibid.

Chapter 4 An assessment of Parsons' scheme

1 See *Sociology Today*, op. cit., ch. 2.
2 *SS*, 3.
3 *TS*, 30.
4 Black, M., op. cit., 321.
5 *SA*, 697.
6 Ibid., 721.
7 See Rapoport, A., *Operational Philosophy*, New York: Harper & Bros, 1953.
8 See Nisbet, R. A., *Emile Durkheim*, Englewood Cliffs: Prentice-Hall, 1965, esp. Part II, ch. 2, and Green, R., *Protestantism and Capitalism: The Max Weber Thesis and Its Critics*, London: Harrap, 1959.
9 *TGA*, 50.
10 *Physics in Canada*, Science Secretariat, Privy Council Office, Ottawa: Special Study No. 2, May 1967, 283–5. Italics added.
11 Hanson, N. R., *Patterns of Discovery*, Cambridge University Press, 1965, 112.
12 *TGA*, 50.
13 Printed in the first edition of Bendix, R., and Lipset, S. M., eds., *Class, Status and Power*, London: Routledge, 1953. Cited below as *RTS*.
14 *RTS*, 128.
15 Black, M., op. cit., 341.
16 *RTS*, 128.
17 Ibid., 93.
18 Ibid., 116.
19 Ibid., 115.
20 See Buckley, W., *Sociology and Modern Systems Theory*, op. cit.; Mills, C. Wright, *The Sociological Imagination*, New York: Oxford University Press, 1959, ch. 2. Mills, however, tends to misrepresent Parsons' theoretical strategy. Thus he writes: 'Claiming to set forth "a general sociological theory" the grand theorist in fact sets forth a realm of concepts. . . .' Also Moore, Barrington, 'The New Scholasticism and the Study of Politics', *World Politics*, October 1953.
21 Black, M., op. cit., 280–1.
22 *RTS*, 103.
23 Ibid., 116.
24 Black, M., op. cit., 341.
25 Koch, S., ed., *Psychology, a Study of a Science*, op. cit., 700.
26 See *Sociology Today*, op. cit., 22.
27 *RTS*, 128.
28 See Bendix, R., and Lipset, S. M., op. cit.
29 See Dahrendorf, R., 'Out of Utopia', *American Journal of Sociology*,

lxiv (September 1968), 115–27, and Lockwood, D., 'Some Remarks on "The Social System"', *British Journal of Sociology*, vii (June 1956), 134–46. Both of these articles are printed in *System, Change and Conflict*, op. cit.

30 Those who are dubious about this statement should refer to p. 3 of Durkheim's last major work, *The Elementary Forms of The Religious Life*, op. cit., where he writes as follows: 'Every time that we undertake to explain something human, taken at a given moment in history . . . it is necessary to commence by going back to its most primitive and simple form, to try to account for the characteristics by which it was marked at that time, and then to show how it developed and became . . . that which it is at the moment in question.'

31 Homoeostatic systems are those which operate to maintain certain 'end states', such as body temperature or the sugar-level of the blood. See Cannon, W., op. cit., and *SS*, 482.

32 *TS*, 70–1.

33 See Swanson, G. E., 'The Approach to a General Theory of Action by Parsons and Shils', *American Sociological Review*, xviii (1953), 125–34.

34 *TS*, 44–79; *SS*, ch. 11; Etzioni, A. and E., *Social Change*, New York: Basic Books, 1964, chapter by Parsons; and Parsons, T., *Societies: Evolutionary and Comparative Perspectives*, Englewood Cliffs: Prentice-Hall, 1966.

35 *TS*, 71. Italics added.

36 See Dahrendorf, R., *Class and Class Conflict in Industrial Society*, Stanford University Press, 1959.

37 *TS*, 59.

38 Ibid.

39 *RTS*, 100–1. Italics added.

40 See Essien-Udom, E. U., *Black Nationalism*, Penguin Books, 1966.

41 This, of course, is largely due to Parsons' lack of precision and the extreme generality of his analyses. Let me give one further example, selected at random. In discussing the position of Christianity in modern America, he argues that despite considerable religious differences there is a common matrix of religious values shared by Protestants, Catholics, Jews and those without formal denominational affiliation. He continues: 'To deny that this underlying consensus exists would be to claim that American society stood in a state of latent religious war. Of the fact that there are considerable tensions every responsible student of the situation is aware. Institutionalization is incomplete, but the consensus is very much a reality.' With respect to religious differences, Parsons is simply repeating what every responsible student knows, while his contention about shared values amounts to no more than a denial that there is a latent religious war. Parsons' involved discussion conveys very little actual information, and precisely what this information is depends on the recipient's interpretation of such vague phrases as 'latent religious war'. Parsons, T., *Sociological Theory and Modern Society*, New York: The Free Press, 1967, 414. For further 'empirical' studies see *Structure and Process in Modern Societies*, Glencoe: The Free Press, 1960.

42 Merton, R. K., *Social Theory and Social Structure*, New York: The Free Press, revised and enlarged edition, 1957, 10.

NOTES

Chapter 5 A second functional alternative: Merton

1 Merton, R. K., *Social Theory and Social Structure*, op. cit., 6. Cited below as *ST*.
2 *ST*, 9.
3 Ibid., 5.
4 Ibid., 10.
5 Ibid., 103.
6 Ibid., 115.
7 See *ST*, chs. 4, 6.
8 See Brown, R., *Explanation in Social Science*, London: Routledge, 1963.
9 See Malinowski, B., *Argonauts of the Western Pacific*, London: Routledge, reprint, 1964.
10 See Radcliffe-Brown, A. R., *A Natural Science of Society*, Glencoe: The Free Press, 1957. Radcliffe-Brown's theoretical perspective is more sophisticated than Merton implies.
11 *ST*, 25.
12 Ibid., 33.
13 Ibid., 52.
14 See Hempel, C. G., 'The Logic of Functional Analysis', in Gross, L., ed., *Symposium on Sociological Theory*, New York: Harper & Row, 1959, ch. 9.
15 *ST*, 33–4.
16 Radcliffe-Brown, A. R., *Structure and Function in Primitive Society*, op. cit., 181.
17 Radcliffe-Brown does himself occasionally use the term 'disfunction', but without developing the notion systematically. For example, *Structure and Function in Primitive Society*, 182.
18 *ST*, 30.
19 Ibid., 32.
20 Ibid., ch. 4.
21 See above, ch. II, sec. IV.
22 *ST*, 121–2.
23 Ibid., 141.
24 Ibid., 146.
25 Ibid., 142–3.
26 Most attempts to develop Merton's scheme have either implicitly or explicitly recognized its tendency toward radical simplification and conceptual imprecision. For example, in the following article, Merton's fourfold classification of deviant responses is extended into a typology with fourteen categories, Dubin, R., 'Deviant Behaviour and Social Structure', *American Sociological Review*, April 1959, 147–64.
27 The official criminal statistics appear to exaggerate the relatively higher incidence of criminal acts among the lower strata, if we can presume that 'self-reporting techniques' are a more reliable source of information about actual behaviour. See Short, J. F., and Nye, F. I., 'Reported Behaviour as a Criterion of Deviant Behaviour', in *Social Problems*, Winter 1957, 207–13.
28 *ST*, 151.
29 Ibid., 153.
30 Ibid., 191.
31 Cohen, A. K., *Delinquent Boys*, Glencoe: The Free Press, 1955, 36.
32 *ST*, 178.

33 Ibid., 160. Italics added.
34 Blau, P., *The Dynamics of Bureaucracy*, University of Chicago Press, revised edition, 1963.
35 *ST*, 99.
36 Ibid., 98.
37 Ch. V, sec. II.
38 Nagel, E., *Logic Without Metaphysics*, New York: The Free Press, 1956, 251. Nagel offers an extensive and detailed critique of Merton's paradigm for functional analysis. Part of it is reprinted in *System, Change and Conflict*, op. cit.
39 For example, Radcliffe-Brown writes: 'The concept of function applied to human societies is based on an analogy between social life and organic life', *Structure and Function in Primitive Society*, op. cit., 178.
40 See Cannon, W., op. cit.
41 *ST*, 73.
42 Ibid., 80.
43 Gouldner, A. W., 'Reciprocity and Autonomy in Functional Theory', in L. Gross, op. cit., 249. The most direct *substantive* link between functionalism and exchange theory is to be found in the article cited above and in Gouldner, A. W., 'The Norm of Reciprocity', *American Sociological Review*, XXV (1960), 161–78. Links between Merton's brand of functionalism and exchange analysis can also be seen in Blau, P., *The Dynamics of Bureaucracy*, op. cit., and Hagstrom, W. O., *The Scientific Community*, New York: Basic Books, 1965.
44 *ST*, 19.
45 Homans, G. C., *Sentiments and Activities*, Glencoe: The Free Press, 1962, 43, 44, 46.

Chapter 6   Functionalism rejected: Homans:

1 Faris, R. E. L., *Handbook of Modern Sociology*, Chicago: Rand McNally & Co., 1964, ch. 25.
2 Durkheim, E., *Suicide*, Glencoe: The Free Press, 1951.
3 The deductive schema given here is a simplified version of that formulated by Homans in Faris, op. cit., 951.
4 Homans, G. C., *Social Behaviour: Its Elementary Forms*, New York: Harcourt, Brace & World, Inc., 1961, 205. Cited below as *SB*.
5 There are many resemblances between Homans' work and that of Pareto. This is not surprising, for Homans was introduced to sociology by way of an intensive study of Pareto's writings. See Homans, G. C., and Curtis, C. P., *An Introduction to Pareto*, New York: Knopf, 1934, and Homans, G. C., *Sentiments and Activities*, Glencoe: The Free Press, 1962, 3–5. Cited below as *S & A*.
6 Faris, op. cit., 953.
7 Lévi-Strauss, C., *Les structures élémentaires de la parenté*, Paris: Presses Universitaires de France, 1949; Homans, G. C., and Schneider, D. M., *Marriage, Authority and Final Causes*, New York: The Free Press, 1955. Quotations from this paper by Homans and Schneider are taken from the version in *S & A*, ch. 14.
8 For an alternative interpretation and a critique of Homans and Schneider, see Needham, R., *Structure and Sentiment*, University of Chicago Press, 1960.
9 *S & A*, 212.

10 Ibid., 24–8.
11 Ibid., 28–9. See Malinowski, B., *The Father in Primitive Psychology*, London, 1927, and Firth, R., *We, the Tikopia*, New York: Macmillan, 1936.
12 *S & A*, 247.
13 Ibid.
14 Ibid., 33.
15 See Murdoch, G. P., 'World Ethnographic Sample', in *American Anthropologist*, lix (1957), 664–87.
16 *S & A*, 248.
17 Homans, G. C., *The Human Group*, New York: Harcourt, Brace & World, Inc., 1950. Cited below as *HG*.
18 Ibid., 12.
19 Ibid., 13.
20 Ibid., 34.
21 Ibid., 36.
22 Ibid., 38.
23 Ibid., 3.
24 *SB*, 7.
25 *HG*, 90.
26 Ibid., 109–10.
27 *SB*, 230–1.
28 *HG*, 19.
29 Ibid., 112, 133. Homans' sources are noted on p. 48 of *HG*.
30 Ibid., 118, 134.
31 Ibid., 120, 135.
32 Ibid., 141.
33 Ibid., 145.
34 Ibid., 112.
35 Ibid., 118.
36 Ibid., 175. See Whyte, W. F., *Street Corner Society*, Chicago University Press, 1943.
37 *HG*, 177.
38 Ibid., 182.
39 Ibid.
40 Ibid., 184.
41 Ibid., 182.
42 Ibid., 183.
43 Firth, R., op. cit.
44 *HG*, 231.
45 Ibid., 243.
46 Ibid. 247.
47 Ibid., 242–3.
48 Ibid., 47.

Chapter 7 A theory of social exchange: Homans

1 *HG*, 296. Italics added.
2 Ibid., 298.
3 Ibid., 361.
4 The source of Homans' empirical material is Hatch, D. L., 'Changes in the Structure and Function of a Rural New England Community since 1900', Ph.D. thesis, Harvard University, 1948.
5 *HG*, 359.

6 Ibid.
7 Homans relies heavily on the work of Skinner, B. F. See *The Behavior of Organisms*, New York, 1938; also Deutsch, M., and Krauss, R., *Theories in Social Psychology*, New York: Basic Books, 1965.
8 *SB*, 13.
9 Ibid., 33–4.
10 Ibid., 35.
11 Ibid., 46.
12 Ibid., 41.
13 Ibid., 45.
14 Ibid., 53–60. As in ch. VI, Homans' propositions have been made simpler and more explicit.
15 Ch. VI, sec. IV.
16 Jennings, H. H., *Leadership and Isolation*, New York, second edition, 1950.
17 Newcomb, T. M., *Personality and Social Change*, New York, 1943.
18 *SB*, 339.
19 Ibid., 354.
20 Blau, P., op. cit.
21 *HG*, 37.
22 Ibid.
23 Ibid., 241.
24 Ibid.
25 Ibid.
26 Ibid., 16.
27 See ibid., 118–19.
28 E.g. ibid., 102.
29 Ibid., 359.
30 Ibid.
31 Ibid., 360.
32 Ibid.
33 Ibid.
34 Ibid., 34.
35 *SB*, 10.
36 See ibid, ch. 2; also Deutsch, M., and Krauss, R., op. cit.
37 *SB*, 60.
38 Ibid.
39 Ibid., 93–9; Gerard, H. B., 'The Anchorage of Opinions in Face-to-face Groups', in *Human Relations*, vii (1954), 313–25.
40 *SB*, 96.
41 Ibid., 97.
42 Deutsch, M., Krauss, R., op. cit., 114–15.
43 *SB*, 221.
44 Ibid., 222.
45 Ibid., 220.
46 Ibid., 223.
47 Ibid.
48 Ibid., 223–4.
49 Ibid., 208.
50 Ibid., 3, 5.
51 Ibid., 5–6.
52 Ibid., 380.
53 Blau, P., *Exchange and Power in Social Life*, New York: John Wiley, 1964, 3.

Chapter 8 A conceptual elaboration of exchange theory: Blau

1. Blau, P., op. cit. Cited below as *EP*.
2. Ibid., 6.
3. Ibid., 2.
4. Ibid.
5. Ibid.
6. Blau's debt to Gouldner and the latter's criticisms of functional analysis are clearly evident at this point. See *EP*, 92, Gouldner, A. W., 'The Norm of Reciprocity', in *American Sociological Review*, op. cit., and 'Autonomy and Reciprocity in Functional Theory', op. cit.
7. *EP*, 88.
8. Ibid., 90.
9. Ibid., 88.
10. Ibid., 6.
11. Ibid.
12. Ibid., 93.
13. Ibid., 95.
14. Ibid., 96.
15. Ibid., 97.
16. Ibid., 13
17. Ibid., 316.
18. Ibid., 26.
19. Ibid., 21.
20. For a discussion of power by Parsons, see *Sociological Theory and Modern Society*, op. cit., ch. 10; also Giddens, A., ' "Power" in the recent writings of Talcott Parsons', *Sociology*, September 1968, 257–72.
21. *EP*, 32.
22. Goffman, E., *The Presentation of Self in Everyday Life*, University of Edinburgh Social Science Research Centre, 1956.
23. *EP*, 129.
24. Ibid., 1178
25. Ibid., 141–2
26. Ibid., 258.
27. Cf. *SB*, ch. 12.
28. *EP*, 161–2.
29. Ibid., 202.
30. Ibid., 213.
31. Ibid., 214.
32. Ibid., 219.
33. Ibid., 255.
34. Ibid., 266.
35. Ibid., 271.
36. Ibid., 280.
37. Ibid., 285.
38. Ibid.
39. Ibid., 310.
40. Ibid., 334.
41. Cf. Pareto's broadly similar analysis of élite circulation.
42. *EP*, 338.
43. Ibid., 50–1.
44. Ibid., 49.
45. Ibid., 51.

46 Sec. II.
47 *EP*, 52, footnote. For a critique of certain aspects of Blau's analysis at the level of microstructures, see Heath, A., 'Economic Theory and Sociology', *Sociology*, September 1968, 273–92.
48 For two interpretations of Blau's theoretical logic, see MacIntyre, A., book review of *Exchange and Power in Sociology*, May 1967, 199–210, and Heath, A., 'MacIntyre on Blau', *Sociology*, January 1968, 93–6. The interpretation offered here is closer to that of Heath.
49 *EP*, 333. Italics added.
50 See Dahrendorf, R., *Class and Class Conflict in Industrial Society*, op. cit.

Chapter 9 Sociological theory and theoretical strategy

1 Toulmin, S., *Foresight and Understanding*, Harper Torchbooks edition, 1963, 108.
2 See Moore, Barrington, Jr., 'The New Scholasticism and the Study of Politics', op. cit.
3 Kuhn, T. S., *The Structure of Scientific Revolutions*, University of Chicago Press, 1962.
4 van den Berghe, P. L., 'Dialectic and Functionalism', in Demerath and Peterson, op. cit., 293. Italics added.
5 Dahrendorf uses a similar technique in arguing that functionalism and conflict theory are distinct, but complementary, theoretical models, op. cit., 161; see also Demerath, N. J., 'Synecdoche and Structural-Functionalism', in Demerath and Peterson, op. cit.
6 Bottomore, T. B., *Sociology*, London: Allen & Unwin, 1962, 25.
7 This is also true of Homans.
8 *ST*, 10.
9 There are good grounds for regarding the cross-fertilization of ideas as a fundamental source of intellectual development. For this reason, it should form a part of any comprehensive theoretical strategy. See Koestler, A., *The Act of Creation*, London: Hutchinson, 1964, especially ch. 10.
10 One of the few types of empirical study provoked by Pareto's work has been that of élite mobility. See Kolabinska, *La circulation des élites en France*.
11 For example, see ch. 7 of *Sociological Theory and Modern Society*, op. cit.
12 See Mills, C. W., op. cit., for an account of differentiation within academic sociology.

Bibliography

Included in this bibliography are all the main sources cited above, plus certain additional references which might prove useful to students of functionalism and exchange.

BALES, R. F., *Interaction Process Analysis*, Cambridge, Mass.: Addison Wesley, 1951.

BARBER, B., 'Structural-Functional Analysis: Some Problems and Misunderstandings', *American Sociological Review*, April 1965, 129–35.

BENDIX, R. and LIPSET, S. M., eds., *Class, Status and Power*, London: Routledge, 1953.

BLACK, M., ed., *The Social Theories of Talcott Parsons*, Englewood Cliffs, N. J.: Prentice-Hall, 1961.

BLAU, P., *Exchange and Power in Social Life*, New York: John Wiley, 1964.

BLAU, P., *The Dynamics of Bureaucracy*, University of Chicago Press, revised edition, 1963.

BORKENAU, F., *Pareto*, London, 1936.

BOTTOMORE, T. B., *Sociology*, London: Allen & Unwin, 1961.

BRAITHWAITE, R. B., *Scientific Explanation*, London: Cambridge University Press, 1953.

BREDEMEIER, H. C., 'The Methodology of Functionalism', *American Sociological Review*, April 1955, 173–80.

BROWN, P. and BROWN, R., 'A Note on Hypotheses in Homans' *The Human Group*', *American Sociological Review*, February 1955, 83–5.

BROWN, R., *Explanation in Social Science*, London: Routledge, 1963.

BUCKLEY, W., *Sociology and Modern Systems Theory*, Englewood Cliffs, N. J.: Prentice-Hall, 1967.

COHEN, P., *Modern Social Theory*, London: Heinemann, 1967.

DAHRENDORF, R., *Class and Class Conflict in Industrial Society*, London: Routledge, 1959.

DAHRENDORF, R., 'Out of Utopia', *American Journal of Sociology*, September, 1968, 115–27.

DAVIS, K., 'The Myth of Functional Analysis as a Special Method in Sociology and Anthropology', *American Sociological Review*, December 1959, 752–72.

BIBLIOGRAPHY

DEMERATH, N. J., and PETERSON, R. A., eds., *System, Change and Conflict*, New York: Free Press, 1967.

DEUTSCH, M., and KRAUSS, R., *Theories in Social Psychology*, New York: Basic Books, 1965.

DORE, R., 'Function and Cause', *American Sociological Review*, December 1961, 843–53.

DUBIN, R., 'Deviant Behavior and Social Structure', *American Sociological Review*, April 1959, 147–64.

FIRTH, R., *We, the Tikopia*, London: Allen & Unwin 1936.

GIDDENS, A., ' "Power" in the recent writings of Talcott Parsons', *Sociology*, September 1968, 257–72.

GLASER, B. G., and STRAUSS, A. L., *The Discovery of Grounded Theory*, London: Weidenfeld & Nicolson, 1968.

GOULDNER, A. W., 'The Norm of Reciprocity', *American Sociological Review*, 1960, 161–78.

GOULDNER, A. W., 'Reciprocity and Autonomy in Functional Theory', in Gross, L., ed., *Symposium on Sociological Theory*, New York: Harper & Row, 1959.

HANSON, N. R., *Patterns of Discovery*, Cambridge University Press, 1965.

HEATH, A., 'Economic Theory and Sociology: a Critique of P. M. Blau's *Exchange and Power in Social Life*', *Sociology*, September 1968, 273–92.

HEMPEL, C. G., 'The Logic of Functional Analysis', in Gross, L., ed., *Symposium on Sociological Theory*, New York: Harper & Row, 1959.

HOMANS, G. C., 'Bringing Men Back In', *American Sociological Review*, December 1964, 809–18.

HOMANS, G. C., *The Human Group*, London: Routledge, 1950.

HOMANS, G. C., *The Nature of Social Science*, New York: Harcourt, Brace & World, 1967.

HOMANS, G. C., *Sentiments and Activities*, Glencoe: The Free Press, 1962.

HOMANS, G. C., *Social Behaviour: Its Elementary Forms*, London: Routledge, 1961.

HOMANS, G. C., and CURTIS, C. P., *An Introduction to Pareto*, New York: Knopf, 1934.

HOMANS, G. C., and SCHNEIDER, D. M., *Marriage, Authority and Final Causes*, New York: The Free Press, 1955.

ISAJIW, W. W., *Causation and Functionalism in Sociology*, London: Routledge, 1968.

KUHN, T. S., *The Structure of Scientific Revolutions*, University of Chicago Press, 1962.

LÉVI-STRAUSS, C., *Les structures élémentaires de la parenté*, Paris: Presses Universitaires de France, 1949.

LOCKWOOD, D., 'Some Remarks on *The Social System*', *British Journal of Sociology*, June 1956, 134–46.

MALINOWSKI, B., *Argonauts of the Western Pacific*, London: Routledge, reprint, 1964.

MANDELBAUM, M., 'A Note on Homans' Functionalism', *British Journal of Sociology*, xiv (1963), 113–17.

MARTINDALE, D., ed., *Functionalism in the Social Sciences*, American Academy of Political and Social Sciences, 1965.

MERTON, R. K., *Social Theory and Social Structure*, New York: The Free Press, revised and enlarged edition, 1957.

MERTON, R. K., BROWN, L., and COTTRELL, L. S., eds., *Sociology Today*, Harper Torchbooks, 1965.

BIBLIOGRAPHY

MILLS, C. W., *The Sociological Imagination*, New York: Oxford University Press, 1959.
MITCHELL, W. C., *Sociological Analysis and Politics: the theories of Talcott Parsons*, Englewood-Cliffs, N. J.: Prentice-Hall, 1967.
MOSER, C. A., *Survey Methods in Social Investigation*, London: William Heinemann, 1958.
NAGEL, E., *Logic Without Metaphysics*, New York: The Free Press, 1956.
PARETO, V., *The Mind and Society*, New York: Dover Publications, 1963.
PARSONS, T., *Essays in Sociological Theory*, New York: The Free Press, 1949.
PARSONS, T., *The Structure of Social Action*, New York: McGraw Hill, 1937.
PARSONS, T., *The Social System*, London: Tavistock, 1951.
PARSONS, T., *Sociological Theory and Modern Society*, New York: The Free Press, 1967. Contains a full bibliography of Parsons' work to date.
PARSONS, T., *Structure and Process in Modern Society*, New York: The Free Press, 1960.
PARSONS, T., and SHILS, E. A., eds., *Toward a General Theory of Action*, Cambridge: Harvard University Press, 1951.
PARSONS, T., SHILS, E., NAEGELE, D., and PITTS, J., eds., *Theories of Society*, New York: The Free Press, 1961.
PARSONS, T., and SMELSER, N. J., *Economy and Society*, London: Routledge, 1956.
PIERCE, A., 'Empiricism and the Social Sciences', *American Sociological Review*, April 1956.
RADCLIFFE-BROWN, A. R., *A Natural Science of Society*, Glencoe: The Free Press, 1957.
RADCLIFFE-BROWN, A. R., *Structure and Function in Primitive Society*, London: Cohen & West, 1952.
REX, J., *Key Problems in Sociological Theory*, London: Routledge, 1961.
SPROTT, W. J. H., 'Principia Sociologica', *British Journal of Sociology*, iii (1952).
SPROTT, W. J. H., 'Principia Sociologica, II', *British Journal of Sociology*, xiv (1963), 307–20.
STARK, W., *The Fundamental Forms of Social Thought*, London: Routledge, 1962.
SWANSON, G. E., 'The Approach to a General Theory of Action by Parsons and Shils', *American Sociological Review*, April 1953.
TOULMIN, S., *Foresight and Understanding*, Indiana University Press, 1961.
ZETTERBERG, H. L., *On Theory and Verification in Sociology*, New York: The Bedminster Press, third enlarged edition, 1964.

Index

Activity: assessment of concept, 160–6, 168; definition, 131–2; in empirical generalizations, 135–152
Ad hoc classificatory system, 36
American class structure, 84, 91, 106–8
American paramount value system, 77
American political machine, 116–17
Authority, 190–200, 203–6

Bales, R., 53
Bank Wiring Room, 136–40, 146–7, 150
Black, M., 80
Blau, P., 3, 6, 7, 111, 157–9, 178, 179–212, 224–5, 227, 229–30, 233, 235, 237–8
Bottomore, T. B., 229
Boyle's Law, 144

Categorial knowledge, 37
Categorial system: Blau, 180, 184, 207; Parsons, 36–8, 40, 47, 55, 63–4, 67, 70, 72–6, 78, 80, 82, 216
Cathectivity, 45–6
Cognition, 46, 48–9
Cohen, A. K., 108–9
Collectivity: Blau, 191–4, 201, 206; definition, 51; Parsons, 54–5, 57
Competition, 188–95, 202–7
Complementarity of expectations, 48, 85

Conceptual formalism, 68, 72, 92, 97, 180, 218, 237
Conflict theory, 89–90, 212, 228–9
Criminality: Merton, 104–5, 107–9; Pareto, 33
Cross-cousin marriage, 125–30, 177
Cross-fertilization of ideas, 237
Culture: discrepancy between culture and social structure, 105; Pareto, 33; Parsons, 43–5
Cultural system: as alternative to instinct, 42–3; and input-output analysis, 59; as ready-made solutions to problems of choice, 46–8, 58, 74, 217
Cycles of interdependence, 12–13, 15–16, 20, 22, 24, 41, 214, 222

Dahrendorf, R., 229
Deductive system, 6–7; Blau, 210–1; Homans, 122–5, 128, 143, 154–9, 167–75, 222; Merton, 94, 110, 220; Pareto, 10, 15, 27, 214
Derivations, 16–18, 20–3, 25, 27, 28, 32, 214–15
Deutsch, M., and Krauss, R., 171
Deviance: Homans, 156–7; Merton, 104–5; Parsons, 88
Dialectical pattern of change, 194–195, 204–6
Dilemmas, 185–7, 194, 204–6
Disequilibrium: Blau, 186; Homans, 148–50; Pareto, 14, 23, 32; Parsons, 89

257

INDEX

Double exchange paradigm, 60–4, 75, 91, 218
Durkheim, E., 38, 68, 85, 98, 122–3, 232
Dysfunction, 102–4, 112, 115

Economic exchange, 183
Elementary social behaviour, 132, 134, 145, 150–60, 167–78
Élite: definition, 21; èlite cycle, 22–7, 54
Empirical specification of theoretical terms: Blau, 207–12; Homans, 129–32, 160–75, 223; Merton, 94–7, 101, 107–12, 118, 219–21; Pareto, 11, 29–31, 34–5, 216; Parsons, 37–9, 55, 69, 73–82, 91–2, 218–9; and theoretical strategy, 229–39
Empirical-theoretical system, 36–7, 67
Equilibrium: Blau, 186–7; Homans, 148; Pareto, 4, 13–18, 21, 24; Parsons, 54, 57, 59, 86–8
Evaluation, 46, 48–9
Evolutionary theory, in anthropology, 98–9; Darwinian, 88
Explanation, genetic, 99; Blau, 211; Homans, 1, 6, 122–4, 128–30, 134, 143, 166–75, 222; Merton, 112–8, 221; Pareto, 4, 9–11, 27, 30–2; Parsons, 66–7
External system, 133–4

Fashion, 19, 29
First-order abstractions, 131, 143, 161–3
Firth, R., 141, 162
Formal organizations, 194–5, 201–6
Function, concept of, 40, 78, 98–104, 112–18; anthropological functionalism, 98–102, 115, 119; functional alternatives, 101, 104, 113, 117; functional contribution, 77, 79, 81; functional differentiation, 52, 57, 79, 188, 206; functional explanation, 100–1, 112–118; functional imperatives, 42–3, 50, 52–5, 58, 64, 75, 77–9, 86, 89, 100–3, 113, 115, 117, 119, 133, 200, 218; functional indispensability, 99–103; functional unity, 99–103; latent function, 102–4, 112; manifest function, 102–4, 112; paradigm for functional analysis, 98–113, 119, 219–21; structural-functionalism, 4–5, 39–41, 64, 76–91, 216; universal functionalism, 99–103

General theory, 1, 9, 11, 22, 24, 34, 73, 81, 94–6, 98, 122–4, 201, 206, 219, 226, 233, 235, 239
Gerard, H. B., 168–70
Givens, 122–4, 128, 133–4, 175–8, 180, 188
Gouldner, A. W., 117
Governing èlite, 21, 24–7, 217
Group differentiation, 137–42, 159, 187–95
Group elaboration, 137–42, 159, 180, 187–95

Hanson, N. R., 71
Hilltown, 149–50, 164–5
Homans, G. C., 3, 6, 7, 119–20, 122–78, 179–81, 184, 187, 210, 212–13, 221–5, 234–5, 237–8
Homans-Schneider hypothesis, 127–31, 141–2, 177
Homeostasis, 86–7

Impartial observer, 18, 45
Indirect exchange, 194–8, 203, 206, 224
Induction: Homans, 123–4, 130, 134–45, 154, 160–7, 222; Merton, 96–8; Pareto, 10, 17, 24, 27–8, 213; Parsons, 68–72
Inductive-deductive strategy, 9–10, 34, 122–4, 144–5, 213, 222, 233–4
Industrial protection, 22–4
Instinct, 19–20, 33, 43
Institution: and functional differentiation, 55; institutions as given, 176–7; and macrostructures, 198–201; and pattern variables, 57; Parsons' definition, 50–1
Interaction, 131–2, 135–45, 146–52, 160–6
Interests, 16, 18, 20–3, 26–8, 44, 214
Internal system, 133

Kuhn, T. S., 228

Lévi-Strauss, C., 125–30
Logical action, 17–18, 20

INDEX

Logical priority of concepts, 38, 70–1
Logico-deductive system, 4, 67, 216, 225

Macrostructures, 195–207, 210–12, 224
Malinowski, B., 127
Marshall, A., 68
Marx, K., 212
Marxism, 12; Hegelian-Marxian dialectic, 228; Marxian analysis of 'social stratification', 89
Merton, R. K., 3–5, 93, 94–121, 123, 125, 128, 130, 134, 144, 219–223, 227, 230–2, 235–6, 239
Microstructures, 187–95, 201, 204–211
Middle range theory, 22, 93, 95–6, 97–8, 110–12, 118, 219–21, 230–3, 236
Moreno, J. L., 155

Nagel, E., 114
Negative feedback, 114–19, 221
Newcomb, T. M., 156
Non-logical action, 17–18, 29, 43–4
Non-logical theories, 17–18, 28, 32, 68
Norm: behaviourist definition, 168; in empirical generalizations, 136–152; of fairness, 191–4, 205; as first-order abstraction, 131–2; and indirect exchange, 177, 196–197; and social action, 41–5, 51
Normative theories, 45
Norton Street Gang, 138–41

Opposition, 25, 194–5, 198, 200, 204–7

Pareto, V., 3–7, 9–35, 36–41, 43–5, 47, 54, 58, 64, 66, 68–9, 72–3, 78, 80, 85, 90, 93–7, 104, 110–11, 113, 120, 123–4, 134–5, 144–5, 160–1, 210, 212–20, 222–4, 226–7, 229–230, 233–5
Parsons, T., 3–5, 34–5, 36–93, 94–8, 104–5, 110–11, 115, 119–20, 125, 129, 144, 171, 180, 184–5, 191, 196, 201, 207, 211–13, 216–24, 227–30, 232, 235–8
Pattern variables, 55–6, 77, 197–8, 200

Personality system, 42–3, 46, 57, 59, 74, 105
Power, 6, 62–3, 185–7, 189–92, 206
Prediction: Blau, 180, 184, 206–10; Homans, 124, 172–5, 223; Pareto, 9–11, 27, 31–2; Parsons, 66–7
Preparatory strategy, 229–39
Presentation of self, 188, 207
Psychic profit, 153

Quantity, 152–3

Radcliffe-Brown, A. R., 102
Reciprocity, principle of, 181–2, 185–9
Reduction, 124
Residual categories, 29, 44, 220
Residues, 16–29, 32, 214–15, 218; combinations, 19, 22–4, 29–31, 66; integrity of the individual and his possessions, 19; need for activity, 19; persistence of aggregates, 19, 22–4, 26–7, 29–31, 66; sexuality, 19, 29; sociability, 19, 29
Reward/cost, 138–9, 143, 147–60, 167–78, 181–211
Role: Homans, 131, 145, 176; Parsons, 50–1, 54–5, 76–81
Role-differentiation in sociology 239

Schneider, D., 127–9
Second-order abstractions, 131–2
Segmentation of collectivities, 52
Sentiments: assessment of concept, 160–6, 168; behaviourist redefinition, 152; definition, 132; in empirical generalizations, 135–51
Shares values: in American society, 76–80; in complex systems, 51–4; as media of indirect exchange, 196–8; and pattern variables, 57; and social change, 86–90; and social exchange, 185; as sources of opposition, 199–201, 204–5; success goal as cultural value, 105; in two-actor situation, 48–50
Social action, 41–4, 47, 51, 53, 57, 64, 68, 75–6, 217
Social change: Blau, 186–7, 204–6; Homans, 137, 148–50; Pareto, 13–4, 25; Parsons, 85–91

INDEX

Social control, 6, 146–8
Social exchange, 5–8; Blau, 180–212, 225; Homans, 150–60, 166–178, 225; Lévi-Strauss, 125; Merton, 103, 117–18, 221; Parsons, 57–64, 75, 82–3, 88–9, 218
Social heterogeneity, 16, 21–2, 26, 28, 214–15
Socialization, 43, 46, 54, 199
Social order, problem of, 85
Social ranking: Blau, 188–94; Homans, 136–44, 146–7, 154–9, 173–175
Social solidarity, 125–6, 129
Social stratification: Parsons, 73, 76–81, 83–4, 89–90
Social structure, 33, 35, 50–1, 86, 127–9, 130, 132, 145, 217–18; and anomie, 104–13, 116, 118; structural categories, 39–40; structural constraint, 101, 104, 113
Social system: Blau, 201; and functional analysis, 7, 145; Pareto, 4, 7, 12–16, 21, 26–7, 32–4, 215; Parsons, 40, 42–50, 59, 64, 74, 86–7, 217–8
Sociological universals, 7, 145
Solid state physics: research strategy, 70–1; role-differentiation in, 239

Specification of normative culture, 52, 75, 86, 88
Strategical dialectic, 3, 8, 212, 226, 238–9
Sub-institutional behaviour, 176–8
Suicide, 122–3

Theoretical content, 1, 2, 7, 84
Theoretical convergence, 37–8, 41, 44, 68–9, 95, 228–9
Theoretical goal, 1, 2, 10, 14, 21, 36–7, 122, 179
Theoretical prolegomenon, 179–80, 184, 207, 225
Theoretical strategy, 1–7, 213–40; Blau, 178–81; Homans, 119–24, 144–5; Merton, 93–8, 110–12; Pareto, 10, 14–15, 27; Parsons, 34–6, 38, 50, 67, 71–2
Tikopia, 127, 141–2
Toulmin, S., 225–6, 231
Trobriand Islanders, 127

Unexpected insights, 73–4, 83–4

Value, in exchange, 152–60, 168–72

Weber, M., 38, 44, 68, 85, 98